Building Urban Resilience

DIRECTIONS IN DEVELOPMENT
Environment and Sustainable Development

Building Urban Resilience

Principles, Tools, and Practice

Abhas K. Jha, Todd W. Miner, and Zuzana Stanton-Geddes, Editors

THE WORLD BANK
Washington, D.C.

Australian AID

Contents

Boxes

Figures

Tables

Foreword

In the context of emerging demographic, urbanization, and climatic trends, policy makers in East Asia face difficult decisions about medium- and long-term investments in public infrastructure and urban management.

Recent tragic events in the region, among them the Great East Japan earthquake and tsunami, the widespread flooding in Thailand, and the tropical storm Washi in the Philippines, illustrate the devastation, economic damage, and loss of human life that result from disasters. They add a sense of urgency to the challenge of preparing for and managing disasters and offer important lessons for urban disaster risk management practitioners.

There are concrete ways to improve the decision-making process to guide cities toward the aspired benefits. This report guides readers in finding ways to avoid the mistakes of the past and build resilience into urban management, critical infrastructure investments, and disaster and climate risk mitigation measures that stretch across sectors and jurisdictions all the way to communities and the most vulnerable.

First, there are principles that can guide those who make decisions about public finances. One of these is investing in quality data on risk and in tools that facilitate the use of data across sectors and jurisdictions. Cities that are better able to define and communicate their risks do a better job of preparing for and managing the impacts of natural disasters in a complex and uncertain environment.

Second, there are concrete tools that can support preparation for decisions and their implementation. For example, integrating risk-based approaches into urban governance and planning processes can help national and municipal stakeholders to make complex decisions in a smarter, more forward-looking, and more sustainable way that increases resilience.

Finally, key economic sectors—especially water, energy, and transport systems—deserve particular attention. They are not only vital if cities and communities are to deal with a disaster and recover quickly, they are also sectors where careful investments—those that pay attention to the principles and make full use of the tools available—can make a real difference in people's lives.

The *Building Urban Resilience in East Asia* initiative encourages cities to invest in risk-based approaches and make better use of the technologies and tools available to manage disaster risks. This report is an example of the commitment of the World Bank and the Australian Agency for International Development (AusAID) to support cities in East Asia to be better prepared for the development challenges of today as well as tomorrow.

John Roome
Director
Sustainable Development
East Asia and the Pacific
The World Bank

Preface

About Building Urban Resilience in East Asia

Building Urban Resilience in East Asia is a World Bank program that aims to increase the resilience of cities to disasters and the impacts of climate change by using a risk-based approach to making public investment decisions. The objective is to demonstrate a scalable methodology and practical tools for risk assessment that can be used for city-level investment decisions.

Working closely with the stakeholders involved in land use planning and infrastructure development, Phase I of this program identified the major challenges facing urban decision makers in terms of risks from natural disasters and climate change and now offers open-source risk assessment tools that can be used by city-level institutions, other communities, private investors, and planners of infrastructure services. Phase II explores different investment options, management plans, and capacity building needs.

Building Urban Resilience in East Asia is part of a World Bank effort to encourage governments to use risk information effectively. The Open Data for Resilience Initiative (OpenDRI) is intended to reduce the impact of disasters by empowering decision makers with better information and the tools to support their responsibilities. InaSAFE (the Indonesia Scenario Assessment for Emergencies) is one of those tools, developed through a partnership with the Indonesian National Disaster Management Agency (BNPB), the Australia-Indonesia Facility for Disaster Reduction (AIFDR), and the Global Facility for Disaster Reduction and Recovery (GFDRR) Labs team.

Getting Started—How to Use This Handbook

The three major sections of this report are designed to give urban planners and practitioners an intuitive way to build elements of resilience into their urban governance and city planning.

- *Chapter 1: Principles of Urban Resilience* presents guiding principles for resilient cities in terms of today's urban development; risk, uncertainty, and complexity; disaster risk management; social resilience; land use planning; urban ecosystems; urban upgrading; and incorporating resilience into the project cycle.

- *Chapter 2: Tools for Building Urban Resilience* focuses on how to use the most common and effective tools and methodologies available, among them risk assessment; risk-based land use planning; urban ecosystem management; urban upgrading; community and stakeholder participation; disaster management systems; data gathering, analysis, and application; and risk financing and transfer approaches.

- *Chapter 3: The Practice of Urban Resilience* provides guidance on identifying, planning, and implementing urban investment projects in three major sectors. The section on water supply and wastewater systems details the importance of these systems, especially resilience to flooding—an increasing challenge to cities around the world. Energy and communications apply to both national and subnational systems. The section on transportation systems discusses how to enhance disaster resilience in road, rail, and air systems.

The handbook contains case studies and tables that provide further details and examples of good practice. Each chapter ends with a comprehensive reference list, and the most important resources are emphasized throughout. The appendixes provide general disaster definitions and classifications, a checklist for infrastructure owners and operators, a comparison of spatial plans for urban infrastructure, and guidelines for collecting data.

Acknowledgments

Building Urban Resilience: Principles, Tools, and Practice was prepared by a team led by Abhas K. Jha and composed of Abigail Baca, Meskerem Brhane, Cynthia Burton, Soumya Dharmavaram, Todd W. Miner, Artessa Niccola Saldivar-Sali, Charles Scawthorn, and Zuzana Stanton-Geddes. Technical editing was done by Todd W. Miner.

The team would like to thank John Roome and Vijay Jagannathan for their support and guidance, and Victor Vazquez Alvarez, Bernard Baratz, Laura Elizabeth Boudreau, Bernice K. Van Bronkhorst, Alan Coulthart, Henrike Brecht, Vivien Foster, Stéphane Hallegatte, Hitoshi Baba, Shomik Raj Mehndiratta, Liana Zanarisoa Razafindrazay, Robert John Soden, Victor Vergara, and Reindert Westra for their constructive comments.

The team acknowledges with gratitude the generous support from the Australian Agency for International Development (AusAID) provided through the World Bank East Asia and Pacific Infrastructure for Growth Trust Fund (EAAIG), which enabled the technical work to take place.

Editors and Contributors

Editors

Abhas K. Jha is the Sector Manager for Transport, Urban and Disaster Risk Management in East Asia and the Pacific at the World Bank. In this capacity, he is responsible for the overall technical quality control of World Bank operations, strategic staffing, and the provision of high-quality knowledge and services in these sectors to World Bank clients. Mr. Jha's core interests are smart cities, urban resilience, and the use of open data for better service delivery. He has been with the World Bank since 2001, leading the urban, housing, and disaster risk management work in Turkey, Mexico, Jamaica, and Peru, as well as serving as the Regional Coordinator for Disaster Risk Management for Europe and Central Asia. He has also served as Adviser to the World Bank Executive Director for India, Bangladesh, Sri Lanka, and Bhutan on issues related to urban development, infrastructure, and climate finance. Prior to joining the World Bank, Mr. Jha served for 12 years in the Indian Administrative Service of the government of India in the Federal Ministry of Finance and in the state of Bihar. Mr. Jha is the lead author of the World Bank publications, *Safer Homes, Stronger Communities: A Handbook for Reconstructing after Disasters* and *Cities and Flooding: A Guide to Integrated Urban Flood Risk Management*.

Todd W. Miner is a Consultant specializing in disaster risk management, resilience, and environmental conflict. He has worked on projects with the World Bank, the United Nations Mission in Liberia, the Extractive Industries Transparency Initiative, the Federal Emergency Management Agency, the New York City Mayor's Office of Long-Term Planning and Sustainability, Population Services International, and the Center for International Earth Science Information Network. He was directly involved with the response and recovery effort in New York City following Hurricane Sandy and 9/11 and on the Gulf Coast following Hurricanes Katrina and Rita, and he has extensive experience in South Sudan, Mali, Senegal, and Liberia. He is the co-author of *Enhancing the Feasibility of Electric Vehicles in New York City* and *A Conceptual Framework for a Global Resilience Index*, serves on the Environment and Peace Working Group at Columbia University, and is a member of the New York Resilience System.

Zuzana Stanton-Geddes is a Disaster Risk Management Consultant at the Sustainable Development Department in the East Asia and the Pacific Disaster Risk Management team where, since 2010, she supports operational and analytical work related to urban resilience, urban flood risk management, disaster risk financing, and gender concerns. Prior to joining the World Bank, she worked at the Friedrich Foundation in Berlin, the European Commission Permanent Representation to Germany, and IBM in Slovakia. Ms. Stanton-Geddes conducted research in Valparaiso, Chile, concerning conditions of local micro-entrepreneurs and their financing and business needs, and she worked as a short-term researcher for the Center for Transatlantic Relations in Washington, DC. A native of the Slovak Republic, Ms. Stanton-Geddes holds a master's degree in international economics and international affairs from Johns Hopkins School of Advanced International Studies (SAIS), a master's degree in European studies from Humboldt University in Berlin, and a bachelor's degree from the University of Cambridge in the United Kingdom.

Contributors

Abby Baca is a Disaster Risk Management Specialist in the World Bank's East Asia and the Pacific Disaster Risk Management team. Since joining the World Bank's Global Facility for Disaster Reduction and Recovery (GFDRR) in 2010, she has supported multiple projects, including the Pacific Catastrophe Risk Assessment and Financing Initiative, Building Urban Resilience in East Asia, and GFDRR's Open Data for Resilience Initiative (OpenDRI), including the InaSAFE development in partnership with the Australia-Indonesia Facility for Disaster Reduction (AIFDR). Prior to that, she worked as a natural catastrophe risk modeler and product manager, gaining six years of international, multi-peril modeling experience at Risk Management Solutions Inc. (RMS). Ms. Baca served as a vulnerability engineer for multiple projects, including probabilistic earthquake and climate risk models for the Americas and Europe. She earned a bachelor's in civil and environmental engineering from Stanford University and a master's in structural engineering from the University of California, San Diego.

Laura Boudreau is a Disaster Risk Financing and Insurance Analyst working for the World Bank's Global Facility for Disaster Reduction and Recovery (GFDRR) Disaster Risk Financing and Insurance (DRFI) Program. Ms. Boudreau provides technical assistance on disaster risk financing and insurance in low- and middle-income countries, specifically, technical assistance for sovereign disaster risk financing and insurance for middle-income countries, with a regional focus on the Latin American and the Caribbean region, although she is also involved in the DRFI Program's larger portfolio. Ms. Boudreau has formerly worked as a research assistant at the Wharton Risk Management and Decision Processes Center and at the Europa Reinsurance Facility Ltd. She is an American national with a background in applied economics, risk analysis, and globalization, and she graduated with a business degree from The Wharton School of the University of Pennsylvania.

Meskerem Brhane is Senior Urban Specialist in the Sustainable Development Department in the East Asia and the Pacific Region of the World Bank. She currently leads urban development projects in China and is Senior Adviser on the World Bank's urban development program in Mongolia. Her areas of focus include urban regeneration/slum upgrading, urban planning, flood risk management, infrastructure improvement, and community participation. Her current analytical work focuses on affordable housing and municipal finance. Earlier, she worked in the Middle East and North Africa Region, where she most recently served as Senior Urban Specialist and Sustainable Development Coordinator in the Country Office for the West Bank and Gaza, leading operations in community-driven development, municipal infrastructure provision and governance, and NGO-led service delivery. She has led analytical work on gender and conflict, youth and development, municipal finance, and poverty and social impact analysis in the water and energy sectors. Dr. Brhane speaks French, Arabic, Hebrew, and Amharic and holds a doctorate in political science from the University of Chicago.

Cynthia Burton is a Technical Specialist in disaster risk management and social equality, with more than 30 years of international development and humanitarian experience. She has worked with a diverse range of organizations, including the Australian Agency for International Development (AusAID), the Canadian International Development Agency, the International Federation of Red Cross and Red Crescent Societies (IFRC), the World Food Programme, and the World Bank. Ms. Burton has conducted numerous studies, disaster needs assessments and evaluations, and social equality and protection programs, and she has contributed to the design of major programs, such as the AusAID large-scale urban disaster risk management and climate change adaptation initiative in the Philippines. She also has played a lead role in the development of many disaster risk management and social/gender analyses, learning methodologies, and other tools, such as the World Bank Toolkit on Building Resilient Communities: Risk Management and Response to Natural Disasters through Social Funds and Community-Driven Development Operations. Ms. Burton is currently a key technical adviser for a World Bank project to develop the capacity of staff and partner governments to integrate disaster risk management and climate change adaptation approaches into national social protection systems.

Soumya Dharmavaram is an Urban Planner-Architect with 20 years of experience in land management, low-income housing, and sustainable building design/technology. Ms. Dharmavaram has worked in India, where her work included field research on resettlements related to large infrastructure projects, slum upgrading, gender issues in low-income housing, training needs assessments for sustainable building technologies for international/national agencies, and participatory building design using energy-efficient and culturally sensitive technologies for NGOs and the private sector. In addition to teaching at the national planning school, she has conducted technical/design workshops and prepared curricula for the training of trainers as well as construction manuals for the Indian Institute for

Human Settlements and NGOs. More recently, Ms. Dharmavaram contributed to a World Bank handbook on climate change, disaster risks, and the urban poor. She has also contributed to content development on urban flood risk management, post-disaster reconstruction, disaster prevention, and land use planning for urban infrastructure, peri-urban areas, local economic development, and social equity for the World Bank Institute's global e-learning courses on disaster risk management, safe and resilient cities, and sustainable urban land use planning. She has managed the implementation of these courses for policy makers and practitioners.

Artessa Saldivar-Sali is a Resilience Engineering Specialist working on the World Bank's East Asia and the Pacific Disaster Risk Management team. Previously, she worked on the Sustainable Cities and Climate Change team of the Urban Development and Local Government Unit. Before joining the World Bank, she worked at the Office of the President of the Philippines, assessing government policy and programs on urban development and disaster risk management. Ms. Saldivar-Sali was also a faculty member for three years at the Department of Civil Engineering of the University of the Philippines. A graduate of the Massachusetts Institute of Technology, she holds master's degrees in both civil and environmental engineering and building technology.

Charles Scawthorn is internationally recognized as an authority on the analysis and mitigation of natural and technological hazards. He retired as Professor and Head of the Earthquake Disaster Prevention Systems Laboratory, Kyoto University (Japan) and currently has visiting academic appointments at several universities. He teaches a course on Disaster Risk Assessment, Mitigation, and Financing at the World Bank, and he chairs the Hazus Open Source Committee. He is also a member of the Multihazard Mitigation Council. As President of SPA Risk LLC, he consults to the global insurance industry, the World Bank, local/state/federal agencies, and Global 1000 corporations.

Abbreviations

ACCCRN   Asian Cities Climate Change Resilience Network
AIDMI   All India Disaster Mitigation Institute
AIFDR   Australia-Indonesia Facility for Disaster Reduction
AKOM   Disaster Management Centre of Istanbul City
ATC   Air Traffic Control
BNPB   Indonesia's National Disaster Management Agency
BPPTK   Office for the Study and Development of Volcanic Technology, National Ministry for Energy and Mineral Resources
BRACE   Building the Resilience and Awareness of Metro Manila Communities to Natural Disaster and Climate Change Impacts
CAEP   City-Assisted Evacuation Plan
CAS   Country Assistance Strategy
CAT DDO Catastrophe Deferred Drawdown Option
CBDRM   Community-Based Disaster Risk Management
CCA   Climate Change Adaptation
CDD   Social Fund/Community-Driven Development
CDMP   Comprehensive Disaster Management Programme
CDP   Community Development Plans
CIESIN   Center for International Earth Science Information Network
COWS   Cell on Wheels
CPS   Country Partnership Strategy
CSO   Civil Society Organization
DEM   Digital Elevation Model
DPL   Development Policy Loan
DRFI   Disaster Risk Financing and Insurance
DRM   Disaster Risk Management
DRR   Disaster Risk Reduction
EEWS   Earthquake Early Warning Systems
EHV   Extra High Voltage
EMPI   Earthquake Mitigation Plan for Istanbul

EOC	Emergency Operations Centers
FEWS	Famine Early Warning Systems
GFDRR	Global Facility for Disaster Reduction and Recovery
GHG	Greenhouse Gas
GIS	Geographic Information System
GLTN	Global Land Tools Network
GUO	Global Urban Observatory
HABISP	Information System for Social Housing in the City of São Paulo
HOT	Humanitarian Open Street Map Team
IDRM	Integrated Disaster Risk Management
IIED	International Institute for Environment and Development
IMM	Istanbul Metropolitan Municipality
IRM	Immediate Response Mechanism
ITC	International Institute for Geoinformation Science and Earth Observation
JFPR	Japan Fund for Poverty Reduction
KAPAWA	Maasin People's Organization Federation
KVERMP	Kathmandu Valley Earthquake Risk Management Project
LDCF	Least Developed Countries Fund
LNG	Liquid Natural Gas
LRAP	Local Resilience Action Plans
MIS	Management Information Systems
MIWD	Metro Iloilo Water District
MOU	Memoranda of Understanding
NGO	Non-Governmental Organization
OCHA	Office for the Coordination of Humanitarian Affairs
PAD	Project Appraisal Document
PAS 200	Publically Available Specification in Crisis Management
PCN	Project Concept Note
PCRAFI	Pacific Catastrophe Risk Assessment and Financing Initiative
PDI	Project Development Indicator
PDNA	Post-Disaster Needs Analysis
PDO	Project Development Objective
PID	Project Information Document
RRTI	Regional Risk Transfer Initiative
SCBA	Socioeconomic Cost Benefit Analysis
SDI	Shack/Slum Dwellers International
SMS	Short Message Service
STDM	Social Tenure Domain Model

UNEP	United Nations Environment Programme
UrEDAS	Urgent Earthquake Detection and Alarm System
VCA	Vulnerability and Capacity Assessment
VHR	Very High Resolution
VOIP	Voice Over Internet Protocols
VTC	Volunteer Technical Communities
WBI	World Bank Institute
WFP	World Food Programme
WRI	World Resources Institute

Executive Summary

This handbook is a resource for enhancing disaster resilience in urban areas. It summarizes the guiding principles, tools, and practices in key economic sectors that can facilitate incorporation of resilience concepts into the decisions about infrastructure investments and general urban management that are integral to reducing disaster and climate risks.

Resilience is the ability of a system, community, or society exposed to hazards to resist, absorb, accommodate to, and recover from the effects of a hazard in a timely and efficient manner (UNISDR 2011).

In the context of cities, resilience translates into a new paradigm for urbanization and influences the way we understand and manage urban hazards, as well as urban planning in general. It provides practical rules of thumb that can guide stakeholders' decisions to incorporate the management of disasters and climate risks into urban investments. In practice, *operationalizing* resilience is challenging (Upton and Ibrahim 2012). To facilitate this process, this handbook provides guidance on how to build urban resilience into critical infrastructure and the social realm by taking advantage of available methodologies, tools, and resources.

Focus on Cities

In the next decades, the major driver of the increasing damages and losses from disasters will be the growth of people and assets in harm's way, especially in urban areas (IPCC 2012). Cities are the quintessential complex adaptive systems (Montenegro 2010). By 2050, the United Nations expects 80 percent of the world's population to live in urban areas (United Nations 2009). In East Asia, the urban population is expected to double between 1994 and 2025 (Jha and Brecht 2011). Often located along the coastline, in flood plains, or along seismic rifts, cities with their concentration of assets and people are vulnerable to disasters. Rapid and unplanned urbanization, which takes place on marginal lands and hazardous areas, in combination with poorly constructed settlements and degraded ecosystems, puts more people and more assets in harm's way.

Rapidly growing peri-urban, small, and middle-sized cities are particularly at risk. They often lack not only financial resources, infrastructure, and services but also the capacity to manage the increase in urban population even as their exposure is increasing. This will translate into heavy loss of life and property if there are climate and disaster events unless proactive measures are mainstreamed into urban governance and planning processes.

East Asia and the Pacific, along with South Asia, are particularly vulnerable to natural disasters. Globally, Asia Pacific is the region most affected in terms of economic impact and numbers of people. In the past year, the earthquake and tsunami in Japan, large-scale floods in Thailand, and the tropical storm in the Philippines have been tragic reminders of the devastation, economic and social damages, and loss of human life disasters cause. They offer valuable lessons to urban disaster risk management practitioners.

Risk and Uncertainty

Urbanization, environmental degradation, climate change, and development-related processes and planning shape and configure hazards. The complexity of systems and uncertainty about the impact of development and climate change affect the way we understand and manage risks when we build and expand cities. It is necessary to recognize that our underlying assumptions could be wrong, and in any case the risks of disasters cannot be eliminated completely. This has two implications for cities:

1. Rather than focusing on "optimal engineering design," cities ought to adopt a robust approach to uncertainty and unknown risks that uses a balance of ecosystem measures and land use options that incorporate more flexibility into engineering designs and take into account potential weak spots and failure. Urban planners must understand and incorporate natural ecosystem services into infrastructure and resilience projects. This approach will help keep cities from being locked in to financing large-scale investments that might prove obsolete if in future the risks change.
2. Recognition of residual risks implies that cities must continuously improve their risk communication, early warning systems, and emergency contingency, evacuation, and recovery planning.

The risks of disasters and climate change are highly uncertain. While long-term trends in losses have not yet been attributed to natural or anthropogenic climate change, it does add a layer of additional risk and uncertainty (IPCC 2012). Climate change can have a compounding effect on, for example, the risk of floods from sea level rises, changing rainfall patterns, and more storm surges.

Both physical and nonphysical features of the urban environment change, sometimes naturally, sometimes by design. Development-related processes, such as planning and management of urban growth and settlements, environmental and ecosystem degradation, and poverty, already affect city risk profiles, with serious consequences. For instance, city decision makers must consider a range of time horizons, from budgeting priorities each year to 20–30 years for spatial plans and some 50 years for infrastructure design. Urban planning methods may support this longer-term view of a city's needs; however, the output of the planning process may often be incomplete or inconsistent, and it can rapidly become outdated and limited in its usefulness for guiding the city to a more resilient future.

Facing these challenges, there is a critical need for a flexible and dynamic approach to building resilience that goes beyond risk mitigation.

Building Urban Resilience: Principles, Tools, and Practice

Building resilience in cities relies on investment decisions that prioritize spending on activities that offer alternatives that perform well in different scenarios. In managing risks today and planning for the future, a balance must be struck between, on the one hand, common-sense approaches that minimize impact through better urban management and maintenance of existing mitigation measures and, on the other hand, far-sighted approaches. Long-term views anticipate, defend against, and build resilience in the face of future hazards by investing in new infrastructure or by altering the urban landscape. The balance will be different for each urban settlement. The goal is to formulate a strategy in which flexible and "low-regret" measures can be cost-effective even when risks are uncertain (World Bank 2012).

Taking into account future risks and uncertainties, resilience relies on redundancy. Cities facing difficult decisions about scarce resources and investments strive for efficiency. The quest often results in trade-offs between resilience and redundancy (Montenegro 2010). Resilience does not strive for efficiency but for "ways to build into near-term investments and choices appropriate consideration of long-term trends and worst-case scenarios" (Revkin 2011).

Because all governments have an obligation to protect their citizens, resilience can be seen as a public good (Lall and Deichmann 2009) that is dependent on public funding. For city and municipal governments, this implies planning development; providing safe and affordable infrastructure and services; regulating building design and construction; regulating hazardous activities; influencing land availability and construction requirements; encouraging and supporting household and community actions to reduce risk; and finally, putting in place effective disaster early warning, preparedness, and response systems. Doing all these can reduce risk for both populations and economies.

The disaster risk management framework—the mitigation, preparedness, disaster, response, recovery, and reconstruction phases—offers practical opportunities for enhancing resilience. Risk is the uncertainty of loss, and loss is the convolution of hazard, assets, and the vulnerability of these assets to hazards. Risk can be reduced by approaches focusing on location, structure, operational aspects, and risk financing and transfer options. To reduce risk and enhance resiliency, government and donor-led projects should implement a balanced combination of these approaches.

Urban infrastructure—water, sanitation, energy, communications, and transportation systems—is critically important for emergency response and quick recovery of the community and its economy. Where there is vulnerability to a wide range of natural hazards, there are opportunities for enhancing the resilience of critical systems. Residual risks have to be managed in ways that are both flexible and robust. Traditional cost-benefit analysis does not deal well with catastrophic tail risk. Critical systems therefore need to be designed so that they fail "gracefully," the goal being a robust design that builds on investments in risk information, strategic communication, cross-sectoral coordination, and a well-planned response and recovery strategy.

Social resilience is the capacity of a community or society to cope with, and adapt to, disturbances or changes. It includes the ability of communities and society as a whole to absorb disturbances, self-organize to adjust to current and new stresses, and build and increase capacity for learning and adaptation. A resilient community is able to respond positively to changes or stress and despite them maintain its core functions as a community. Policy makers should strive to create an environment that enables communities to participate and make decisions. This increases collective resilience and facilitates the work of public authorities in both creating and disseminating risk information.

Risk-based land use planning identifies the safest areas to prioritize immediate investments in urban development and infrastructure projects. Land use plans influence the location, type, design, quality, and timing of development. Mainstreaming land use planning in infrastructure projects reduces risk, both episodic and everyday, in rapidly growing urban centers in hazard-prone areas. While land use planning informs urban spatial development, comprehensive risk reduction requires social and economic policies and programs that will increase the capacity of the urban population to adapt to risks.

Combined with land use planning, ecosystem management approaches to promote resilience in urban areas make use of the natural landscape and can significantly decrease the cost of urban infrastructure projects. Ecosystem management requires an understanding of ecosystem services and the local urban environment. Methodological tools can help to integrate ecology into urban resilience. A number of ecosystem management strategies are relevant to urban resilience, and more broadly to disaster risk reduction, among them watershed management (e.g., coastal zone management); urban landscape design; green and blue infrastructure; and environmental buffers.

Urban upgrading prioritizes infrastructure, housing, livelihoods, and social networks for highly vulnerable households living in slum settlements. Most slum settlements are located on relatively inexpensive but hazard-prone sites. Poorly built and overcrowded structures, lack of basic services and secure tenure, and their socio-spatial exclusion make the urban poor vulnerable to disasters. However, variations in slum conditions create different degrees of risk. Strategic urban upgrading can manage risks by (a) regulating slum development in hazard-prone areas through planned resettlement and building codes; (b) reducing losses by prioritizing critical infrastructure, escape routes, and community refuges in slums; and (c) promoting safe and socioeconomically viable low-income neighborhoods in accordance with a city-wide plan.

Reaching decisions on how to prioritize resilience efforts requires an understanding of both current and future risks. Risk information forms the basis for prioritizing different risk reduction measures. By highlighting trade-offs between policy options, indicators and visualization tools guide investment and development decisions. Risk assessments are important disaster and climate risk management tools for identifying and quantifying potential impacts and prioritizing mitigation measures. Geographic information systems (GIS) are instrumental in identifying assets at risk. Sharing hazard and risk information is critical for assessing potential hazards and identifying the vulnerabilities of different urban communities and sectors. Building on this, innovative approaches to managing capital and risk, including risk financing and transfer mechanisms, can reinforce fiscal resilience and make better use of public and private capital.

Emergency and disaster planning is crucial: Risk can never be totally eliminated. Emergency response, continuity, and recovery planning are ways to buffer the impact, easing the reconstruction and recovery process after a disaster. Investments in early warning systems are among the most cost-effective measures that any country can undertake. An integrated warning system consists of scientifically designed and located sensors, a facility for analyzing data and making decisions about warnings, the warning message, dissemination capacity, and a public educated to understand the message and take appropriate action.

Financial approaches to urban disaster resilience should reduce the negative impacts of disasters on individuals and communities, the private sector, and public entities. They allow for an increase in financial response capacity after disasters and reduce the economic and fiscal burden of disasters by transferring excess losses to private capital and insurance markets. While the primary clients of disaster-risk financing programs have traditionally been national governments, cities and local governments can also build up their resilience through principles and instruments that apply widely.

Looking Forward

To prepare effectively to respond to disasters, it is helpful for preparedness planners to:

- Take the rapid expansion of urban built-up areas as an opportunity to incorporate resilience at the outset as they build and manage new settlements as part of standard urban planning. The aftermath of a natural disaster often gives decision makers an opening to push through corrective and preventive actions. Resilience goes beyond risk migration; it increases not just preparedness but also capacity to respond to a disaster and swiftly recover from it. Resilience has to be part of everyday urban development, medium- and long-term

Building Urban Resilience • http://dx.doi.org/10.1596/978-0-8213-8865-5

investment and planning, urban governance, and hazard management. This report makes recommendations on how to enhance resilience, particularly in critical infrastructure and the social realm.

• Invest in sustainable risk information systems and analytical tools that allow for systemic and evidence-based understanding and communication of risk. Quantifying the impacts of planned or proposed investments is critical to reduce risk.

• Integrate risk assessment and cost-benefit analysis within a dynamic decision making process in order to incorporate resilience into urban investments. This requires (a) technical tools to perform risk assessment and cost-benefit analyses; (b) institutional arrangements for incorporating these analyses into decision making; (c) political will to adopt institutional tools for risk assessment; and (d) the capacity of all stakeholders to be able to access and use risk information and tools effectively.

• Identify consistent quantitative tools to evaluate public investments in order to make sound budgetary and investment decisions. Integrating risk-based methods into cost-benefit approaches makes it possible to consider the probable impacts of climate change and disasters by quantifying the economic consequences of these events. Among these tools are
  – risk assessment,
  – risk-based land use planning,
  – urban ecosystem management,
  – urban upgrading,
  – community and stakeholder participation,
  – disaster management systems,
  – data gathering, analysis, and application, and
  – risk financing and transfer approaches.

References

IPCC (Intergovernmental Panel on Climate Change). 2012. *Managing the Risks of Extreme Events and Disasters to Advance Climate Change Adaptation*, by C. B. Field, V. Barros, T. F. Stocker, D. Qin, D. J. Dokken, K. L. Ebi, M. D. Mastrandrea, K. J. Mach, G.-K. Plattner, S. K. Allen, M. Tignor, and P. M. Midgley. Special Report of Working Groups I and II of the Intergovernmental Panel on Climate Change, Cambridge University Press, Cambridge, U.K.

Jha, A., and H. Brecht. 2011. *An Eye on East Asia and Pacific.* Building Urban Resilience in East Asia, Issue 8. Washington, DC: World Bank. http://siteresources.worldbank .org/INTEASTASIAPACIFIC/Resources/226262-1291126731435/EOEA_Abhas_ Jha_April2011.pdf.

Lall, S. V., and U. Deichmann. 2009. "Density and Disasters: Economics of Urban Hazard Risk." Policy Research Working Paper 5161, World Bank, Washington, DC.

Montenegro, M. 2010. "Urban Resilience." *Seeds Magazine*, February 16. http://seedmagazine.com/content/print/urban_resilience/.

Revkin, A. 2011. "Dot Earth." *New York Times* (blog), August 30. http://dotearth.blogs.nytimes.com/author/andrew-c-revkin.

United Nations. 2009. *World Urbanization Prospects: The 2009 Revision*. New York, NY: UN Department of Economic and Social Affairs, Population Division.

UNISDR (United Nations International Strategy for Disaster Reduction). 2011. *Global Assessment Report on Disaster Risk Reduction: Revealing Risk, Redefining Development*. Geneva. http://www.unisdr.org/we/inform/publications/19846.

Upton, S., and M. Ibrahim. 2012. "Resilience in Practice." Programme Briefing Paper, Practical Action, Rugby, U.K. http://practicalaction.org/resilience-in-practice.

World Bank. 2012. *Cities and Flooding. A Guide to Integrated Urban Flood Risk Management for the 21st Century*. Washington, DC: World Bank/IBDR. http://www.gfdrr.org/gfdrr/urbanfloods.

CHAPTER 1

Principles of Urban Resilience

Key Points

- *Resilience* is the ability of a system, community, or society exposed to hazards to resist, absorb, accommodate, and recover from the effects of a hazard promptly and efficiently.
- *Residual risk and uncertainty* have to be managed in a way that is both flexible and robust, using design solutions that build on investments in risk information, strategic communication, cross-sectoral coordination, and a well-planned response and recovery strategy.
- *The urban poor* are particularly vulnerable to the impacts of climate change and natural hazards due to the location of their homes and livelihoods and the lack of reliable basic services.
- *The phases of disaster risk management*—mitigation, preparedness, disaster, response, recovery, and reconstruction—each offer practical opportunities to enhance resilience.
- *Risk mitigation* is part of the resilience approach. With the general aim of increasing preparedness and the capacity to respond to a disaster and swiftly recover from its impacts, resilience goes beyond mere mitigation.
- *Risk* can be reduced by reducing the exposure and vulnerability of people or assets that are linked to their geographical location, the structure of the built and natural environment, operational and institutional arrangements, and management of the fiscal impacts of natural hazards.
- *Social resilience* is the capacity of individuals within a community or society to cope with and adapt to disturbances or changes.
- *Land use planning and ecosystem management* are relatively low-cost "no-regrets" approaches to managing disaster risks effectively, especially for small- and medium-sized urban centers that lack resources and capacity.
- *The resilience of urban infrastructure and services* is critically important for emergency response and the quick recovery of a community and its economy. The design of critical systems needs to take into account the possibility of failure through redundant and backup measures so that they can deal with failure in ways that are least damaging to the society.

- *Risk information* provides a basis for prioritizing risk reduction measures. Sharing hazard and risk information with stakeholders is critical in managing the risks facing urban communities and sectors.
- *Creating an enabling environment* for communities to participate and make decisions based on adequate risk information and tools fosters the collective resilience of an urban system.

Key Resources

Section	Resource
Urban Disaster Resilience	*Natural Hazards, Unnatural Disaster: The Economics of Effective Prevention.* World Bank 2010.
Risk, Uncertainty, and Complexity	Lall, S. V., and U. Deichmann. "Density and Disasters: Economics of Urban Hazard Risk." Policy Research Working Paper 5161, World Bank 2009.
Disaster Risk Management and Opportunities for Resilience	*Improving the Assessment of Disaster Risks to Strengthen Financial Resilience: A Special Joint G20 Publication by the Government of Mexico and the World Bank.* World Bank 2012. *Hyogo Framework for Action 2005–2015: Building Resilience of Nations and Communities to Disasters.* UNISDR 2006.
Social Resilience	*Climate Resilience and Social Change: Operational Toolkit.* World Bank 2011.
Land Use Planning	"The Role of Land-Use Planning in Flood Management: A Tool for Integrated Flood Management." *APFM Technical Document No. 12, Flood Management Tools Series.* World Meteorological Association 2008.
Urban Ecosystems	*NYC Green Infrastructure Plan.* New York City Department of Environmental Protection 2010.
Urban Upgrading	*Climate Change, Disaster Risk, and the Urban Poor: Cities Building Resilience for a Changing World.* World Bank Urban Development Series. World Bank 2011.
Incorporating Resilience into the Project Cycle	Jha, Abhas, and Henrike Brecht, "Building Urban Resilience in East Asia," *Eye on East Asia and Pacific,* Issue 8. World Bank 2011.

Urban Disaster Resilience

Resilience is the ability of a system, community, or society exposed to hazards to resist, absorb, accommodate to, and recover from the effects of a hazard promptly and efficiently by preserving and restoring essential basic structures (UNISDR 2011b). A resilient community is one that can absorb disturbances, change, reorganize, and still retain the same basic structures and provide the same services (Resilience Alliance 2002). As a concept, *resilience* can be applied to any community and any type of disturbance: natural, man-made, or a combination of the two. Disaster resilience can be seen as a public good that builds an appropriate amount of redundancy into urban systems and encourages communities to plan how to deal with disruptions.

In practice, finding ways to operationalize resilience is not easy (Upton and Ibrahim 2012). Addressing disaster risk in the context of resilience encourages urban planners to look at the many impacts of disasters and build the long-term capacity of communities to both adapt to and cope with uncertain risks. The goal is for communities to prepare for an earthquake as much as they prepare for a drought or flooding. By breaking urban resilience down into four components, *infrastructural, institutional, economic,* and *social,* underlying issues can be addressed and capacity can be deepened. While this report addresses all components of disaster resilience, the focus is on the infrastructure and social aspects.

Components of Urban Disaster Resilience

Infrastructural	Institutional	Economic	Social

- *Infrastructural resilience* refers to a reduction in the vulnerability of built structures, such as buildings and transportation systems. It also refers to sheltering capacity, health care facilities, the vulnerability of buildings to hazards, critical infrastructure, and the availability of roads for evacuations and post-disaster supply lines. Infrastructural resilience also refers to a community's capacity for response and recovery.
- *Institutional resilience* refers to the systems, governmental and nongovernmental, that administer a community.
- *Economic resilience* refers to a community's economic diversity in such areas as employment, number of businesses, and their ability to function after a disaster.
- *Social resilience* refers to the demographic profile of a community by sex, age, ethnicity, disability, socioeconomic status, and other groupings, and the profile of its social capital. Although difficult to quantify, social capital refers to a sense of community, the ability of groups of citizens to adapt, and a sense of attachment to a place (Cutter, Burton, and Emrich 2010).

The following sections set the context for integrating resilience into urban areas and summarize the guiding principles. Techniques and tools for building and enhancing resilience are discussed in chapter 2.

Risk, Uncertainty, and Complexity

Drivers of risk, such as rapid urbanization, environmental degradation, development-related processes, and the effects of climate change, shape and configure hazards. The shift of populations from rural to urban areas is largely driven by economic opportunity. Development in high-risk areas, such as hillside slopes, floodplains, or subsiding land, is often uncontrolled, with the poor and the vulnerable settling in hazardous areas because they are more affordable. In extreme cases, vulnerable populations living in slum settlements trade off environmental and disaster safety for living in proximity to the economic opportunities urban environments offer (Lall and Deichmann 2009).

Uncertainty is an essential element of any disaster; it refers to disaster impacts that cannot be quantified or are completely unknown. To cope with uncertainty cities need a robust approach to decision making. This means taking into account potential weak spots and system failures and preparing for a wide range of futures rather than focusing on optimal design solutions.

Climate change adds an additional layer of uncertainty. The 2012 Special Report of the Intergovernmental Panel on Climate Change (IPCC) on Managing the Risks of Extreme Events and Disasters to Advance Climate Change Adaptation states that "long-term trends in normalized losses have not been attributed to natural or anthropogenic climate change" (IPCC 2012, 9). In the foreseeable future, population and asset growth in hazardous areas will be by far the biggest driver of fatalities and damages from extreme weather events.

Urban infrastructure refers to the systems and services that are critically important for emergency response and the quick recovery of a community and its economy. The design and maintenance of these systems—water, sanitation, energy, communications, and transportation—need to take into account the possibility of failure, and find ways to operate through redundant and backup measures so they are able to shut down gracefully in a way that is least damaging to the society. Traditional cost-benefit analysis, for instance, does not work well for dealing with catastrophic tail risk. A different approach is needed, one that focuses on robust design and builds on investments in risk information, strategic communication, cross-sectoral cooperation, and well-planned response.

The ability to be flexible to adapt to disturbances both known and unknown is central to a resilient system. In planning for disasters there is always an element of uncertainty that requires redundancy in system design. Enhancing resilience relies on having enough redundancy and flexibility to continue providing for essential needs given known and future risks and uncertainty. Poor urban planning often sets minimum critical needs as the objectives of any project. However, given the degree of uncertainty linked to disasters, such an approach often fails to meet those critical needs, whereas resilience approaches go beyond them.

The need for redundancy and alternatives increases with the size and complexity of an urban area. The complexity of urban infrastructure increases exponentially as population and density expand. As an urban area grows, the transportation available will quickly reach capacity and cannot address the basic community needs. After a disaster, this can lead to cascading or co-location failures.

• *Cascading failures* occur in a series in which specific system components overload and fail. Major electrical blackouts are typical cascading failures. Disasters can cause several components to fail simultaneously, triggering the *cascade*. Cascading failures can also jump from one system to another—failure of the electrical grid can cause major traffic disruptions and destroy communications, compounding the disaster.

- *Co-location failures* occur when a catastrophic failure of one lifeline, such as a water main, undermines or otherwise affects neighboring utilities, such as gas mains, power cables, or road infrastructure.

Resilience goes beyond risk mitigation in order to enhance capacity. Due to land use pressures, complex failures are difficult to mitigate. Redundancy planning and designing for failure during the early stages of development of an urban region is ideal but can be difficult to achieve in practice. Resilience measures can be perceived as reducing the efficiency of urban systems and increasing costs. Helping communities to understand the long-term cost savings of resilience is central to addressing issues of risk and uncertainty. Box 1.1 describes steps in enhancing resilience for the water, food, and transport sectors.

Box 1.1 Enhancing Resilience in an Urban Region: Examples

1. Identify and prioritize the most important needs for the region, the sector, or the system concerned. For example:
   - *Potable water* might be the most crucial need after a disaster. Food is generally a lower priority, although still crucial, especially for the elderly, children, pregnant women, and the sick.
   - *Refrigeration* may be a critical need in terms of food—without power, inventory sufficient for days or even weeks can be lost within a day or so. Ensuring relatively modest but highly reliable electric power at major warehouses enhances resiliency.
   - *For the highway department,* there may be a few critical links (e.g., bridges, mountain passes) whose failure will cause major disruption. Understanding where important links are and why they may be vulnerable is a valuable step toward enhanced resiliency.
2. Identify ways to better meet these needs. To the maximum extent feasible, reducing vulnerabilities by strengthening, relocating, or building in redundancy is highly desirable. Because resources are scarce, vulnerabilities typically can only be reduced *as low as reasonably possible* (the ALARP principle). Even so, to reduce uncertainty, resilience can be enhanced by using alternative approaches in parallel, such as
   - *Potable water:* Educate people about its necessity, how to conserve water, and ways to purify questionable water; and identify technologies, stockpile equipment, and make plans for portable water purification and distribution.
   - *Refrigerated food:* Identify major warehouses and help them to upgrade backup power generators and fuel supplies; make emergency plans for replenishing their fuel quickly after a disaster.
   - *Highway department:* Identify alternative ways to re-establish the disrupted link. For example, when the Bay Bridge in San Francisco was out of service for 30 days after the 1989 Loma Prieta Earthquake, temporary ferry service was established to get commuters to work.

Disaster Risk Management and Opportunities for Resilience

All governments have an obligation to protect their citizens. Because local govern-ments are the first institutions to respond to disasters, they have a particular obligation to reduce risk and build resilience within their communities (UNISDR 2011b). For city and municipal governments, this means guiding where develop-ment takes place; providing safe and affordable infrastructure and services; regu-lating building design and construction; regulating hazardous activities that can lead to disasters; influencing land availability and what can be built where; encouraging and supporting household and community action that reduces risk; and providing adequate disaster early warning, preparedness, and response systems. When urban governments fulfill these roles, risks to their populations and economies are much reduced; urbanization is then associated with much lower risks (Satterthwaite et al. 2007).

Public institutions are accountable for managing and communicating risk. Creating and enforcing the accountability of city and municipal governments to effectively manage and communicate risk can be challenging, in part because it requires a perspective that stretches beyond elected terms. Authorities must balance a multiplicity of competing economic, political, and social interests, for example, whether to protect mangroves that buffer storm surges or allow indus-trial development in coastal areas; or whether to try to control population movements to high-risk sites or to direct incentives and infrastructure invest-ments to guide population movements toward safer sites (Satterthwaite et al. 2007). Some decisions and resources also are beyond local control, at regional or national levels, or beyond their jurisdiction.

A combination of measures is needed to ensure that local government is accountable for the safety of its citizens, namely:

- *Adoption and enforcement of a legal and institutional framework*—including performance goals—for disaster and climate-related risk management, in cooperation with civil society, the private sector, and regional and national governments.
- *Promotion of meaningful participation by community* and other interest groups in the design, delivery, and monitoring of disaster and climate-related risk management, including the use of such tools as social audits. Box 1.2 gives an example from the Philippines.
- *Clear delineation of the responsibilities* of all levels of government and civil society actors for disaster and climate-related risk management.

The disaster risk management framework offers many opportunities for enhanc-ing resilience. Disaster risk management (DRM) relies on the coordination of different sectors. Measures adopted should be guided by the principles set out in the Hyogo Framework for Action (HFA), accepted by 168 countries. A comprehensive DRM strategy is based on five pillars: (a) identifying, assessing, and monitoring risk; (b) reducing risk through prevention and mitigation measures;

Box 1.2 Increasing Accountability in the Philippines

The Mindanao Summit on Disaster Risk Reduction and Geo-Hazard Awareness in Cagayan do Oro City was called by two Philippines Government senators after a devastating tropical storm hit Mindanao and nearby areas. It brought together a range of government and civil society stakeholders to discuss how to reduce disaster risks. They identified specific legislative, communication, planning, and response priorities for disaster risk reduction, among them creation of a disaster response and an accountability rating system for local government units.

Source: Mindanao Declaration on Disaster Risk Reduction Priorities 2012.

Figure 1.1 The Six Phases of the Disaster Cycle

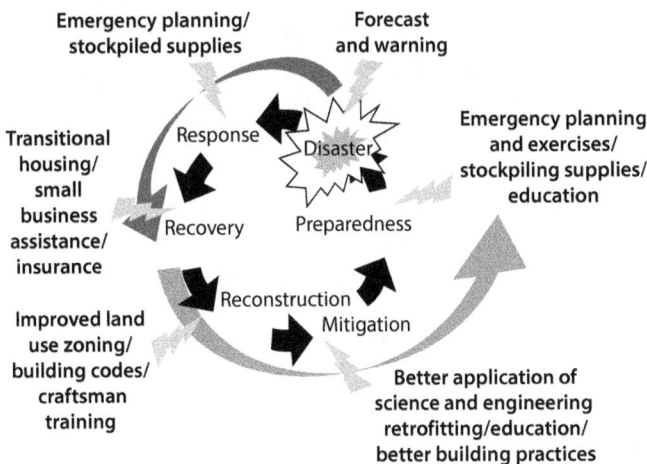

(c) disaster risk financing and insurance; (d) emergency preparedness; and (e) post-disaster response, recovery, and reconstruction that reduces risk from future events (World Bank 2012b).

From the perspective of urban planning, decision makers face a trade-off between adequate preparedness and the potential future costs associated with response, recovery, and reconstruction after a disaster. The aftermath of a natural disaster often provides an opportunity for decision makers to take corrective and preventive actions. A World Bank report on the economics of natural disasters presents empirical evidence of large returns from preventive measures (World Bank 2010). Throughout this handbook, the resilience tools and sectoral practice are geared toward the long-term mitigation and planning component of the disaster cycle, depicted in figure 1.1.

Analyzing disasters in terms of the disaster cycle identifies opportunities to break the chain of causation to build up disaster resilience. It is useful, however, to bear in mind that the cycle is only a schematic representation; in reality phases may take place in parallel.

In the *Mitigation Phase*, strengthening community ties, social organizations, and the economic base enhances resilience. Learning from the lessons of previous disasters encourages present and future urban development and growth that is sustainable.

The *Preparedness Phase* focuses on getting ready for the next disaster. Typical activities are disaster and evacuation planning, training and exercises, and stockpiling of supplies. Box 1.3 provides an example of the earthquake drills that are regularly conducted in California.

In the *Disaster Phase*, warnings and evacuation help to reduce losses and prepare the community to respond more quickly. Warnings not only allow people to seek shelter for personal safety but, if the warning period allows, also permit quick movement of valuable goods, foodstuffs, animals, and vehicles to safer locations.

The *Response Phase* may last hours to weeks, depending on the scale and type of disaster and the capacity of the areas affected. This phase focuses on people through rescue operations, public health precautions, shelter arrangements, and food distribution. Interventions are made only to prevent major destruction: containing fires and release of hazardous materials, emergency repairs to prevent further infrastructure failures, and restoration of crucial services, such as emergency communications.

The *Recovery Phase* can last months, depending on the size and scale of the disaster. In this phase, social and economic functions are restored, using temporary measures as needed. Communities are moved out of temporary structures into

---

Box 1.3 The Great California Shake-Out

In November 2008 the largest earthquake drill in U.S. history to that date took place; it had 5.3 million participants. The drill, organized by the Earthquake Country Alliance, took place in homes, businesses, schools, places of worship, and communities across the state. Week-long events connected Southern California communities with preparedness resources and gave residents the information and knowledge they needed to prepare for, respond to, and recover from a disaster. The drill is now an annual event—in 2009 it attracted 6.9 million participants, and in 2011 more than 8.6 million Californians plus another 800,000 people in Oregon, Nevada, Idaho, Guam, and British Columbia. Encouraged by live drill broadcasts on more than 55 California radio and television stations, participants simultaneously practiced the "Drop, Cover, and Hold On" drill recommended by experts as essential for avoiding injury and even death during a major earthquake.

Source: The Great California Shake-Out n.d.

semi-permanent housing, schools are reopened, and community organization is restored. At this point, noncritical as well as critical infrastructure is rebuilt so the economy can begin to function again.

The *Reconstruction Phase* fully restores what was lost, to the extent possible, and typically takes months to years. The transition from emergency responders to normal government agencies occurs early in the phase. In most disasters, residential housing reconstruction is crucial for addressing long-term needs of the community. Central decision making tends to remain in place to restore permanent infrastructure and economic sectors, but residential housing presents complexities, such as resettlement in hazard-free zones, payment for private reconstruction, and setting and applying construction standards. Introducing new building technologies in response to pressure to rebuild quickly makes *building back better* more difficult. In extraordinary cases, a special government agency may be created, such as the Queensland Reconstruction Authority described in box 1.4.

Disaster Risk Information and Mitigation

Sharing data and creating open systems promotes transparency and accountability and ensures that a wide range of actors enhance resilience. As a knowledge institution, the World Bank has a mandate to share its information freely, widely, and in accessible ways.

Risk information provides the basis for prioritizing risk reduction measures. Indicators and visualization tools can highlight trade-offs between various policy options and guide investment and development decisions. The Open Data for Resilience Initiative (OpenDRI), led by the Global Facility for Disaster Reduction and Recovery (GFDRR) in partnership with the World Bank and other development institutions, aims to reduce the impact of disasters by empowering decision makers with better information and the tools to support their decisions.

Box 1.4 The Queensland Reconstruction Authority

In Queensland, Australia, after the 2010/2011 floods the Queensland Reconstruction Authority (QldRA) was formed for a term of two years. The QldRA's mission was to reconnect, rebuild, and improve Queensland communities and the economy. It was vested with the power and authority to take charge of the reconstruction process and facilitate interaction between state and local line departments in coordination with local councils. This approach ensures that reconstruction will continue to be part of normal government business for the line departments concerned. The QldRA also supports local councils in pushing forward their own recovery and development agendas within the broader state reconstruction policy, especially with regard to disaster mitigation, reconnecting the community, and rebuilding the local economy. This approach not only promotes ownership by local councils and their constituents, it will also empower them to incorporate resilience into future planning and investment decisions.

Source: World Bank/Queensland Reconstruction Authority 2012. More information about the Queensland Reconstruction Authority: http://www.qldreconstruction.org.au/.

Figure 1.2 illustrates the virtuous cycle of improving risk information for better decision making.

Figure 1.2 Open Data for Resilience Cycle

Better decisions · Better data · Better tools and analytics

Smarter management of information within a city's institutions can greatly enhance decision making capacity and therefore resilience. There is a critical need for systems at the city level to manage and share geospatial data and information associated with technical disaster and climate risk studies. The main objective of data-sharing is to promote open and efficient exchange of information between government stakeholders. The OpenDRI approach promotes creation of tools to assist with sharing data and enabling resilient decision making.

A core task of the urban public sector is the collection of information that is relevant to urban planning and management—producing credible information on hazard risk and making it easily available to all stakeholders (Lall and Deichmann 2009). Full openness of data has many benefits; however, it can be recognized as a continuing process that evolves through discussion between government stakeholders and their constituents. Opening access to information allows more stakeholders, academic institutions, individual citizens, and the private sector to incorporate risk reduction elements into their decision making. This increases collective resilience and supports city authorities in creating and then disseminating risk information.

Risk is the probability of an event with negative consequences—in other words, the likelihood of an uncertain amount of loss or damage in a given period. Disaster risk is a function of hazard,[1] exposure, and vulnerability. While some perceive vulnerability as the opposite of resilience (Bahadur, Ibrahim, and Tanner 2010, 5), they can be distinguished as follows: resilience refers to the capacity of systems to absorb, buffer, and recover from shocks; vulnerability refers to the susceptibility of people and assets to damage or losses due to certain conditions, such as poor living conditions. Vulnerability is linked to exposure; the location of people or economic assets creates conditions for vulnerability, such as the quality of housing standards. Figure 1.3 depicts the elements of risk calculation.

Figure 1.3 Elements of Risk Calculation

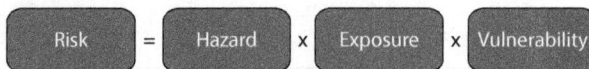

Risk = Hazard x Exposure x Vulnerability

Building Urban Resilience · http://dx.doi.org/10.1596/978-0-8213-8865-5

Disaster impacts can be mitigated using risk reduction approaches directed to location, structure, operational capacity, and fiscal strength and exposure (see figure 1.4).

- *Locational approaches* avoid hazards through land use planning or resettlement.
- *Structural approaches* increase resistance by hazard-proofing buildings, retrofitting, and refining building codes.
- *Operational approaches* focus on contingency and emergency planning, such as arranging for temporary evacuation.
- *Fiscal approaches* include risk financing and transfer mechanisms, such as contingent financing, budget relief, and other instruments and services to share or transfer financial exposure through public or private entities.

Figure 1.4 Elements of Risk Reduction

| Locational | Structural | Operational | Fiscal |

Chapter 2 provides information about tools to increase resilience. Chapter 3 explains how to use these tools in key sectors.

Locational Mitigation

Locational mitigation physically avoids the impacts of natural hazards. When natural hazards occur in a geographically defined manner so that their likely location can be defined, population and assets can be guided to safer areas where disaster impacts are lower or nonexistent. *Land use planning* and *ecosystem management* are relatively low-cost approaches to managing disaster risks effectively, especially for small and medium urban centers that lack resources and capacity. The most common modality for the locational approach is *hazard mapping for land use planning*. Though mapping hazards does require a significant investment of scarce resources, international organizations or national geologic agencies can assist in the process and help build local capacity.

Hazard maps can take many forms, depending on hazard definition; for instance a given locality might have unique multi-hazard maps. Flood hazard maps are the most common type of hazard map, but many countries have also begun to map earthquake faults, seismic liquefaction zones, landslide potential, tsunami inundation zones, cyclone storm surge zones, and volcanic hazards. In urban areas development projects should consider hazard identification and mapping as part of project technical work, taking into consideration land use policies. Maps need to be widely disseminated and used to support land use policies. Community-directed household, settlement and/or city surveys are useful in helping communities to look at their own situations and consider their priorities, as well as providing government and other external providers with detailed community level data and hazard maps (d'Cruz and Satterthwaite 2005; UN-HABITAT 2010).

Another modality of the locational approach is *building in redundancy*. Infrastructure projects should enhance the reliability of redundant facilities within complex systems, as by having two water tanks or water treatment plants at different sites, rather than one large tank or plant. Having excess water or power capacity is not wasteful if it makes the systems more reliable—the costs of outages are far greater than would be a modest investment at the time of construction. Redundancy is most effective when geographically dispersed.

Structural Mitigation

Addressing mitigation from a structural perspective deals with the physical impacts of natural hazards. Natural hazards are physical phenomena whose forces and energy can to some extent be physically managed. Traditional structural mitigation has dealt with resisting forces like earthquakes in buildings via structural *bracing, frames,* or *shear walls*. More recently, reducing forces rather than resisting them has emerged as a viable alternative. Earthquake forces are reduced by the technique of *base isolation* by placing the structure on a series of flexible foundations like rubber pads, which isolate the building from motions in the ground beneath the pads. Another technique for reducing forces is *enhanced structural damping*, which is analogous to shock absorbers in an automobile. When building displacements caused by ground motions are damped to acceptable levels, damage is avoided. Structural approaches are not limited to dealing with earthquakes or winds. Floods have traditionally been mitigated by building levees and floodwalls, which hold back or resist floodwaters. *Flood-proofing* buildings and elevating them above the floodplain, check dams, holding ponds, bypasses, and wetland buffers are other structural approaches to reducing rather than resisting flood impacts.

Structural approaches are most effective when they are addressed during initial design and construction using a thoughtful combination of local building practices, such as land use regulations and building codes that address modern design technologies. When the original design does not address hazard risk, *retrofitting*, although it can be expensive, can be an option for structural mitigation. Given the time and resource limitations of replacing building stock with new structures that address hazards, cities often choose to invest in retrofitting critical public structures, such as schools, hospitals, and fire stations. In the long term, structural mitigation is most effective when urban authorities build their capacity to understand risks and incorporate what they know into urban infrastructure through building codes and land use regulations.

Operational Mitigation

Rather than permanent structural or locational mitigation, operational mitigation uses temporary measures to reduce the impact of specific disasters. Because natural hazards cannot be prevented, it is usually not possible to foresee all potential damage. Operational capability to respond is necessary.

The most common modalities for operational mitigation are *emergency plans* and *disaster management systems*, which typically

- Define critical functions in order to maintain their continuity.
- Assign responsibility for specific actions at projected times and places where capabilities are exceeded.
- Define lines of authority and relationships.
- Show how actions will be coordinated.
- Describe how people and property will be protected.
- Identify resources for response and recovery operations.
- Address mitigation concerns during response and recovery activities.

Since risks cannot be entirely eliminated or failures prevented, investing in emergency planning, early warning systems, and response capacity cannot be neglected. *Early warning systems* are among the most cost-effective measures any town or country can undertake. Weather services significantly support efforts to reduce disaster risks, alleviate poverty, enhance food security, and protect health. Early warning systems (see figure 1.5) have been used increasingly across the world since the mid-20th century to anticipate tropical cyclones, flash floods, volcanoes, and tsunamis. To make such a system effective, authorities need to train personnel, support emergency planning and exercises, enhance emergency

Figure 1.5 Tsunami Early Warning System

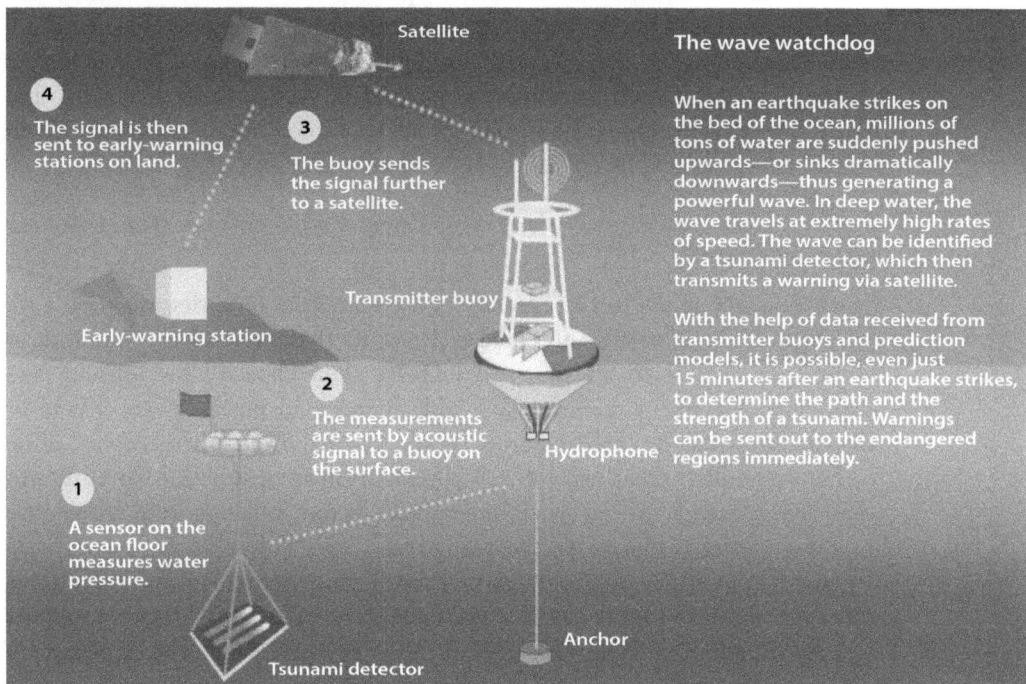

Satellite

The wave watchdog

4
The signal is then sent to early-warning stations on land.

3
The buoy sends the signal further to a satellite.

When an earthquake strikes on the bed of the ocean, millions of tons of water are suddenly pushed upwards—or sinks dramatically downwards—thus generating a powerful wave. In deep water, the wave travels at extremely high rates of speed. The wave can be identified by a tsunami detector, which then transmits a warning via satellite.

Transmitter buoy

Early-warning station

With the help of data received from transmitter buoys and prediction models, it is possible, even just 15 minutes after an earthquake strikes, to determine the path and the strength of a tsunami. Warnings can be sent out to the endangered regions immediately.

2
The measurements are sent by acoustic signal to a buoy on the surface.

Hydrophone

1
A sensor on the ocean floor measures water pressure.

Anchor

Tsunami detector

Source: Der Spiegel/NOAA.

Building Urban Resilience · http://dx.doi.org/10.1596/978-0-8213-8865-5

communications systems, and improve the emergency response and logistical capabilities of all stakeholders. Often coordinated by a dedicated emergency operations center, these measures are best undertaken routinely so that prepared-ness is entrenched before a disaster.

Fiscal Mitigation

Disasters place a significant fiscal burden on governments, businesses, house-holds, and individuals. They are considered a contingent liability because directly and indirectly disasters can undermine the economic development of communities and countries (World Bank 2012b). After a disaster, quick access and the ability to disburse funding to affected communities is of vital impor-tance. In the immediate aftermath and the early recovery phases, ex ante financing mechanisms can be used, such as budget reserves, contingent credit lines, and transfer mechanisms like catastrophic risk insurance, risk pools, weather derivatives, and catastrophe bonds. For the recovery and reconstruc-tion phases, governments typically mobilize funds through deficit spending, tax increases, spending cuts, and loans.

Financial approaches to urban resilience can spread disaster risk to soften the impact of a disaster. Policy makers should strive to create a comprehensive plan for dealing with disaster risk that addresses high-impact low-probability events as well as medium- and low-impact high-frequency events. The choice of finan-cial instruments would correspond to specific disaster phases: relief, recovery, and reconstruction. The area's socioeconomic situation and the products available on national and international markets also shape selection of the mix of risk instru-ments. While traditionally the primary clients for disaster risk financing are national governments, city and other local governments can also reinforce their resilience by using such principles. In chapter 2, section "Risk Financing and Transfer Approaches" provides further information on disaster risk financing and insurance.

Social Resilience

Social resilience refers to the capacity of a community or society to cope with and adapt to disturbances and changes. It covers the ability of communities to self-organize, adjust to stresses, and increase their capacity for learning and adaptation. A resilient community is able to respond positively to change or stress and maintain its core functions. People affected by an emergency are often the first responders and the most critical partners in reconstruction. Any attempt to build resilience thus has to consider social factors, utilizing local knowledge and networks for managing and reducing risk.

Efforts to quantify and create a methodology to score a country's relative resilience tend to break social resilience into two separate components (Cutter, Burton, and Emrich 2010). The first explains the amount of participation and engagement of communities and the second the demographic distribution of the entire society. The first component will rely on indicators like political engagement and participation in elections, while the second will take into account demographic indicators like sex and age distribution, socioeconomic status, ethnicity, and disability. For our purposes, these components have been combined into a single group that explains traditional social development themes and goals. Table 1.1 lists major challenges in integrating social resilience into urban projects. A more comprehensive description can be found in section "Community and Stakeholder Participation" of chapter 2.

The most cost-effective, useful, and sustainable urban investments in building social resilience are those that meet basic development or poverty reduction needs while simultaneously reducing vulnerability to disasters (Pasteur 2011; Pelling 2010; Venton 2010). The urban poor are particularly vulnerable to climate change and natural hazards as a result of where they live within cities and their lack of reliable basic services (World Bank 2011). Collaboration between local governments and citizens has been found to substantially reduce the costs of risk reduction, ensure local acceptance, and build social capital (UNISDR/ILO/UNDP 2010). The benefits can extend to general improvements in urban governance, infrastructure, and services.

Within urban governments, social resilience is well-suited to be integrated into project cycles because it parallels social development goals. To maximize the chances that investments in building sustainable resilience will be successful, urban planners must understand the relationships and institutions that protect against and encourage adaptation to the shocks and hazards urban areas face.

Government and donor-financed projects can support effective participation and help build social resilience at both neighborhood and municipal levels. Projects should promote and enhance community and stakeholder participation to the extent possible, regardless of whether the proposed investment focuses on the community or the government. While it is still difficult to include stakeholders at the community level effectively, a number of strategies have been tested. The sections below summarize how promotion of social resilience will

Table 1.1 Challenges in Integrating Social Resilience

Stakeholder/community participation	Vulnerable and marginalized populations
• Limited awareness of the impact of disaster risk and climate change. • No priority given to reducing disaster risk and adapting to climate change. • Lack of political will within local government units. • Vested political or commercial interests. • Poor coordination between local government units, civil society organizations, and private stakeholders. • Limited resources. • No support for participatory decision making and local resilience planning.	• Competing priorities. • Lack of legitimacy and trust. • No history of collective organization. • Discrimination within communities. • Gender inequality.

Box 1.5 Combining Resources to Reduce Flood Impacts

In Quelimane City, Mozambique, local informal communities partnered with the City Council and several international organizations (Cities Alliance, World Bank, DANIDA, UNICEF, WaterAid) to work on upgrading communities that are particularly affected by cyclical floods because of a high water table and heavy rains. City and communities worked together to formulate a participatory urban development strategy for informal neighborhoods, where about 80 percent of the population live, with special attention to water and sanitation conditions.

The participatory planning process led to joint action to improve conditions in densely populated peri-urban slum belts. The City Council made an in-kind contribution of US$100,000 by providing office space, equipment, a meeting room, technical/administrative staff, and vehicles. The community provided an in-kind contribution of US$150,000 by providing subsidized labor, conducting awareness campaigns, forming operational management teams, and reducing plot sizes or, in extreme cases, moving to another area. UN-HABITAT, the World Bank, DANIDA, UNICEF, and WaterAid together contributed US$440,000 in cash and in kind. Other in-kind contributions totaling US$30,000 were secured from a state water supply institution and a private firm that made its trucks available on weekends in exchange only for payment for the fuel and the driver.

The results achieved through these combined efforts included a City Council that was better equipped to work with informal settlements; construction of two community centers; cleaning of 10 km of drainage channels with 1 km paved; widening and improvement of 20 km of unpaved roads; installation of 10 new water points in the most densely populated areas; and construction of 20 rainwater collection systems and four public lavatories—all mainly through planned labor-intensive activities. The endeavor also produced greater government and community awareness of water, sanitation, and drainage maintenance issues and improved planning for sanitation and expansion of the water supply network to densely populated peri-urban slum belts.

Sources: Jha et al. 2011, 20, 21; UN-HABITAT n.d.

---

produce better results, lower costs, and improve the livelihoods of poor and vulnerable populations. Box 1.5 provides an example of a participatory process in Mozambique.

Better Results

Enhancing the social resilience of urban areas helps governments to achieve urban development goals. It has often been demonstrated that prioritizing social development produces better results that are more sustainable. In 2005 the World Bank reviewed 2,507 projects in nine thematic portfolios and found a strong positive association between social development themes and project success. Projects that addressed at least one social development theme were rated 3–4 percent higher on outcome, sustainability, and institutional development impact than the average of all Bank projects over a 30-year period. Projects that addressed multiple social development themes concurrently performed even better. The study also highlighted that subnational institutions were central to long-term sustainability, noting the role of local government and community institutions (World Bank 2005a, xiv, xv).

When diverse stakeholders collaborate on project planning, design, and implementation they produce more options and create a better platform for decision making. International experience also has shown the importance of bringing local government units, civil society organizations (CSOs), and the local private sector in on efforts to make cities more resilient to natural hazards and climate change. While local communities often already have grassroots adaptation strategies, local government units and organizations may not be familiar with using urban resilience strategies in a broader context. Interventions to reinforce physical infrastructure, service delivery, or government capacity for disaster risk reduction and climate change adaptation have the biggest impact when implemented in partnership with communities (World Bank 2011, 11).

Without government support, there are limits to what household and community action can do to reduce disaster risk. Much of what is needed to reduce risk in low-income urban communities depends on financing or providing infrastructure that residents cannot provide alone, such as road networks and a full range of health care services. The scale and range of what CSOs can achieve are significantly increased when they work with government agencies (Moser and Satterthwaite 2010, 246).

When local communities and businesses are not consulted and not involved in urban investment projects, efforts to build resilience can become fragmented and even counter-productive. In extreme cases, poor planning and communication have even led to popular protests and riots, as was seen with the privatization of many urban water systems in the 1990s (Pelling and Wisner 2009).

Lower Costs

There is considerable evidence that building up social resilience is cost-effective. Communities and local businesses that can see the potential benefits of a project are more likely to support it by entering into cost-sharing arrangements. One study on community-based and community-driven development found such projects generally had better outcome ratings than other types of projects and helped lower the cost to government of delivering infrastructure (World Bank 2005b, xii). This is an especially important consideration for local government units that have limited financial and management capacities.

There are also significant potential benefits from combining investments in physical infrastructure with investments in building household and community resilience. A 2008 cost-benefit study of flood and drought risk reduction in urban and rural locations in India, Nepal, and Pakistan found approaches that took a people-centered resilience-driven flood risk reduction approach had cost-benefit ratios that ranged from 2 to 2.5 in both current and future climate change scenarios (Khan et al. 2008, 1–2). The study concluded that the most economically effective risk reduction strategies were those to increase the resilience of livelihoods, housing, and other infrastructure at the household and community level (Khan et al. 2008).

Improved Outreach to the Poor and Vulnerable

Urban infrastructure projects improve the livelihood of poor and vulnerable populations by building up the relationship between at-risk populations and government stakeholders. Poor and vulnerable populations are most at risk from disasters and climate change. The creation of opportunities for communities, local businesses, and CSOs to engage with local government can bring about better-informed and more appropriate policy decisions. When communities and other stakeholders are engaged in their own governance, they have more capacity to shape mitigation and adaptation measures to the shocks, whether from natural hazards or other causes (see also Twigg and Bottomley 2011). Conversely, people who are not able to engage in governance are more likely to be negatively impacted by forces outside their control (Venton 2010).

The disproportionately high adverse impact of disasters on women is well-documented. Gender analysis of all proposed urban interventions is essential to assess how men and women will be differently affected and to identify actions to promote the full and active participation of both genders in project decision making and equal access to project benefits. Gender-sensitive programming recognizes the conditions that allow women, men, boys, and girls to fully contribute to building resilience to disasters and climate change, thereby benefitting both households and the entire community.

Land Use Planning

Risk-based land use planning identifies the safest areas in order to prioritize immediate investments in urban development and infrastructure projects. Land use plans influence the location, type, design, quality, and timing of development. Mainstreaming risk-based land use planning in infrastructure projects reduces risk in the rapidly urbanizing centers that are prevalent in hazard-prone areas and exposes where high concentrations of population and economic assets are at risk. Risk-based land use plans must inform all infrastructure projects.

Historically, urban centers have been located in naturally hazardous zones. Cities have arisen at sites of agricultural surplus, such as fertile volcanic soils, or along major trade and transportation routes, such as coasts and river systems that are prone to flooding and coastal erosion (Dilley et al. 2005); they are often located on seismic faults. Close to 650 million people in dense urban centers in East and South Asia, Central America, and Western and South America are exposed to geophysical and hydrometeorological hazards (Dilley et al. 2005). High densities of population and economic assets increase losses during catastrophic events. Climate change is said to exacerbate these risks while also creating new risks in zones previously considered safe.

Land use planning efforts have not responded to rapid urban growth and the spatial expansion that is exposing more people and economic assets to disasters. More than half the global population now lives in urban centers; fastest-growing are small and medium urban centers in low- and middle-income countries (UNECOSOC 2009). While the urban population is expected to double by 2025, land settled in urban areas is expected to triple by then (Angel, Sheppard, and Civco 2005). Land use planning spatially directs projected growth by allocating zones for specific uses that meet stated community socioeconomic goals. In practice, however, the typically long planning cycles in low- and middle-income countries do not garner political support; land use plans are prepared by technical experts without effective community consultation; and land use plans are rarely implemented fully because most municipalities have limited technical capacity and resources to invest in land and infrastructure. Consequently, the plans follow rapid urban growth rather than direct it; and unplanned developments (often informal settlements on hazard-prone sites) are common and increase hazard risk. For example, unplanned land development can heighten flood risk by increasing impervious surfaces and consequent water runoff (see box 1.6), besides extending habitation beyond flood defenses (Jha et al. 2011). Intensified urban energy consumption and the heat island effect associated with spatial expansion also contribute to climate change.

Land development based on promises that large engineering works will offer safety from episodic risks can instead exacerbate disaster risks. Traditionally, development ignores the hazard characteristics of land and assumes that large engineering works will ensure safety for future residents. Since urban land values are high, it is common for development to occur on floodplains, wetlands, steep slopes, and seismic fault lines. For example, in the U.S. city of New Orleans, which has been historically susceptible to floods and hurricanes, the $200 billion in losses from Hurricane Katrina is largely attributed to expansion onto former wetlands that were deemed safe through the construction of levees; in fact, levee failures contribute to about a third of all flood disasters in the United States (Burby 2006).

Risk-based land use planning can reduce both episodic and everyday risks. While risks from catastrophic events like earthquakes and volcanic eruptions may not be predictable, relatively small and frequent events that cause localized damage though few injuries and deaths constitute a considerable proportion of hazard risks (Bull-Kamanga et al. 2003). Analysis of detailed records of 126,000 hazardous events in Latin America showed that 99 percent of the events reported accounted for 51.3 percent of housing damage (UNISDR 2009). Small hazards can turn into disasters if many people occupy hazard-prone areas, critical infrastructure is inadequate, and so is emergency response. While it is important to plan large structural measures to contain risk from catastrophic events, locating development safely through land use planning can reduce risks from

---

Box 1.6 Urbanization and Flood Risk

Urban expansion, particularly in flood-prone areas, alters the path of natural water-courses, increases impermeable surfaces that reduce rainwater infiltration, and increases overland flows beyond the capacity of drainage systems. Poor sanitation and solid waste management in most cities in developing countries exacerbate health risks when there are floods. The figure below illustrates the differences in infiltration in rural and urban areas.

Change in watershed characteristics after urbanization

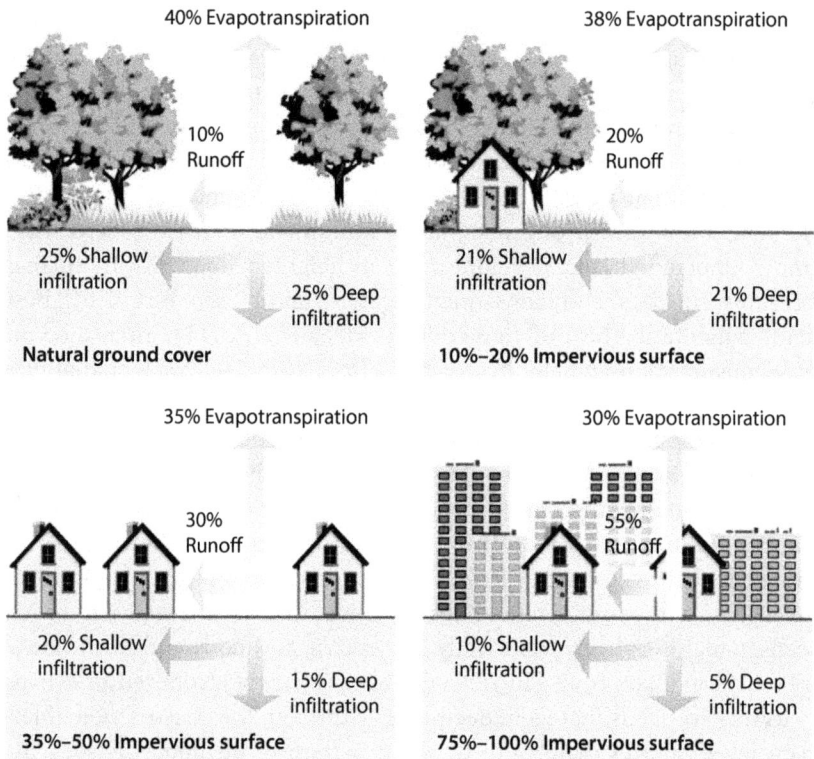

40% Evapotranspiration

10% Runoff

25% Shallow infiltration

25% Deep infiltration

Natural ground cover

38% Evapotranspiration

20% Runoff

21% Shallow infiltration

21% Deep infiltration

10%–20% Impervious surface

35% Evapotranspiration

30% Runoff

20% Shallow infiltration

15% Deep infiltration

35%–50% Impervious surface

30% Evapotranspiration

55% Runoff

10% Shallow infiltration

5% Deep infiltration

75%–100% Impervious surface

Source: Jha et al. 2011.

---

both episodic events and frequent everyday events; a study of National Flood Insurance Program claims and payments in the U.S. showed that state governments that had comprehensive planning requirements reduced losses from flooding (Burby 2006).

The HFA for disaster resilience emphasizes the need to incorporate risk reduction into urban planning. Its priority area 4 identifies the need for risk-based land use planning and building codes in urban infrastructure projects to reduce risk factors.

Building Urban Resilience • http://dx.doi.org/10.1596/978-0-8213-8865-5

Urban Ecosystems

From an ecological perspective, an urban area is its own fully functioning ecosystem. An ecosystem is defined as a biological community of interacting organisms and their physical environment, a concept that clearly applies to urban areas. The major difference between our traditional understanding of ecosystems and one that covers urban areas is that the physical environment in cities has human-made as well as natural elements that are affected not only by the natural environment but also by culture, personal behavior, politics, economics, and social organization. The urban ecosystem thus contains both individual and nested systems from three spheres: the natural, the built, and the socioeconomic environments (see figure 1.6).

Urban planners need to incorporate natural ecosystem services into urban infrastructure and resilience projects. Urban ecosystems are intertwined systems of natural and man-made services so that it can be difficult to understand how new infrastructure will impact natural systems. Urban planners can work with local stakeholders and experts to attempt to understand positive externalities, like ecosystem services, that may not be fully understood. The goal is not to stop new infrastructure projects but to ensure that the complexity of an urban ecosystem is recognized in government and donor-supported projects.

To formulate policies and programs that build resiliency and promote sustainable development, systems need to be dynamically balanced as well as integrated. Issues like biological diversity, water filtration, soil depletion, and deforestation must be dealt with as part of issues like sewerage, water supply, transportation, social/political institutions, and norms and values. This means that because urban ecosystem management is multidisciplinary it requires a composite of social, environmental, economic, and decision making tools and institutions that are flexible enough to adapt to changes in one or several systems. An integrated urban ecosystem approach generates information for policy makers so that trade-offs and synergies between options (in terms of social, economic, and ecological values) can be addressed at various spatial, temporal, and management scales (UNU/IAS 2003).

Pro-Poor and Community-Focused Ecosystem Management

The poor are forced to draw upon the natural resources within and around cities because of structural and institutional problems. These include inadequacies in governance structures, land tenure arrangements, and access to financial resources. As noted, many of the urban poor live in informal settlements located in less desirable and consequently more hazardous locations. In search of living space, biofuels for cooking or sale, and water for daily needs, they uncover and degrade the landscape (UNU/IAS 2003). The lack of public health resources adds to their difficulties; in low-income countries public health spending averages just 1 percent of gross domestic product (GDP), compared to 6 percent in high-income countries (IFRC 2002).

Building Urban Resilience • http://dx.doi.org/10.1596/978-0-8213-8865-5

Figure 1.6 The Human Ecosystem

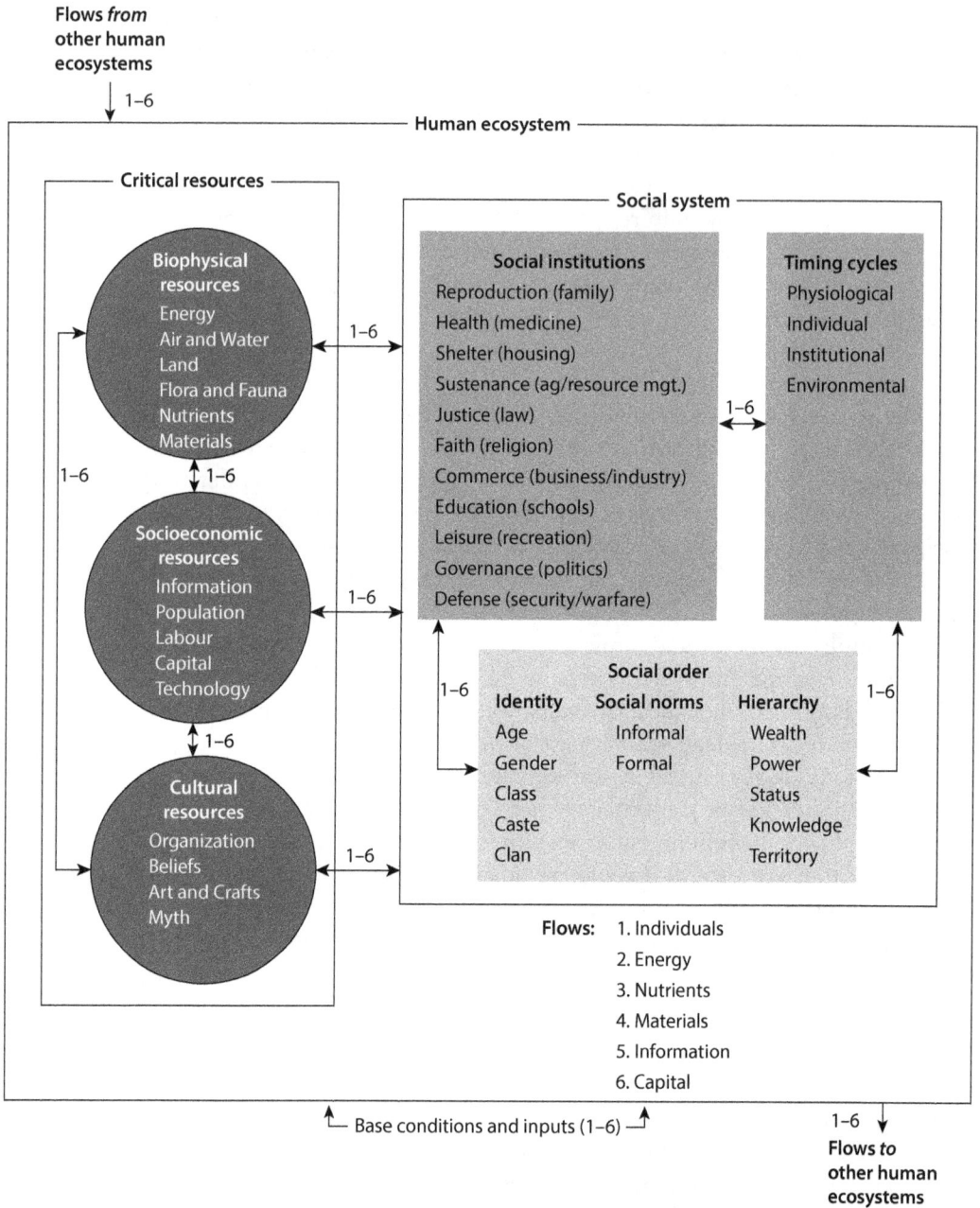

Flows *from* other human ecosystems

1–6

Human ecosystem

Critical resources

Biophysical resources
Energy
Air and Water
Land
Flora and Fauna
Nutrients
Materials

1–6

Socioeconomic resources
Information
Population
Labour
Capital
Technology

1–6

Cultural resources
Organization
Beliefs
Art and Crafts
Myth

1–6

1–6

Social system

Social institutions
Reproduction (family)
Health (medicine)
Shelter (housing)
Sustenance (ag/resource mgt.)
Justice (law)
Faith (religion)
Commerce (business/industry)
Education (schools)
Leisure (recreation)
Governance (politics)
Defense (security/warfare)

Timing cycles
Physiological
Individual
Institutional
Environmental

1–6

Social order

Identity	Social norms	Hierarchy
Age	Informal	Wealth
Gender	Formal	Power
Class		Status
Caste		Knowledge
Clan		Territory

1–6

1–6

Flows:
1. Individuals
2. Energy
3. Nutrients
4. Materials
5. Information
6. Capital

Base conditions and inputs (1–6)

1–6
Flows *to* other human ecosystems

Source: Machlis 2008.

In order to be successful and equitable, ecosystem management must be linked to poverty reduction. Urban infrastructure projects need to address the trade-offs between conservation, livelihoods, and equitable distribution of resources. Historically there has been tension when conservation models that create protected areas are perceived as inaccessible to communities. Often, these models are implemented at the expense of poor and marginalized residents and users of resources from the areas. Social, economic, and environmental development programs have become impediments to sustainable development because there is no balance between the need to protect ecosystem services and the desire to use resources to address community needs. Communities need to be allowed to identify and negotiate their own options and to increase their flexibility to cope with unexpected change (White et al. 2010).

Community-centered approaches to ecosystem management recognize that human impact and activities are elements of any urban area. Initiatives directed to achieving environmental protection and allowing humans to benefit from natural resources are considered more sustainable (see box 1.7).

Box 1.7 Using Vegetation to Limit Landslide Hazards in Seattle

Intense precipitation and steep slopes mean that landslides are a common hazard in Seattle, Washington, and the impacts on transportation systems can be heavy. Landslides are also a secondary hazard from earthquakes and volcanic activity. In the 1990s, a city government study found that a lack of vegetative cover was a major cause of slope instability, and new regulations were added to the Seattle Municipal Code pertaining to maintenance and restoration of vegetation.

The starting point of this project was a landslide map of Seattle that showed detailed information on landslide susceptibility, and a database of 1,400 landslides in the City of Seattle over the previous 100 years. This provided an evidence base for decision making and drafting of policy for resilience against landslides. These policies are now embodied in the Seattle Municipal Code. The Regulations for Environmentally Critical Areas specify use of vegetation on steep slopes and their buffer zones, and further mandate that construction methods should minimize the disruption of vegetation. Removal of trees or vegetation requires city approval; there must be a tree and restoration plan that uses native vegetation.

Stakeholder Engagement: Seattle's Department of Planning and Development enforces the regulations on the use of vegetation in landslide-prone areas. However, the data to identify hazard areas and effective prevention measures were identified collaboratively by local, state, and national governments, together with research institutes and consultants. During the research phase, public outreach was conducted to gather citizen opinions on the scientific approach to hazard mapping. The studies arising from the U.S. Geological Survey Seattle Landslide Project were made available to the public, particularly to communities interested in working on landslide reduction. Since 1997, workshops on landslide hazards and mitigation have been held for Seattle residents and developers. The workshops discuss the causes of landslides, proper drainage for sloping sites, and how to maintain vegetation on slopes.

box continues next page

Box 1.7 Using Vegetation to Limit Landslide Hazards in Seattle *(continued)*

The Department of Planning and Development also produces Client Assistance Memos that detail the regulations affecting property owners and developers, particularly where grading is necessary for constructing roads.

The Client Assistance Memo on "Environmentally Critical Areas: Vegetation Restoration" gives step-by-step instructions on designing and effecting vegetation restoration projects (assessment of location, preparation of a plan, choosing the plants, preparing the site, planting, monitoring, and maintenance). It is emphasized that the ecological function of mature trees should be considered, and removal of tree canopy cover should be avoided when possible.

Lessons learned:

1. The development of a landslide hazard map and a database of historical landslide events provided a systematic knowledge base for determining where policies should be applied to manage risk.
2. The hazard to be mitigated (here, landslides causing destruction of infrastructure and disrupting the road network) was discussed fully with the community before the green infrastructure regulations were presented.
3. Stakeholder engagement and dissemination of policies in the Seattle Municipal Code through useful Client Assistance Memos ensured that developers were familiar with the city's green infrastructure regulations for increasing landslide resilience.
4. Collaboration with the U.S. Geological Survey and private consulting firms made it possible to use the best available data, methods, and experts from both the private and the public sectors.

Source: GRaBS 2010.

Issues of Governance

The political economy of land use and ownership, which is often marked by vested interests, creates tension between the economic, commercial, environmental protection, and social equity objectives of land use planning. In all land systems some actors stand to benefit from extending control over land and natural resources, often to the detriment of others, usually the poor and the vulnerable. Addressing vulnerability and promoting disaster resilience can therefore be perceived as threatening by government agencies or vested professional, commercial, and other interests (UN-HABITAT 2010). All levels of government need to balance these competing interests and ensure that ecosystem management planning is informed by socioeconomic, political, and stakeholder analyses (see figure 1.7).

In recent years a number of governments and international agencies have taken a land governance approach to urban policy development and planning. Land governance refers to the process by which decisions are made about access to and use of land and how conflicting interests are reconciled. A land governance approach to urban planning takes into account the different institutions and stakeholders that affect land use patterns. This information is then combined with risk analysis and land use planning to inform a general strategy for urban ecosystem management. Risk, land use, and community participation are discussed in chapter 2.

Figure 1.7 Competing Interests in Land Use

Social justice

Property conflict   Development conflict

Land

The resource conflict

Economic growth   Environmental
and efficiency   protection

Source: UN-HABITAT 1999, citing D. Campbell, 1999.

Urban Upgrading

Urban upgrading prioritizes the infrastructure, housing, livelihoods, and social networks of the most vulnerable households living in slum settlements. Strategic upgrading can manage disaster risks by (a) regulating slum development in hazard-prone areas; (b) reducing losses by planning evacuation routes and community refuges; and (c) promoting safe and socioeconomically viable low-income neighborhoods as part of a city-wide plan.

In fast-growing cities, poor planning for low-income households creates slum conditions that transfer a disproportionate burden of disaster risk to the poor. Most slum settlements are not planned, slum structures are not durable, and they tend to be located on hazard-prone sites because those are relatively inexpensive. The urban poor live in areas they can afford—close to work and where they have kinship ties—and that is usually in slums[2] (see UN-HABITAT 2003), which have the worst urban environmental conditions. Insecure tenure and sociospatial exclusion also reduce the access of slum residents to disaster information and financial assistance (IIED n.d.; Lall and Deichmann 2009). Urban centers contribute to climate change by generating significant greenhouse gas (GHG) emissions from economic activities, transportation, and energy usage (Lall and Deichmann 2009); paradoxically, the urban poor who consume minimal urban resources and contribute least to global warming bear the brunt of its hazards.

The benefits of urban economic densities outweigh the exposure of large numbers of urban poor to disaster risks (Lall and Deichmann 2009). The rural poor move to urban centers in large numbers for higher-wage livelihoods (Lall and Deichmann 2009). Migrants find accommodation in slum pockets, reinforcing the formation and persistence of slums; a third to half of the urban population in low-middle-income countries lives in slums (Kinyanjui 2010). Slums form when a city is unable to provide affordable housing for migrants seeking better economic opportunities. Colonial legacies of land use and housing regulations in most cities in developing countries have been inappropriate; a chronic lack of housing development finance, public or private, skews urban land markets and drives up the price of housing. Density regulations, such as low floor area ratios (FAR) and minimum development and housing standards that are expensive, restrict the supply of land and housing for low-income households (Nallathiga 2003). Consequently, chronic housing scarcities have given entrepreneurs opportunities to collude with real-estate developers, politicians, and local officials to profit from selling to the urban poor, at considerable cost to them, a notion of security against immediate eviction by "allowing" them to squat on or illegally develop vacant urban sites that are hazardous and without services. In Mumbai, India, it is estimated that 60 percent of the population live in slums that occupy only 8 percent of the land area (MCGM n.d.).

For the urban poor, everyday hazards attributed to climate change can become high-impact disasters (Bull-Kamanga 2003; see table 1.2). In slums

Table 1.2 Urban Poverty, Everyday Hazards, and Disaster Risks

Poverty aspect	Everyday risk	Disaster risk
Inadequate and often unstable income; deprivation of basic necessities; indebtedness.	Very limited capacity to pay for housing; living where environmental health risk is very high.	Location on hazard-prone sites, exacerbated by lack of infrastructure and services.
Inadequate safety net; lack of property, skills, savings, and social networks to ensure basic survival and of access to housing and health care during periods when they have no income.	Very limited capacity to cope with financial and health stresses or shocks in everyday life.	Very limited capacity to recover from disasters in terms of food and water, homes and livelihoods; lack of documentation to access post-disaster support; no insurance.
Housing constructed of temporary materials, often insecure and overcrowded, on dangerous sites.	High risk of physical accidents, fires, extreme weather, and infectious diseases.	At risk from storms/high winds, earthquakes, landslides, floods, fires, and epidemic disease.
Inadequate infrastructure: water supply, sanitation, drainage, roads, footpaths, etc.	High level of risk from contaminated water and flooding from lack of drainage.	Lack of protection from flooding; lack of roads, footpaths, and drains inhibit evacuation.
Inadequate basic services: schools, vocational training, health care, emergency services, public transport, communications, and police.	Unnecessarily high health burden from diseases and injuries because of lack of health care and failure of emergency response.	Lack of health care and emergency services to provide rapid response to disaster.
Limited opportunity to negotiate in public projects.	Inappropriate development investments.	Little support for low-income groups to build back better.

Source: Adapted from IFRC 2010.

that lack drainage infrastructure heavy rainfall may become a disastrous flood. For example, in six cities in Bangladesh, more than 50 percent of slum clusters were typically flooded in the monsoon season (Center for Urban Studies 2006). Destruction or damage to infrastructure can lead to water scarcity, contamination, and spread of disease. Lack of access roads can prevent relief efforts from reaching affected households. Lack of income and access to safe housing with adequate water supply, sanitation, health care, and education affects the capacity of slum residents to recover (IFRC 2010).

Variations in slum conditions create different degrees of risk. While some slums are located on hazard-prone sites and lack basic services, others are planned but residents lack security of tenure. Slums are formed as a consequence of neighborhood deterioration, squatting, unplanned development of urban villages,[3] or illegal subdivision of vacant sites (UN-HABITAT 2003). Slum locations dictate access to and type of livelihoods, urban land values, tenure status, housing conditions, mobility, and social capital, as well as access to basic services, all of which make the urban poor more vulnerable to disasters.

Reducing risk for the poor should be a priority in all urban infrastructure investments. Households in informal settlements generally do not benefit from public investments in essential infrastructure (UNISDR 2011a). Given the large numbers of urban poor, the need for upgrading can far exceed the capacity of a local government to undertake comprehensive measures that would prioritize slum upgrading. However, it might be possible to offer incentives for private sector and community engagement that would both reduce disaster risks and expand the supply of affordable housing to prevent formation of new slums, and new risks. The Mayor's Task Force on Climate Change, Disaster Risk and the Urban Poor launched at the United Nations Climate Change Conference in Copenhangen in 2009 urged a focus on disaster risks for the urban poor and provided a forum for policy development and strategic investments.

Incorporating Resilience into the Project Cycle

It is crucial to place resilience at the core of project planning, particularly in regions that are developing rapidly. This handbook emphasizes incorporating resilience from the start into urban investment projects. All projects go through a cycle, and most organizations use variations of the same core phases. Figure 1.8 shows the World Bank's project cycle as an example of the core process and table 1.3 gives examples of how resilience can be incorporated into each phase.

Project interventions are intended to reduce poverty and increase welfare; sustainably manage the environment and natural resources; and reduce disaster risk and improve recovery management. The Philippines offers an example of a Country Assistance Strategy (CAS) that addresses reduction of disaster and climate risk (see box 1.8).

Building Urban Resilience • http://dx.doi.org/10.1596/978-0-8213-8865-5

Figure 1.8 World Bank Project Cycle

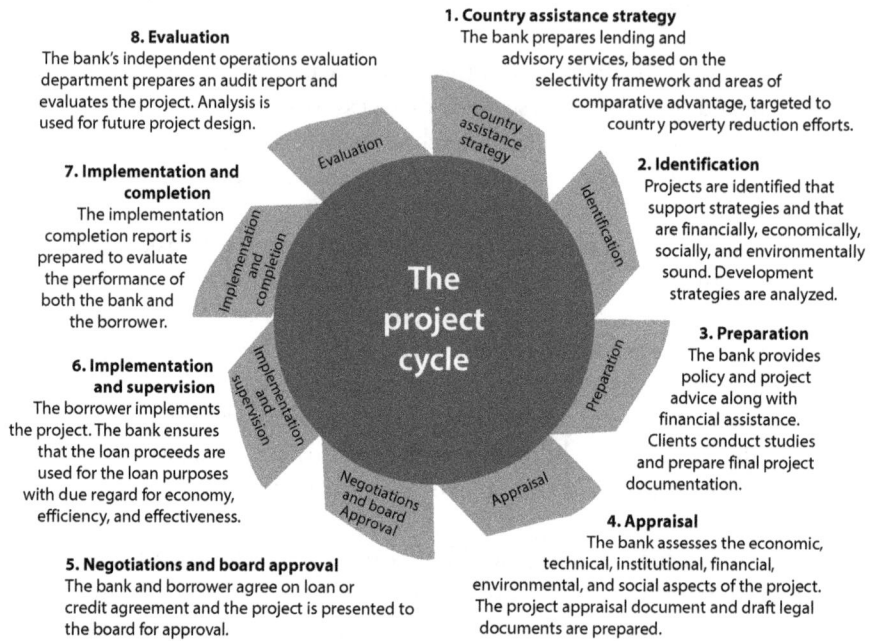

1. Country assistance strategy
The bank prepares lending and
advisory services, based on the
selectivity framework and areas of
comparative advantage, targeted to
country poverty reduction efforts.

8. Evaluation
The bank's independent operations evaluation
department prepares an audit report and
evaluates the project. Analysis is
used for future project design.

**7. Implementation and
completion**
The implementation
completion report is
prepared to evaluate
the performance of
both the bank and
the borrower.

2. Identification
Projects are identified that
support strategies and that
are financially, economically,
socially, and environmentally
sound. Development
strategies are analyzed.

**6. Implementation
and supervision**
The borrower implements
the project. The bank ensures
that the loan proceeds are
used for the loan purposes
with due regard for economy,
efficiency, and effectiveness.

3. Preparation
The bank provides
policy and project
advice along with
financial assistance.
Clients conduct studies
and prepare final project
documentation.

**The
project
cycle**

4. Appraisal
The bank assesses the economic,
technical, institutional, financial,
environmental, and social aspects of the project.
The project appraisal document and draft legal
documents are prepared.

5. Negotiations and board approval
The bank and borrower agree on loan or
credit agreement and the project is presented to
the board for approval.

Source: World Bank n.d. "Projects Website."

Indicators for Monitoring and Evaluation

Although there have recently been a number of high-profile efforts to find
indicators for components of disaster resilience, the most consistent and effective
indicators are produced within urban infrastructure projects. Most of these
efforts have ignored urban areas to focus either on country-level resilience or on
very small areas. Two new indexes, the *Social Vulnerability Index* and the *Resilience
Capacity Index*, though so far only applied in the United States, have been
successful at monitoring disaster resilience and may be useful in understanding
what indicators might be useful for evaluating urban infrastructure projects.

Though individual indicators can be helpful for monitoring and evaluation,
they are not necessarily sufficient in themselves for evaluating projects that
enhance urban resilience. Though single indicators cannot describe all the
components of urban resilience, indicators like *Sheltering Capacity* or *Number of
Hospital Beds* help greatly in understanding the state of resilience in a given area
and evaluating how a community will respond to a disaster. For this reason, it is
suggested that urban planners formulate practical indicators for each infrastructure
project.

Urban planners can base urban resilience indicators on the risk assessment and
the risk-based land use plan. These often provide helpful data, though being
hazard-specific most will address only a small area of urban resilience. Urban
planners should try to create indicators geared to a market basket of hazards so

Table 1.3 World Bank Project Cycle: Opportunities for Enhancing Resilience

Project phase	Opportunities for enhancing resilience
Country Assistance Strategy (CAS) or Country Partnership Strategy (CPS)	The CAS/CPS is the master plan for formulating individual projects, each of which contributes to meeting the goals of the master plan during a given period, normally 3–4 years. Because the CAS is the foundation on which everything else is built, it offers powerful opportunities for enhancing resilience. For example: To place a high value on resilience, the CAS/CPS policy statement might stress redundancy, avoidance of co-location, and performance- or risk-based design for physical projects. In the social realm, it might give priority to education and development of human capital to promote resilience, decentralized decision making, and adaptive management. At this stage a national disaster risk assessment should be drafted to serve as a fundamental criterion guiding the CAS, which would recognize the social and economic impacts of potential disasters on a country.
Identification	Using the social and economic impacts recognized in the national risk assessment, in this phase are specified disaster-related infrastructure or other projects that can readily reduce disaster risk, such as flood, storm, and tsunami warning and planning systems; erecting flood levees; and building earthquake resistance into existing buildings and infrastructure. In this phase *all* projects would be required to employ performance- or risk-based design for mitigating disaster risk.
Preparation	In this phase are performed the studies and ground work on which are based the Project Concept Note, Terms of Reference, Performance Objectives, and other project-specific documents. Disaster-specific projects (e.g., levees) should be designed to ensure that they will actually reduce disaster potential. Other projects (e.g., highway construction or a regional health program) can enhance disaster resilience by considering (a) whether the project might also have a disaster reduction role (e.g., can the highway serve as a flood levee? or be used for evacuation?; can disaster medicine be incorporated into the health program?) and (b) how disasters might affect the project (could it be destroyed?) and what cost-effective measures can be incorporated to reduce this risk, such as exceeding minimum requirements for earthquake design, elevating buildings above likely flood level, or placing electrical and other equipment on or above the second floor to avoid flood damage. Possible economic resilience measures in project design might be contingent emergency components that accord with World Bank Operational Policy 8.0 Operation Rapid Response to Crises and Emergencies.
Appraisal	At this point project preparations are reviewed to assure that they are both consistent with the CAS/CPS and cost-beneficial. In terms of resilience the questions might be: Has the project considered disaster resilience? Is it vulnerable to disasters? If so, are planned mitigation measures sufficient and cost-effective?
Negotiations and Board Approval	This phase consists of an audit and confirmation of what has been done to this point, with inquiries similar to the Appraisal phase.
Implementation and Supervision	Provisions in the project performance documents can be crafted to ensure that mitigation and resilience-enhancing measures are executed effectively.
Implementation and Completion	As the project ends, the questions become: Did the project consider disaster resilience? If it was vulnerable to disasters, were the mitigation measures sufficient and cost-effective?
Monitoring and Evaluation	Here the final question is asked: Is there a program to maintain resilience and mitigation measures?

Source: World Bank n.d. "Projects Website."

Box 1.8 Country Assistance Strategy in the Philippines

The Country Assistance Strategy (CAS) is a three-year plan the World Bank draws up with a country's authorities for allocating support according to country priorities. The 2010–12 CAS for the Philippines outlines four strategic objectives, one of which is to reduce vulnerability. The CAS gave priority to three areas: (a) social protection; (b) disaster risk management and climate change; and (c) stability and peace. As part of disaster risk management and climate change, the following goals were identified:

Outcome 1: Reduction of disaster- and climate change–related risks. The Philippines is extremely vulnerable to natural disasters due to a high incidence of severe weather—especially floods, typhoons, and drought—and a large number of earthquakes and active volcanoes. The effects of global climate change are likely to exacerbate this inherently high disaster risk. The resultant human and economic costs are significant; estimates suggest that every year natural disasters cost the Philippines 0.5 percent of gross domestic product (GDP). The country has thus begun to adopt more intensified strategies for disaster risk management and climate change adaptation so as to (a) build up local preparedness and adaptation by improving planning capacity, knowledge, and understanding of measures to reduce disaster risk, such as adaptation to climate variability; (b) reduce farmer vulnerability to crop risk by supporting innovative solutions, such as weather risk insurance to help small farmers cope with economic losses from disasters; and (c) improve national and local disaster risk financing strategy by helping identify instruments and establish new financing windows for preparedness, response, and recovery. The World Bank supports these initiatives through Global Facility for Disaster Reduction and Recovery (GFDRR) technical assistance for formulating better disaster risk management and climate change strategies; new financing instruments, such as a Catastrophe Deferred Drawdown Option (Cat-DDO); and Global Environmental Facility (GEF) grant-funded activities, including a possible climate change adaptation project that would integrate climate risk management into national and local agriculture and natural resource management planning and would demonstrate cost-effective adaptation measures. These measures might be expanded to other vulnerable sectors or regions, such as coastal areas, where an integrated coastal zone management approach could help reduce vulnerability to natural disasters and other hazards while promoting sustainable livelihoods and reducing poverty.

Outcome 2: Greenhouse gas emissions are reduced through expansion of mitigation programs in key sectors and local government units. While the Philippines is only a minor emitter of greenhouse gases, it is committed to pursuing cost-effective solutions for reducing emissions. The emergence of new mitigation financing instruments—particularly the Carbon Partnership Facility and the Clean Technology Fund—opens up potential for mitigation programs in areas like renewable energy, reducing air and water pollution, and solid waste management. Building on the experience and successes of Bank-supported mitigation projects in the Philippines, such as geothermal, wind, and wastewater treatment projects, that have already committed to reducing emissions by about 2 Mt CO_2e, opportunities will be pursued in the power, transport, and waste management sectors. In cooperation with other development partners, the World Bank will help the Philippines to mobilize sources of international financing.

Source: World Bank n.d. *Country Assistance Strategy for the Republic of the Philippines for 2010–2012.*

Table 1.4 Disaster Resilience Indicators

Social resilience	Economic resilience	Institutional resilience	Infrastructure resilience	Community capital
• Age • Educational equity • Transportation access • Communicatizxon capacity • Language competency • Special needs • Health coverage	• Housing capital • Employment • Income and equality • Single sector employment dependence • Employment • Business size • Health access	• Mitigation • Flood coverage • Municipal services • Political fragmentation • Previous disaster experience • Mitigation and social connectivity	• Housing type • Shelter capacity • Medical capacity • Access/evacuation potential • Housing age • Sheltering needs • Recovery	• Place attachment • Political engagement • Social capital—religion • Social capital—civic involvement • Social capital—advocacy • Social capital—innovation

Source: Adapted from Cutter, Burton, and Emrich 2010—variables used to construct disaster resilience index by sub-components.

that they better explain resilience (see table 1.4). It is probable that not all indicators will be collected during a single urban infrastructure project, but it is important to encourage better data collection. Table 1.5 shows examples of resilience components in World Bank projects.

Concluding Remarks

The rapid expansion of urban built-up areas offers an opportunity to develop and manage new settlements so that at the outset resilience is incorporated into urban planning. Resilience goes beyond risk migration; it increases preparedness and the capacity to respond swiftly to a disaster and recover from it faster. It has to be part of everyday urban development, medium- and long-term investment and planning, urban governance, and hazard management.

To make effective budgetary decisions, decision makers need consistent and quantitative tools to evaluate public investments. Integrating risk-based methods into cost-benefit approaches makes it possible to consider the impacts of climate change and disasters by quantifying their economic consequences (see chapter 2).

Further Reading

- *Using High Resolution Satellite Data for the Identification of Urban Natural Disaster Risk* (Deichmann et al. 2011).
- *Making Women's Voices Count: Integrating Gender Issues in DRM – set of Guidance Notes* (World Bank 2011).
- *Climate Change, Disaster Risk, and the Urban Poor: Cities Building Resilience for a Changing World.* The World Bank Urban Development Series (World Bank 2011).
- *Cities and Flooding. A Guide to Integrated Urban Flood Risk Management for the 21st Century* (World Bank 2012a).
- *The Role of Land-Use Planning in Flood Management: A Tool for Integrated Flood Management* (World Meteorological Association 2008).

Table 1.5 Resilience Components in World Bank Projects: Examples

Country	Project	Project development objective (PDO)	PDO/results indicators
Indonesia	Third National Program for Community Empowerment in Urban Areas III (P118113)	Assist the government of Indonesia in ensuring that the urban poor benefit from improved socioeconomic and local governance conditions. One of the activities to achieve this objective will be to increase awareness of disaster risk mitigation and mainstream resilience measures.	PDO indicators • Improved access to infrastructure, economic, and social services in agreed % wards (*kelurahans*). • Minimum agreed % satisfaction among beneficiaries with improved local services. • Infrastructure built is % less expensive than that built by noncommunity-based approaches in % of participating wards. • Minimum of agreed % of complaints are resolved. • Number of people in urban areas having access to all-season roads within a 500-meter range. Intermediate results indicators • Minimum of agreed % participation of poorest and vulnerable community members in planning and decision making meetings. • Minimum of agreed % participation of women in planning and decision making meetings. • Minimum of agreed % of the adult population voting in neighborhood Badan Keswadayan Masyarakat elections. • Badan Keswadayan Masyarakat formed in at least % of wards. • Minimum of agreed % of wards with Community Development Plans (CDPs) completed and ratified.
Timor-Leste	Road Climate Resilience Project (P125032)	Built sustainable climate-resilient road infrastructure in the Dili-Ainaro corridor.	PDO indicators • Improvement in climate resilience of the Dili-Ainaro corridor. • Increase in traffic in the corridor. • Reduction in the number of incidents requiring emergency repairs. • Roads in good and fair condition as a share of total classified roads. Intermediate results indicators • Improvement in road conditions in the corridor measured by reduced road roughness. • Number of linear kilometers of road sections with new or improved drainage. • Number of locations with improved slope protection. • Corridor is adequately maintained. • Percentage of national roads in Aileu and Ainaro Districts covered by multiyear. • Performance-based maintenance and first-line emergency response contracts.

table continues next page

Table 1.5 Resilience Components in World Bank Projects: Examples *(continued)*

Country	Project	Project development objective (PDO)	PDO/results indicators
Nepal	Modernization of Rani Jamara Kulariya Irrigation Scheme Phase 1 (P118179)	Improve delivery of irrigation water to and its management in the command area by improving the performance of irrigation systems and strengthening community-based irrigation management. (These activities are essentially about building resilience against such water-related hazards as droughts, floods, and changes in water availability during agricultural seasons.)	PDO indicators • Resources generated by water users for the operation and maintenance of the modernized irrigation systems (percentage of required resources). • Irrigation service delivery by service providers (water user associations, WUA) assessed as satisfactory by users (% of users). • Increase in irrigated yields of rice, wheat, and maize in % of the command area, at the head of the canal systems (metric tons). • Numbers of female and male water users (members of the WUA) provided with improved water delivery. Intermediate results indicators • Completed structures. • Number of executive committee meetings and general assembly meetings held per WUA (annual, not cumulative). • Number of WUA members trained yearly. • Agriculture Service Center and Agriculture Contact Points actively providing advisory services. • Number of farmer field schools and demonstrations implemented yearly.
Kiribati	Kiribati Adaptation Phase III (LDCF) (P112615)	To improve the resilience of Kiribati to the impacts of climate change on freshwater supply and coastal infrastructure.	Intermediate results indicators • Number of groundwater abstraction systems installed and operating in North Tarawa. • Reduction in total volume of nonrevenue water lost through leaks and wastage in zones treated for leakage reduction in South Tarawa (%). • Frequency of water supply of households increased from a daily average of hours in areas treated for leakage/waste reduction. • National Key Performance Indicators on Climate Change Adaptation and Disaster Risk Management are applied and reported. • Functional plans (under the Disaster Management Plan) relevant to public health and potable water drafted and operational.

table continues next page

Table 1.5 Resilience Components in World Bank Projects: Examples *(continued)*

Country	Project	Project development objective (PDO)	PDO/results indicators
Colombia	First Programmatic Fiscal Sustainability and Growth Resilience Development Policy Loan (DPL; P123267)	Enhanced fiscal sustainability and resilience of economic growth. The programmatic DPL operation supports the long-term CPS outcome of improved fiscal, financial, and social risk management within the "inclusive growth with enhanced productivity" CPS theme.	Results indicators • Central government nonoil tax revenue as share of GDP. • Central government fiscal deficit. • Publication of an annual evaluation report detailing implementation of the medium-term debt management strategy. • Reimbursements to health insurance companies from Fondo de Solidaridad y Garantía (FOSYGA) for medical services (procedures and medicines) outside the mandatory benefit package of the contributive regime. • Number of financial instruments implemented to mitigate national disaster risks.
Papua New Guinea	Building a More Disaster and Climate Resilient Transport Sector (P129322)	Improve PNG's resilience to natural disasters and climate change in the transport sector by building capacity for assessing hazard risks affecting the transport sector to minimize service disruptions and improve transport access.	Provisional indicators • A system of disaster risk assessment is in place. • Number of km of roads and bridges analyzed for disaster risks.

Source: Based on World Bank n.d. "Projects Website."

Notes

1. *Hazard,* as defined by the UNISDR, can refer to a "dangerous phenomenon, substance, human activity or condition that may cause loss of life, injury or other health impacts, property damage, loss of livelihoods and services, social and economic disruption, or environmental damage." According to HFA, hazards can arise from a variety of geological, meteorological, hydrological, oceanic, biological, and technological sources, or a combination of these.

2. All urban poor do not live in slums; many residents of well-planned and serviced neighborhoods have incomes that are far below local poverty lines. And not all slum residents are poor; in cities where housing supply is extremely inadequate, because the cost of housing for even middle-income families is unaffordable, they are forced to live in slums (UN-HABITAT 2003). UN-HABITAT defines a slum household as a group of individuals living under the same roof lacking one or more of the following: (a) access to safe water; (b) access to improved sanitation facilities; (c) sufficient living area (not more than three people sharing the same room); (d) structural quality and durability of dwelling; and (e) security of tenure (Kinyanjui 2010).

3. Envelopment of originally rural communities during urban expansion creates developments that have slum-like living conditions because they lack services. Where customary law overlaps with statutory law, the sale of land, although legal, is not formally registered. Such developments may not comply with official development standards.

References

Angel, S., S. C. Sheppard, and D. L. Civco. 2005. *The Dynamics of Global Urban Expansion.* Washington, DC: Transport and Urban Development Department, World Bank.

Bahadur, A. V., M. Ibrahim, and T. Tanner. 2010. "The Resilience Renaissance? Unpacking of Resilience for Tackling Climate Change and Disasters." Strengthening Climate Resilience Discussion Paper 1, Institute of Development Studies at the University of Sussex, Brighton, U.K.

Bull-Kamanga, L., K. Diagne, A. Lavell, E. Leon, F. Lerise, H. MacGregor, A. Maskrey, M. Meshack, M. Pelling, H. Reid, D. Satterthwaite, J. Songsore, K. Westgate, and A. Yitambe. 2003. "From Everyday Hazards to Disasters: The Accumulation of Risk in Urban Areas." *Environment & Urbanisation* 15 (1): 193–203.

Burby, R. J. 2006. "Hurricane Katrina and the Paradoxes of Government Disaster Policy: Bringing About Wise Governmental Decisions for Hazardous Areas." *Annals of the American Academy of Political and Social Science* 604: 171–91.

Center for Urban Studies. 2006. "Slums of Urban Bangladesh: Mapping and Census, 2005." Dhaka.

Cutter, S. L., C. G. Burton, and C. T. Emrich. 2010. "Disaster Resilience Indicators for Benchmarking Baseline Conditions." *Journal of Homeland Security and Emergency Management* 7 (1): Article 51. http://regionalresiliency.org/library/Diaster_Resilience_Indicators_Susan_Cutter_et_al_2010_1281451159.pdf.

D'Cruz, C., and D. Satterthwaite. 2005. "Building Homes, Changing Official Approaches." Poverty Reduction in Urban Areas Series Working Paper 16, International Institute for Environment and Development, London.

Deichmann, U., D. Ehrlich, C. Small, and G. Zeug. 2011. "Using High Resolution Satellite Data for the Identification of Urban Natural Disaster Risk." European Union and the World Bank, Global Facility for Disaster Reduction and Recovery, Washington, DC.

Dilley, M., R. S. Chen, U. Deichmann, A. L. Lerner-Lam, M. Arnold, with J. Agwe, P. Buys, O. Kjekstad, B. Lyon, and G. Yetman. 2005. "Natural Disaster Hotspots: A Global Risk Analysis." Synthesis report, International Bank for Reconstruction and Development/ The World Bank and Columbia University, Washington, DC.

GRaBS (Green and Blue Space Adaptation for Urban Areas and Eco-Towns). 2010. *Adaptation to Climate Change Using Green and Blue Infrastructure: A Database of Case Studies.* Manchester: University of Manchester.

IFRC (International Federation of Red Cross and Red Crescent Societies). 2002. *World Disasters Report 2002: Focus on Reducing Risk.* Geneva: IFRC.

———. 2010. *World Disasters Report 2010: Focus on Urban Risk.* Geneva: IFRC.

IIED (International Institute for Environment and Development). n.d. "Climate Change and the Urban Poor: Risk and Resilience in 15 of the World's Most Vulnerable Cities." G02597, London.

IPCC (Intergovernmental Panel on Climate Change). 2012. "Managing the Risks of Extreme Events and Disasters to Advance Climate Change Adaptation," by C. B. Field, V. Barros, T. F. Stocker, D. Qin, D. J. Dokken, K. L. Ebi, M. D. Mastrandrea, K. J. Mach, G.-K. Plattner, S. K. Allen, M. Tignor, and P. M. Midgley. Special Report of Working Groups I and II of the Intergovernmental Panel on Climate Change, Cambridge University Press, Cambridge, U.K.

Jha, A., and H. Brecht. 2011. *An Eye on East Asia and Pacific.* Building Urban Resilience in East Asia, Issue 8. Washington, DC: World Bank. http://siteresources.worldbank.org/ INTEASTASIAPACIFIC/Resources/226262-1291126731435/EOEA_Abhas_Jha_ April2011.pdf.

Jha, A., J. Lamond, R. Bloch, N. Bhattacharya, A. Lopez, N. Papachristodoulou, A. Bird, D. Proverbs, J. Davies, and R. Barker. 2011. "Five Feet High and Rising: Cities and Flooding in the 21st Century." Policy Research Working Paper 5648, World Bank, Washington, DC.

Khan, F., D. Mustafa, D. Kull, and The Risk to Resilience Study Team. 2008. "Evaluating the Costs and Benefits of Disaster Risk Reduction under Changing Climatic Conditions: A Pakistan Case Study." From Risk to Resilience Working Paper 7, edited by Moench, E. Caspari, and A. Pokhrel, 24. ProVention Consortium; Institute for Social and Environmental Transition; Institute for Social and Environmental Transition, Kathmandu.

Kinyanjui, M. 2010. "Development Context and the Millenium Agenda." In UN-HABITAT, 2003, *The Challenge of Slums: Global Report on Human Settlements 2003.* Chapter 1. Revised and updated version (April 2010). Nairobi: UN-HABITAT.

Lall, S. V., and U. Deichmann. 2009. "Density and Disasters: Economics of Urban Hazard Risk." Policy Research Working Paper 5161, World Bank, Washington, DC.

Machlis, G. E. 2008. "The Structure of Human Ecosystems: Coupled Systems Thinking for Research and Resource Management." Paper presented at the 2008 Weaver Lecture, Auburn University, School of Forestry and Wildlife Sciences, Auburn, AL. http:// www.uiweb.uidaho.edu/hesg/downloads/HESG.08-01.pdf.

MCGM (Municipal Corporation of Greater Mumbai). n.d. http://www.mcgm.gov.in/.

Mindanao Declaration on Disaster Risk Reduction Priorities. 2012. Cagayan de Oro: Mindanao Summit on DRR and Geo-Hazard Awareness, February 19–20.

Moser, C., and D. Satterthwaite. 2010. "Toward Pro-Poor Adaptation to Climate Change in the Urban Centers of Low- and Middle-Income Countries." In *Social Dimensions of Climate Change: Equity and Vulnerability in a Warming World*, edited by R. Mearns and A. Norton. Washington, DC: IBRD/World Bank, pp. 231–259.

Nallathiga, R. 2003. "The Impacts of Density Regulations on Cities and Markets: Evidence from Mumbai." *International Journal of Regulation and Governance* 5 (1): 13–39.

NISEE (The National Information Service for Earthquake Engineering). 1994. Picture, 1994 Northridge Earthquake, Los Angeles, USA.

Pasteur, K. 2011. *From Vulnerability to Resilience: A Framework for Analysis and Action to Build Community Resilience*. Bourton on Dunsmore, U.K. Practical Action Publishing, Ltd.

Pelling, M. 2010. *Review and Systematization of Disaster Preparedness Experiences in Urban Areas in the Caribbean Region*. Oxford, U.K.: Oxfam.

Pelling, M., and B. Wisner. 2009. *Disaster Risk Reduction: Case Studies from Urban Africa*. London: Earthscan Publications Ltd.

Resilience Alliance. 2002. "Key Concepts." http://www.resalliance.org/index.php/ key_concepts.

Satterthwaite, D., S. Huq, M. Pelling, H. Reid, and P. Lankao. 2007. "Adapting to Climate Change in Urban Areas. The Possibilities and Constraints in Low- and Middle-Income Nations." Human Settlements Discussion Paper Series 1, International Institute for Environment and Development, London.

The Great California Shake-Out. n.d. http://www.shakeout.org/.

Twigg, J., and H. Bottomley. 2011. *Disaster Risk Reduction NGO Inter-Agency Group Learning Review*. ActionAid, London; Christian Aid, London; Plan, London, Practical Action, Rugby, U.K.; Tearfund, Teddington, U.K.

UNECOSOC (United Nations Economic and Social Council). 2008. *World Population Prospects*. New York, NY: Population Division of UNECOSOC, United Nations Secretariat.

———. 2009. *World Urbanization Prospects*. New York, NY: United Nations Secretariat.

UN-HABITAT. 1999. "Good Land Governance Paper." Global Land Tool Network, Nairobi.

———. 2003. "Slums of the World; The Face of Urban Poverty in the New Millennium? Monitoring the Millennium Development Goal, Target 11—Worldwide Slum Dweller Estimation." Working Paper, Earthscan Publications Ltd. Sterling, VA.

———. 2010. *Land and Natural Disasters: Guidance for Practitioners*. Nairobi: UN-HABITAT.

———. n.d. "Improving Water and Sanitation in Quelimane City." http://www.unhabitat .org/content.asp?cid=7100&catid=220&typeid=13.

UNISDR (United Nations International Strategy for Disaster Reduction). 2006. *Hyogo Framework for Action 2005–2015: Building the Resilience of Nations and Communities to Disasters*. Extract from the final report of the World Conference on Disaster Reduction, UNISDR, Kobe, Japan. Geneva.

———. 2009. *Risk and Poverty in a Changing Climate: Invest Today for a Safer Tomorrow*. 2009 Global Assessment Report on Disaster Risk Reduction, Geneva. http://www .preventionweb.net/english/hyogo/gar/report/index.php?id=1130&pid:34&pif:3.

————. 2011a. *Mayors Statement on Resilient Cities for the 3rd Global Platform for Disaster Risk Reduction.* 13 May 2011. Geneva.

————. 2011b. *Global Assessment Report on Disaster Risk Reduction: Revealing Risk, Redefining Development.* UNISDR Practical Action 2012, Geneva.

UNISDR/ILO/UNDP (International Labour Organization/United Nations Development Programme). 2010. *Local Governments and Disaster Risk Reduction: Good Practices and Lessons Learned.* Geneva: UN-ISDR.

UNU/IAS (United Nations University/Institute of Advanced Studies). 2003. *Biodiversity Access and Benefit-Sharing Policies for Protected Areas: An Introduction.* Tokyo: UNU/IAS.

————. 2010. *Defining an Ecosystem Approach to Urban Management and Policy Development.* Tokyo: UNU/IAS.

Upton, S., and M. Ibrahim. 2012. "Resilience in Practice." Programme Briefing Paper, Practical Action, Rugby, U.K. http://practicalaction.org/resilience-in-practice.

Venton, P. 2010. *Meso Level Partnerships for Disaster Risk Reduction and Climate Change Adaptation and How They Address Underlying Drivers of Risk: Practical Experiences Based on Case Studies in Afghanistan, Peru, Nepal, the Democratic Republic of the Congo, and El Salvador.* Global Assessment Report, Christian Aid, London; Practical Action, Rugby, U.K.; Tearfund, Teddington, U.K.

White, A., J. Hatcher, A. Khare, M. Liddle, A. Molnar, and W. D. Sunderlin. 2010. "Seeing People through the Trees and the Carbon: Mitigating and Adapting to Climate Change without Undermining Rights and Livelihoods." In *Social Dimensions of Climate Change: Equity and Vulnerability in a Warming World,* edited by R. Mearns and A. Norton. Washington, DC: IBRD/World Bank, pp. 277–301.

World Bank. 2005a. *Putting Social Development to Work for the Poor: An OED Review of World Bank Activities.* Washington, DC: World Bank.

————. 2005b. *The Effectiveness of World Bank Support for Community-Based and -Driven Development: An OED Evaluation.* Washington, DC: World Bank.

————. 2010. *Natural Hazards, Unnatural Disasters: The Economics of Effective Prevention.* Washington, DC: World Bank.

————. 2011. *Climate Change, Disaster Risk, and the Urban Poor: Cities Building Resilience for a Changing World.* Washington, DC: World Bank.

————. 2012a. *Cities and Flooding. A Guide to Integrated Urban Flood Risk Management for the 21st Century.* Washington, DC: World Bank.

————. 2012b. "Improving the Assessment of Disaster Risks to Strengthen Financial Resilience. Experience and Policy Lessons from the Work of the World Bank." In *Improving the Assessment of Disaster Risks to Strengthen Financial Resilience: A Special Joint G20 Publication by the Government of Mexico and the World Bank.* Chapter 1, pp. 10–35. Washington, DC: World Bank.

————. n.d. "Projects Website." http://www.worldbank.org/projects.

————. n.d. *Country Assistance Strategy for the Republic of the Philippines 2010–2012.* Manila. http://siteresources.worldbank.org/INTPHILIPPINES/Resources/PhilippinesCASFY20102012Booklet.pdf.

World Bank/Queensland Reconstruction Authority. 2012. *Queensland Recovery and Reconstruction in the Aftermath of the 2010/2011 Flood Events and Cyclone Yasi.* Washington, DC: World Bank. http://www-wds.worldbank.org/external/default/WDSContentServer/WDSP/IB/2011/07/22/000386194_20110722031713/Rendered/PDF/633930revised00BLIC00QUEENSLAND0web.pdf.

Tools for Building Urban Resilience

Key Points

- *Risk assessment* is a technical tool for quantifying the possible impacts of disaster and weather events in terms of the spatial distribution of damage and loss and the probability or likelihood of events occurring.
- *Socioeconomic cost-benefit analysis* is a method to assess a range of positive and negative impacts of a public or private investment.
- *Risk-based land use planning* identifies the safest areas in order to guide the prioritization of investments in urban development and infrastructure projects.
- *Urban upgrading* gives priority to infrastructure investments that benefit the most vulnerable populations living in slum settlements.
- *Ecosystems management* approaches for resilience in urban areas make use of natural infrastructure and can significantly decrease the cost of urban infrastructure projects.
- *Participation of communities and stakeholders* in urban infrastructure projects, including public-private partnerships, is an effective way to build social resilience.
- *Geographic information system (GIS)* software and tools are instrumental in creating and analyzing geospatial data, such as hazard and exposure maps, as part of a risk assessment.
- *Recognition of residual risk* implies that cities have to continue improving the quality of risk communication, early warning systems, and contingency planning for evacuation and recovery.
- *Disaster management frameworks* are an extension of local networks, national systems, and even international regional networks. The key is to create systems that are complementary and encourage collaboration between different levels of authority.
- *Investments in early warning systems* are among the most cost-effective measures a country can undertake.
- *Financial approaches* to urban resilience can spread disaster risk and soften the impact of a disaster.

Key Resources

Section	Resource
Risk Assessment	*Tools for Building Urban Resilience: Integrating Risk Information into Investment Decisions. Pilot Cities Report–Jakarta and Can Tho.* World Bank 2012.
Risk-Based Land Use Planning	*Safer Homes, Stronger Communities: A Handbook for Reconstruction after Natural Disasters,* chapter 5. World Bank 2010b.
Urban Ecosystem Management	*Cost-Effective Green Opportunities to Protect and Improve Upper Neuse Watershed Health—A Survey of the Literature for Beneficiaries.* World Resources Institute 2011.
Urban Upgrading	*Approaches to Urban Slums: Adaptive and Proactive Strategies.* World Bank Institute 2009.
Community and Stakeholder Participation	Participatory Climate Change Assessments. A toolkit based on the Experience of Sorsogon City, Philippines. Toolkit for Participatory Climate Change Assessments in Urban Areas. Cities and Climate Change Initiative Discussion Paper, Number 1. UN-HABITAT 2010.
Disaster Management Systems	*Disaster Risk Management Systems Analysis.* Food and Agriculture Organization 2008.
Data Gathering, Analysis, and Application	*Using High Resolution Data for Identification of Urban Natural Disaster Risk.* World Bank 2012.
Risk Financing and Transfer Approaches	Cummins, J. David, and Olivier Mahul. *Catastrophe Risk Financing in Developing Countries: Principles for Public Intervention—Overview.* World Bank 2009.

Risk Assessment

Institutional   Economic

Key Points
- Risk assessment is a technical tool for quantifying the probability and consequences of disaster and climate events.
- It is the primary tool to understand the levels and types of risk facing urban infrastructure projects.
- A risk assessment is ideally implemented during project identification or preparation.
- Core components of risk assessments are hazard, exposure, and vulnerability.

Summary
The objective of a risk assessment is to provide a quantitative measure of the possible impacts of natural hazards. The results can enhance resilience to disasters and climate change by informing the selection and design of infrastructure and other urban investments. To make budgetary decisions, decision makers seek consistent quantitative tools to evaluate public investments. Integrating risk-based methods into cost-benefit approaches makes it possible to consider the impacts of climate change and disasters by quantifying their likely economic consequences. When such cost-benefit evaluations are used consistently through a standardized project evaluation method, they can stimulate efficient and effective public investments.

Risk assessment lays the factual foundation for integrating disaster risk reduction into urban infrastructure projects. A risk assessment should always be part of the planning process to help communities, property owners, urban planners, and governments at all levels to form an understanding of the underlying and future risk linked to natural hazards and climate change impacts. Depending on the context, a risk assessment can be used to help build social resilience as well, which can greatly enhance the quality of the assessment. In all cases, risk cannot be assessed without inputs from communities and stakeholders in order to define each of the elements of risk.

Risk Assessment and Investment Decisions

Because risk assessment is central to any urban infrastructure project, ideally it should be done whenever an urban project is being prepared. The purpose is to give a comprehensive sense of the expected loss from specific or multiple hazards over a given period. Traditionally, loss referred to human lives and welfare, which includes infrastructure and the economy, but over the years it has also come to cover socioeconomic and institutional factors.

Technical risk information acquired during the project assessment and evaluation stages provides the basis for risk reduction measures. Figure 2.1 gives the elements of a dynamic decision making process that integrates risk assessment and cost-benefit analyses. The process begins with a problem statement specific to the investment decision, and the cycle is repeated for variations in such conditions as climate change scenarios, growth in exposure, and investment options. When investment-related measures reduce the probability or consequences of a disaster, the relative change in risk can be evaluated by comparing the differences in the expected value of the impact. In this way, risk assessment becomes part of a cost-benefit analysis.

Figure 2.1 Dynamic Decision-Making Process

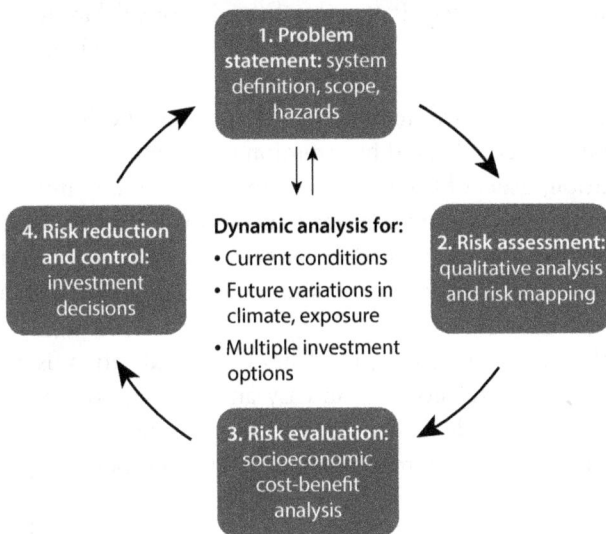

Source: Adapted from World Bank 2012c.

Building Urban Resilience · http://dx.doi.org/10.1596/978-0-8213-8865-5

Methodology

When choosing a method for assessing a particular risk, it is preferable that the method be well-understood and repeatable. In any method, however, the four core elements are *hazard identification, exposure analysis, vulnerability analysis,* and *risk analysis.* The quality of a risk assessment will depend on the availability of data, interaction of multiple hazards, the complexity of disaster effects, and the ability to involve experts in the assessment. As with any urban investment project, community participation is critical to understanding the practical effects of disasters. Community representatives have a role in the risk assessment process at all stages, and community risk mapping can prove to be an invaluable tool for community participation because it grounds the risk analysis in actual rather than assumed or projected risk data (see section "Community and Stakeholder Participation").

Hazard Identification

In urban resilience terms, hazards are defined as disturbances to urban areas that threaten human life and habitation. Disturbances refer not only to natural disasters like earthquakes and flooding but also to events that result from human acts of both omission and commission (World Bank 2010b). In this component of a risk assessment, hazard data are collected and analyzed to produce a probabilistic event set and define localized physical hazard conditions, such as elevation, soil type, and bathymetry.

With usually rare events like earthquakes, a robust probabilistic analysis of the hazard is particularly important. This will yield a characterization of the hazard that extends beyond the limited historical record of observed events. *Probabilistic hazard models* make it possible to quantify how climate change may affect the occurrence of disasters. *Historical event catalogues* are useful as a source of validation benchmarks. The most valuable validation data are empirical measurements or observation points from historical hazard events, which can be used to test down-scaling of the algorithms used to produce event footprints.

The resolution of hazard analysis will determine the fitness-of-use of the risk assessment results. If hazard information is available in only coarse or low-quality resolution, users of the risk assessment need to be informed about the limitations. What results from a hazard analysis is a probabilistic event catalogue defining the frequency and severity of possible events and multiple geospatial data sets defining local site conditions that will affect event footprints.

Mapping, the most common form of hazard identification, is recommended for urban investment projects. It is an easy and intuitive way to identify areas at risk. Identifying hazards recognizes frequency, duration, area extent, speed of onset, spatial dispersion, temporal spacing, and the possibility of secondary hazards. Multiple hazards should be treated separately and identified through parallel processes. Box 2.1 gives an example of a city-wide community risk-mapping exercise in Uganda.

Box 2.1 City-Wide Mapping in Uganda

The government of Uganda, Cities Alliance, and Shack/Slum Dwellers International (SDI) are engaged in a partnership program to transform urban slums in five secondary cities in Uganda (Ninja, Arua, Kabale, Mbale, and Mbarara). The program aims to reach an estimated 200,000 families living in slums and register all informal settlement in these cities.

As part of the program UN-HABITAT's Global Land Tools Network (GLTN) and a social tenure domain model (STDM) were tested in Uganda in 2011; this entailed city-wide enumeration and mapping exercises. The effort was informed by enumeration experiences of STDM developers from slum dweller federations in Mumbai, India; Nairobi, Kenya; and Kisumu, Uganda with the results coded onto an open source Quantum GIS program. The STDM uses GIS and Microsoft Excel to capture enumeration and mapping information at the household level, which is one base lower than plot level cadastre-type information.

Uganda has a complex urban land tenure system. For instance, the land under the Kisenyi slum in Kampala is owned by the Kabaka, the constitutional king of the Buganda kingdom. Over time, the king has given to select landowners grants of land. In turn, they have parceled up the land and given leases to people who among them have built a sprawl of 35,000 shacks that they rent by the month to the city's poor.

SDI's Ugandan affiliate, the Uganda Slum Dwellers Federation, and its supporting NGO, Actogether, plan to use the city-wide enumerations and mapping exercises to determine usage and investment patterns within such informal settlements. In the long run, this work has implications for transformation of the land information system in Uganda, since title deeds could conceivably be supplemented by user deeds. The success of the pilot will depend on persuading Uganda's Ministry of Lands of its use value.

Source: Makau 2011.

Exposure Analysis

Exposure analysis connects identified hazards with the elements at risk, which in urban infrastructure projects are generally human populations and infrastructure. The standard definition of exposure is the collection of threatened assets (such as buildings, infrastructure, crops, and people) that are likely to sustain loss or damage during a disaster. This discussion uses buildings and structures as examples of specific types of exposure.

Exposure is characterized by a combination of physical characteristics (e.g., four-story masonry apartment building); monetary value (replacement cost or actual market value); and location (street address, latitude and longitude coordinates). The accuracy and detail of the exposure data is critical to the risk assessment: location of exposure determines the type and intensity of the hazard, physical characteristics influence vulnerability and therefore potential damage, and finally monetary value coupled with damage potential form the basis for the expected losses a community would incur in recovering.

Understanding how the risk assessment will be applied is important in analyzing exposure. For example, the resources and tools required to assess exposure will change based on whether the assessment is global, regional, national, municipal, or site-specific. Large-scale assessments, from the national on up, often include aggregated exposure data determined by top-down estimates of the numbers of structures and people and assignment of typical characteristics. These aggregate methods contrast with building-specific exposure, where data are collected about individual structures at specified locations.

Vulnerability Analysis

This analysis quantifies how susceptible exposed populations and their assets are to different hazard intensities and identifies elements at risk that can be addressed. It is important that vulnerability relationships are defined in ways that reflect the unique characteristics of the assessed area. Vulnerability analysis must, for instance, estimate likely human casualties based on distribution of population, damage, and loss of assets and capacity (WBI 2009). Historical data on disaster loss are vital for understanding how specific disasters impact populations and infrastructure. Often the necessary data may not exist; however, there are engineering-based analytical models that can estimate disaster impacts.

Risk Analysis

This analysis provides a spatial assessment of risk based on hazards, vulnerable populations, and the ability of the community to cope with disasters. It lays a foundation for determining the acceptable level of risk and related land use planning interventions. It also provides data for calculating the benefits and costs of various interventions (WBI 2009). Figure 2.2 illustrates the flow of information

Figure 2.2 Risk Assessment Model

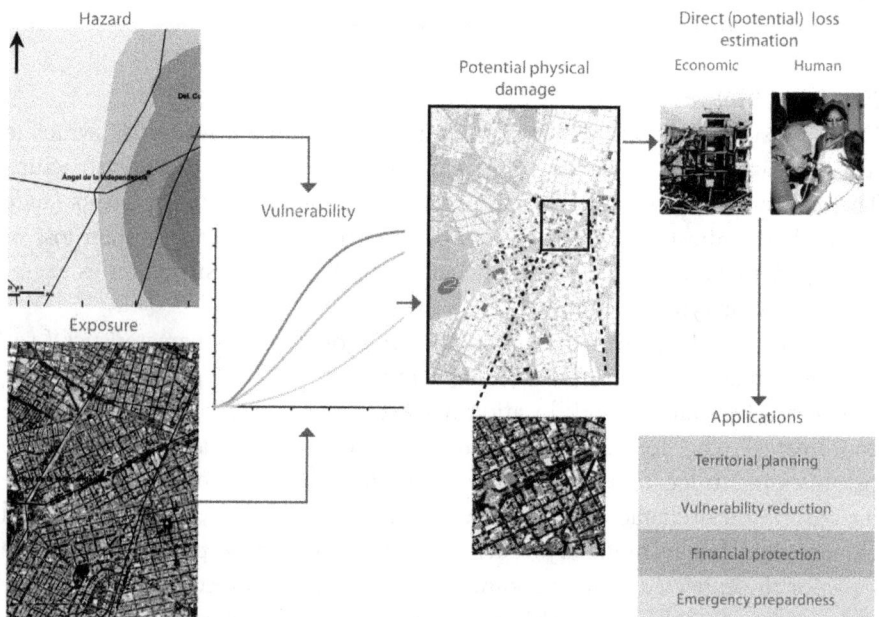

Source: World Bank 2012b.

Table 2.1 Types of Disaster Impact

	Economic	Noneconomic
Direct	• Residences, commercial and industrial buildings • Vehicle stock and supply, other nonstructural property • Agriculture, livestock • Infrastructure and other public facilities • Utilities and communication • Business interruption (inside flooded area) • Evacuation and rescue operations • Clean-up costs	• Population (physical casualties, psychological cost of displacement) • Environmental • Historical and cultural
Indirect	• Business interruption/supply chain disruption outside flooded area • Substitution of production outside flooded area • Extended temporary housing or permanent relocation of evacuees	• Societal disruption • Damage to government capacity

from the hazard and exposure components to the vulnerability function that yields estimated damage as a measure of risk. Risk assessment results can be visualized through risk maps, which are very useful for both making decisions and communicating the risks to stakeholders.

Risk analysis must estimate losses of human life as well as direct and indirect economic losses. The direct losses are more straightforward to evaluate using standard relationships between the severity of the hazard event, location of the damaged assets, and occurrence of damage of certain severity, but other disaster consequences that are harder to quantify can contribute significantly to the risk an urban infrastructure investment seeks to mitigate. The information in table 2.1 gives examples of categories of disaster impacts within a matrix for impact type (direct or indirect) and asset type (economic or noneconomic).

Probabilistic risk modeling, which was developed by the insurance industry, can help decision makers who must deal with the uncertainty of current and future risks. Probabilistic risk assessments can guide urban planning, ensuring that buildings, schools, hospitals, and other assets are located in safe areas. The Central American Probabilistic Risk Assessment (CAPRA) is an example of a probabilistic initiative (see box 2.2).

Probabilistic risk assessments can have many policy applications (World Bank 2012b), for instance:

• Territorial planning to identify, for example, floodplains or scenarios for geographic damage from earthquakes or tsunamis;
• Assessment of expected damage to infrastructure from specific hazard scenarios;
• Cost-benefit analysis for mitigation planning;
• Preparedness for support of emergency and contingency planning for different crisis scenarios; and
• Insurance premium calculations that require accurate information about annual expected loss and probable maximum loss for a specific area.

Cost-Benefit Analysis

A risk assessment used to quantify the added value of a project or measure can become part of the cost-benefit analysis. In the cost-benefit analysis, a range of

Box 2.2 CAPRA: A Probabilistic Risk Assessment Initiative

A free, modular, open-source, and multi-hazard tool for risk assessment, CAPRA is a risk calculation platform that integrates exposure databases, physical vulnerability functions, and hazard assessments to calculate probabilities (see figure below). CAPRA evaluates risk in terms of physical damage and direct economic and human losses using standard risk metrics (Annual Average Loss [AAL] and Probable Maximum Loss [PML]) to visualize hazards and risk in geographical information systems.

Building on—and reinforcing—previous initiatives, CAPRA was developed by Latin American experts with the support of the Central American Coordination Centre for Disaster Prevention, the World Bank, the Inter-American Development Bank, and the International Strategy of United Nations for Disaster Reduction, in partnership with Central American governments. Risk assessment and visualization tools like CAPRA have many applications.

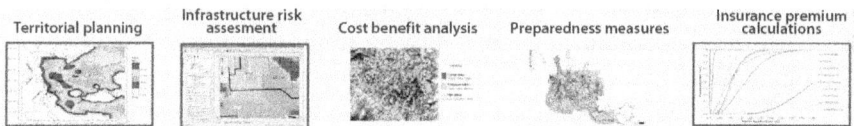

| Territorial planning | Infrastructure risk assesment | Cost benefit analysis | Preparedness measures | Insurance premium calculations |

Source: World Bank 2012b. Further information: http://www.ecapra.org/.

impacts beyond direct damage is assessed, such as costs for mitigation and emergency aid and the relative decrease in damages due to these measures.

Socioeconomic cost-benefit analysis (SCBA) is used to assess a broad range of impacts, positive and negative, that an investment project could have on the public and city government stakeholders. Such analyses express financial, environmental, and social impacts (see table 2.2) in monetary terms. The advantage is that the costs and benefits of all impacts can be summed so that it becomes clear whether an investment will have a positive or negative effect.

Table 2.2 Summary of Socioeconomic Cost-Benefit Analysis

Area of analysis	Socioeconomic factor
Question that the analysis seeks to answer	Example: What is the welfare change for society due to a project?
Perspective (target group)	All actors of a specified society, such as a country, province, or city.
Type of impacts	Human welfare in terms of: • Market, internal and external. • Direct and indirect link to the project.
Time span	• When possible an infinite time span is used. • Later impacts count less than earlier impacts due to discounting.
Reference situation/base line	The current situation plus autonomous developments.

The outcome of the SCBA is usually expressed in terms of net present value or internal rate of return. When on balance a project is positive, the investment is socioeconomically sound. SCBA can be used to enhance sustainable economic development because it reveals the relationship between market and socioeconomic impacts; it thus resembles a financial cost-benefit analysis. The main difference between the SCBA and the standard CBA is the inclusion of nonmarket impacts as well as impacts on market welfare.

For instance, the most common criteria used in evaluating measures to mitigate flood risk are:

- *Economic benefits:* e.g., reduction of direct damage to property, industry, and agriculture, and of indirect damage from loss of business, evacuation costs, and disruption of society;
- *Social benefits:* e.g., reductions in the affected area in terms of assets, people, and vulnerable points (hospitals, police station, power plants); psychological damage; and loss of life;
- *Environmental benefits:* e.g., improvements in water quality or biodiversity; and
- *Costs for construction, operation, and maintenance.*

In ex ante decision making, direct economic damage is usually valued in terms of replacement and productivity costs. Monetizing possible intangible damage is more complicated because market prices are not always available. Among options for estimating the economic value of reducing flood risk, for instance, are these (see Ruijgrok, Brouwer, and Verbruggen 2004; Wagemaker, Leenders, and Huizinga 2008):

- *Damage cost avoided*, estimated in relation to the costs of measures to prevent flooding;
- *Averting behavior method*, estimated in terms of the costs to avoid actual damage and unwanted effects;
- *Replacement costs*, estimated in terms of the costs to repair or compensate for flood damage;
- *Productivity costs*, estimated in terms of the costs of the loss of production of commercially marketed goods; and
- *Conditional valuation method*, estimated by creating a hypothetical market in which people are able to price flood damage.

From the decision making perspective, investments can be evaluated in terms of efficiency, effectiveness, and relative priority:

- *Efficiency:* Will the project achieve more benefits than it costs compared to other projects being considered for the same public financing?
- *Effectiveness:* Is this project the best way to reach the specified goal, or are there less expensive options?
- *Priority:* If a project is efficient and effective, what is the best time to do it?

Concluding Remarks

Risk assessments provide foundational data for understanding and enhancing urban resilience. While attempts have been made to create a single comprehensive risk assessment tool, the debate about the most appropriate methodology continues. Most important is to select a risk assessment methodology that can work both now and in the future, so that urban planners can understand how a given risk is changing over time. Even though methodologies differ, the four core elements of risk assessment are widely accepted and should always be used in quantifying risk. Box 2.3 illustrates a flood risk assessment conducted in Dhaka.

Box 2.3 Flood Risk Assessment for Mitigation Planning in Dhaka, Bangladesh

Dhaka is located on low-lying land at the confluence of two major river systems, the Brahmaputra and the Meghna, and is subject to regular flooding. The death toll and the economic loss can be significant, heavily burdening the national budget, which then requires international support. During the monsoon season, May to August, some 30–70 percent of urbanized and agricultural areas is generally inundated. In addition to the annual flooding, there were extremely serious floods in 1974, 1984, 1987, 1988, and 1998. The 1974 flood caused widespread famine, and the 1988 flood is considered to have been the most devastating flood in recorded history: two-thirds of the country was inundated and more than 30 million people, urban and rural, were directly affected. Millions were displaced from their homes and lost earning opportunities.

Because after a disaster employment opportunities in rural areas are scarce, rural people move to urban areas for jobs and shelter. In this way, natural disasters in Bangladesh are directly linked with the high rate of urbanization.

Further, water retention ponds and lakes that naturally emerged over time are vanishing due to land being filled for urbanization, and as Dhaka's population rises steadily, the city is forced to identify more lands for housing and industry, accelerating urbanization. Waterlogging due to poor drainage compounds the impact of floods.

The flood risk assessment aimed to:

• Map flood vulnerability using remote sensing and GIS technologies.
• Use remote sensing to provide timely and low-cost information on floods and land use status.
• Use GIS for managing information for flood risk mitigation.

Actions taken included:

• A land cover map was generated using satellite data and major land cover classes, which were verified against urban maps for accuracy.
• A flood area map was generated using data from normal floods; a digital elevation model (DEM) clarified flooded and nonflooded areas where there was ambiguity in interpreting satellite data; and optical sensor images were used to identify water features not affected by rainfall.
• The land cover map was combined with population data to produce a map of population distribution by land use type. Since population information was available to the district level, a finer spatial distribution was achieved by combining land use categories with population subdistricts.

---

box continues next page

Box 2.3 Flood Risk Assessment for Mitigation Planning in Dhaka, Bangladesh *(continued)*

- A flood risk map was produced by overlaying the analysis of flood areas and the population distribution map by land use type to show the number of people at risk during the annual flooding season.
- This map was compared with the Dhaka City Master Plan to evaluate the adequacy of the plan for flood mitigation.

Source: WBI 2009.

Risk-Based Land Use Planning

Infrastructural   Institutional   Economic

Key Points

- Risk-based land use planning is a nonstructural approach that identifies the safest locations and regulations for guiding urban development.
- Risk-based land use plans should inform all urban infrastructure projects.
- Mainstreaming land use planning in infrastructure projects reduces episodic and everyday risk in rapidly urbanizing cities and towns in hazard-prone areas that expose a high concentration of economic assets and population, especially the poor, to disaster risks.
- Land use plans control development in hazard-prone zones, facilitate rescue operations, and provide for emergency refuges.
- Land use plans are implemented using a combination of regulations and incentives for private sector and community engagement. This is more difficult if institutional coordination and municipal capacity are lacking.
- Risk-based land use planning should be incorporated into all phases of the urban project cycle.

Summary

Risk-based land use planning identifies the safest areas for prioritizing investments in urban development and infrastructure projects. Land use plans influence the location, type, design, quality, and timing of development. Risk-based land use planning is intended to (a) identify and mitigate the disaster risks embedded in current land development practices through building codes and regulations for use of land in hazard-prone areas; (b) reduce losses by facilitating faster response by providing open spaces and well-planned road networks for rescue operations; and (c) promote controlled urban growth without generating new risks through rebuilding and upgrading infrastructure ("building back better") using hazard-resistant construction according to a comprehensive plan. This section discusses the importance of mainstreaming effective urban land use planning to reduce disaster risk; difficulties in implementation; and how risk-based land use planning can be incorporated into projects.

Mainstreaming Risk-Based Land Use Planning

Risk-based land use planning manages exposure to disaster risks in urban centers and reduces new risks created by rapid and haphazard urban growth, which is common in cities in low- and middle-income countries. The Hyogo Framework for Action (HFA; Priority 4) emphasizes incorporating land use planning and regulations to reduce risk factors. Since then modest progress has been made on planning regulations in some countries; for instance, an Earthquake and Megacities Initiative that focuses on risk-sensitive urban redevelopment planning is being piloted in Makati, Philippines (UNISDR 2011). Even though reducing risk through land use planning and building codes has not been as effective as advances in national legislation, risk assessments, and preparedness, it can inform all urban infrastructure projects (UNISDR 2011).

Implementation Challenges

Despite its evident benefits, risk-based land use planning has not been widely adopted. Although nearly all the Asia-Pacific countries committed to the HFA have land use guidelines and building codes for risk reduction, mechanisms for enforcing the regulations are lacking (UNISDR 2011). In the United States, fewer than half the states require local governments to prepare comprehensive plans, and fewer than 10 incorporate risk resilience; although some local governments have building or zoning regulations to minimize flood losses, building code violations still contribute heavily to losses (Burby 2006). Key concerns are (a) capacity development and resource constraints at subnational levels; (b) national institutional structures that are not connected to local and community processes; and (c) administrative devolution of risk reduction in some countries that is not backed by financial devolution (UNISDR 2011).

Coordination among jurisdictions is necessary. Implementation of risk-based land use plans depends primarily on (a) coordination between sector-specific agencies engaged with land management and cooperation between adjoining jurisdictions when risks extend beyond urban limits; and (b) institutional capacity for good urban management, risk assessment, adequate financing, and compliance with plans. If risk-based land use planning is to be effective, different agencies concerned with land development, such as those responsible for roads and transportation, communication, utilities, and housing, need to share information and coordinate their work using an information management system that can ensure accountability to residents. Risk-based land use planning can encompass areas beyond the city, since risks can be generated upstream; for example, floods in a basin may be the result of land use practices on the hillsides.

Integrating Risk-Based Land Use Planning into the Project Cycle

Risk-based land use planning enables project managers to better guide proposals for infrastructure investments by taking into account the spatial distribution of risk. Risk-based land use planning should be incorporated into all stages of the project cycle (see table 2.3).

Table 2.3   Risk-Based Land Use Planning in Urban Infrastructure Projects

Stage of project cycle	Incorporating risk-based land use planning
Identification	Feasibility assessment and definition of scope for incorporating risk concerns into the local land use planning environment. Stakeholder perceptions of spatial distribution of risk.
Preparation/Appraisal	Preparing a risk-based land use management strategy. Stakeholder appraisal to ensure buy-in for major strategies like resettlement and retrofitting.
Implementation	Building up institutions and capacity for land use planning. Communication of land use plan intent and implications.
Monitoring	Indicators for risk reduction through land use planning. Institutional capacity and community participation in monitoring risk reduction through land use planning.

Project Identification

Risk-based land use planning will be effective if the local political environment and land use planning culture are favorable and if time and resources are available. In many cities, land use plans are poorly prepared and not updated regularly. It is necessary to sensitize politicians and administrators to the possibilities of reducing risk through land use planning. Such planning is typically a slow process that has limited political support because it can outlive political careers. But political support is usually strong after a major disaster; for example, risk reduction was incorporated into post-earthquake reconstruction in Bhutan in 2009 (UNISDR 2011). It must be an integral part of any post-disaster reconstruction plan and whenever any land use plan is updated. Many cities have local resilience action plans (LRAPs) that can emphasize reducing risk through land use planning. Programs to develop, e.g., transportation networks, water supply, housing, commercial centers, and other community amenities can create large additional benefits by reducing risk through land use planning. For example, the Myanmar Action Plan on risk reduction requires a disaster impact study as part of the process for planning and approval of development programs (UNISDR 2011).

The scope of risk-based land use planning activities needs to be defined based on the distribution of local risk, institutional capacity, and community priorities. Lack of robust risk information at the local level is often stated as a reason to forego planning. The lack of spatial distribution and of time and skilled personnel can limit the scope of a risk-based land use plan.

While city-wide comprehensive plans are desirable, where time or finances are scarce a site-specific or hazard-specific land use plan can be effective in reducing the major risks. Planning processes assume that there is a supporting legal and institutional framework and professional capacity; small urban centers typically lack financial and technical capability to undertake preventive measures. A level of institutional capacity is necessary to disseminate risk information, communicate with local stakeholder groups, revise land management strategies as circumstances change, and recommend updates to development regulations. Box 2.4 summarizes questions to ask when preparing a feasibility assessment. An institutional audit is necessary to identify all local agencies involved with land development, including their roles and responsibilities, as well as any coordination or other

Box 2.4 Checklist for Feasibility Assessment and Definition of Scope

- Is there political support for risk-based land use planning? Is it possible to demonstrate short-term gains and garner political support?
- Is local risk concentrated or dispersed? What resources are available to scale down national risk assessments or assess local risk?
- Is there enabling legislation and a comprehensive plan that can incorporate risk-reduction measures into infrastructure projects? If not, is it more feasible to prepare a hazard- or a site-specific plan?
- Does the planning institution have well-trained technical personnel, adequate finances, and capacity to work with the community?

capacity gaps. Community perceptions of risk, goals for urban space, and capacity to accommodate new risk-based guidelines can affect compliance with the municipal plan. (For details on stakeholder consultations, please see section "Community and Stakeholder Participation.")

When initiatives start small and are consistent with local policies and there are opportunities for incremental improvements consistent with the capacities of under-resourced local governments, there is greater possibility of success (UNISDR 2011).

Project Preparation/Appraisal

A risk-based land use plan is prepared by incorporating local risk assessment within a spatial development plan that delineates no-build zones, zones for risk-sensitive development and guidelines for retrofitting, and zones safe for future development. However, spatial development plans alone do not work when municipalities lack funds and when institutional capacity and coordination of land development are weak. Stakeholder appraisal is required to gather feedback and recommendations to ensure buy-in (see section "Community and Stakeholder Participation").

Preparing a Supportive Management Strategy

Step 1: Assess local risk.
Step 2: Prepare a risk-based land use plan.
Step 3: Analyze the costs and benefits of land use measures.
Step 4: Find the right mix of regulations and incentives.

Step 1: Local Risk Assessment. Risk assessment is used to inform, e.g., comprehensive land use plans, hazard-specific plans, and site-specific multihazard plans. It collects information on which parts of the city might be affected, such as a shoreline with tourist facilities or a peri-urban residential community. The outcome of risk assessment is a defined set of risk-based (micro) zones whose characteristics vary. Planners can determine which neighborhood is over time at most risk from a specific hazard or combination of hazards and establish spatial planning standards, zoning regulations, and building codes that correspond to an acceptable level of risk (see also box 2.5). A detailed time-dependent assessment may be needed to justify differential zoning regulations and ensure social equity (WBI 2009). (For more information, see section "Risk Assessment.")

Step 2: Risk-based Land Use Plan: A spatial plan is prepared based on the project scope. Incorporating risk reduction into a comprehensive plan is effective where such a plan already has standing as a policy guide. A spatial plan can take the form of land classification, future land use, a statement of policy, or a land use management plan, or it may be a mix of all these.[1] Since comprehensive plans are common, planners are familiar with their utility, procedures, and limitations. However, in order to be comprehensive, such plans tend to be detailed and time-consuming to draft, making the planning process tedious,

---

Box 2.5 Istanbul Earthquake Risk Reduction Plan

Istanbul, a fast-growing historic, commercial, and cultural center, is close to the North Anatolian Fault Zone and has survived 120 earthquakes over the last 2,000 years. Earthquake risk is increasing because of deteriorating old buildings and poorly constructed newer ones. Probabilistic risk assessment revealed that in the event of a major earthquake, the city would not be able to respond to emergency needs since 30 percent of its hospitals are in the highly vulnerable southwestern part of the city. A study of 1,278 buildings in different locations also found the average concrete quality to be below the 1998 Seismic Code requirements for new buildings.

Scenario analysis: Distribution of peak ground acceleration and number of heavily damaged buildings

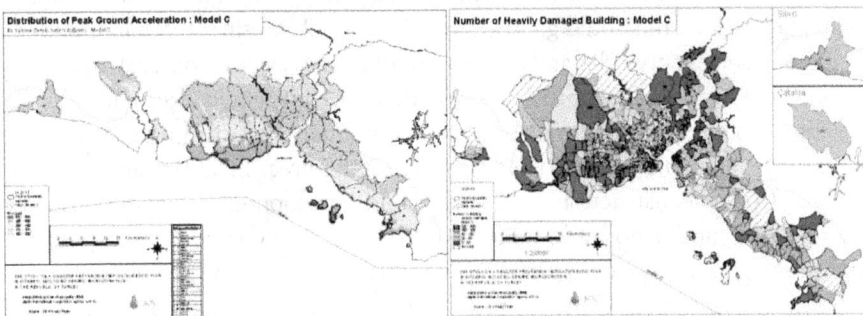

The Istanbul Metropolitan Municipality decided on two parallel risk reduction approaches:

- A strategic plan for disaster mitigation with three types of suggested measures: macro (national, regional, and metropolitan master plans); mezzo (urban redevelopment projects); and micro (urban redevelopment ignition, local development, and land readjustment areas); and
- An Earthquake Mitigation Plan consisting of a city contingency plan and local action plans for high-risk areas.

Sources: Ergenc, Ilkisik, and Murat n.d.; WBI 2009.

---

costly, and difficult to update after a disaster or to anticipate demand for land and changes in land use in rapidly urbanizing areas. When there is no comprehensive plan, or the plan is weak or out of date, a specialized risk reduction plan may be appropriate. This could consist of general policy guidelines or a specific program that addresses specific hazard-prone areas, such as floodplains; it might also take a more community-wide approach. However, stand-alone risk management plans are less effective than adapting development mechanisms to reduce risks (WBI 2009). Site-specific risk reduction plans are appropriate and efficient where there are no broad policies or plans or if risks in a particular location require special attention. Care must be taken that site-specific measures do not create new risks or transfer existing ones to other areas.

Step 3: Cost-benefit analysis of risk reduction options: Options for consideration include planned resettlement, hazard zoning, managing urban form and densities, ecosystem management, critical infrastructure planning, and road network planning. Based on the measures chosen, compatible regulations and incentives need to be identified.

Planned resettlement eliminates exposure to risks and reduces the costs of emergency response and rehabilitation. Resettlement may be the only option where it is not possible to mitigate risks, as in seismic areas with highly liquefiable soil, areas of volcanic flow, and hurricane, flood, or landslide-prone areas (Correa 2011b). More often than not, it is low-income families who occupy hazard-prone sites and need resettlement. (For more details on resettlement, see section "Urban Upgrading.")

Often resettlement is not planned and provides only housing; relocated families then often move back to the location where they had economic or social ties. Planned resettlement should go beyond relocation of housing to rehabilitation of livelihoods, social networks, and access to public services (see box 2.6). In Bogotá, Colombia, emergency relief in 1997 resettled 100 households from an informal settlement in a seismic high-risk and environmentally sensitive micro-watershed zone; however, some households returned to the area. In 2005, an integrated rehabilitation, reconstruction, and sustainable development plan established a hazard buffer and a no-build zone; socioeconomic studies identified potential impacts of displacement (loss of housing, social networks, and livelihoods); the community was engaged in the risk awareness and resettlement process; and there was post-resettlement assistance for education and health care. When implementation was challenged by vested interests, lack of legal tools, and fear of relocation, inter-institutional and inter-sectoral interventions were central to resolving the issues (Correa 2011a).

Hazard zoning enables local authorities to demarcate hazard-prone areas like coastal and seismic zones; regulate land use or prevent development in these areas; demarcate safe land for future infrastructure expansion; set development regulations (rules about location, bulk, height, shape, and use of structures in each zone); and draw up building codes (design, construction specifications) to withstand risk. Examples are flood zone regulations; setbacks from faults, steep

---

Box 2.6 Checklist for a Successful Relocation

Planned resettlement or relocation is a sensitive program that must be implemented carefully, with residents fully involved in the process and the decision to relocate. The following are desirable when implementing a relocation program:

- Affected communities participate in critical relocation and implementation decisions (site selection, identification of basic needs, settlement planning, and housing designs).
- Livelihoods are not site-specific and so are not disrupted.
- Water, public transport, health services, markets, and schools are accessible and affordable.
- People are able to bring with them items of high emotional, spiritual, or cultural value.
- People belonging to the same community are resettled together.
- Emotional, spiritual, and cultural attachment to the old site is not excessively high.
- Housing designs, settlement layouts, natural habitat, and community facilities support the community's way of life.
- Social, environmental, and hazard risk assessments confirm that risk cannot be mitigated in the old location, and the community can be assured of the suitability of the relocation site.
- Communication with target groups is frequent and transparent, and mechanisms to resolve grievances are effective.
- Relocation and assistance to assuage its economic impacts are adequately funded over a reasonable period.

Source: World Bank 2010b, 80.

---

slopes, and coastal erosion areas; and development standards for wetlands, dunes, and hillsides. If hazard zoning is to succeed in areas that are already settled, it must be accompanied by planned resettlement of families located in the no-build zones identified and programs to increase the supply of housing in the city as a whole (see box 2.7 for examples).

Risk-based development regulations and building codes can apply to both new construction and retrofitting when resettlement is not feasible. The Chennai Corporation in India is carrying out a vulnerability analysis of 65,000 buildings taller than one story and recommending retrofitting measures (UNISDR 2011). Development regulations and building codes should incorporate climatic settlement planning and design principles to minimize the fuel and energy consumption that is said to contribute to climate change. The IPCC considers energy efficiency in buildings to be a cost-effective way to reduce greenhouse gas (GHG) emissions among all energy-consuming sectors; India is applying its Energy Conservation Building Code to large commercial buildings, with strenuous measures to ensure compliance (World Bank 2010a).

Although a powerful tool, zoning ordinances are difficult to implement if institutions are weak, technical capacity is limited, and political support is lacking; in Nepal only 4 of 58 municipalities are implementing the Seismic Code (UNISDR 2011).

Box 2.7 Hazard Zoning Initiatives

In Metro Manila, fault zoning in the City of Muntinlupa included demarcation of danger and no-build zones along a 10 km area, with tax relief, relocation, and financial assistance for affected residents. However, land surveys by the Zoning Administration Office were usually unwelcome; notices to vacate danger zones fell on deaf ears; and informal settlements continued to thrive. The government did not acquire land for relocation or provide sufficient assistance for resettlement.

In Istanbul, the municipality launched a micro-zoning project in the high-risk southwestern part of the city; detailed information on local ground conditions were used to draft design parameters and building codes. The figures below indicate vulnerable infrastructure in a district of the city.

**Istanbul: Left: Distribution of vulnerable buildings in the Sumer neighborhood
Right: Distribution of earthquake weakness scores in the Zeytinbumu district**

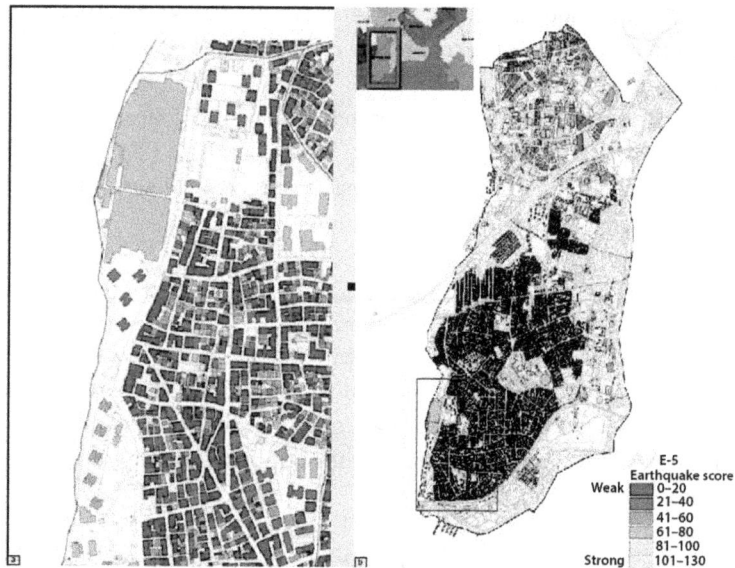

E-5
Earthquake score
Weak   0–20
       21–40
       41–60
       61–80
       81–100
Strong 101–130

Sources: Ergenc, Ilkisik, and Murat n.d.; WBI 2009.

The use of incentives to promote risk-based building codes needs to be encouraged; in Japan, fiscal incentives have been used to promote retrofitting of old buildings in congested areas (UNISDR 2011).

Urban form and densities can be managed to build resilience to risk; among the options are zoning safe land for urban expansion, redeveloping the city center and increasing the supply of housing to control unplanned expansion, facilitating multi-nucleated urbanization with multiple community-based developments that enable faster recovery if an economic center is destroyed during a disaster, and using development incentives to encourage development along safely sited transit corridors. Apart from the environmental and recreational benefits, planning for open spaces can facilitate emergency response and relief operations by housing temporary shelter sites and medical field stations (see box 2.8).

Ecosystem management: Using spatial plans that protect and improve the connectivity of green spaces and minimize impervious surfaces, ecosystem management can effectively reduce disaster risk and enhance the urban environment. For example, protecting wetlands with zoning regulations and demarcating environmental buffer zones produces environmental and health benefits while reducing flood impacts in urban areas (World Bank/GDFRR 2012). (See section "Urban Ecosystem Management" for more information on ecosystem management.)

Critical infrastructure located strategically through land use planning can facilitate quick response and rescue efforts. For example, zoning can locate community amenities like hospitals and schools at locations throughout the city in close proximity to neighborhoods rather than in a central location that could be destroyed by a disaster. Building codes for critical facilities should be based on a higher threshold of acceptable risk. (See section "Urban Upgrading" for more information on upgrading critical urban infrastructure.) *Road networks* that facilitate search and rescue operations and function as evacuation routes in hazard-prone areas can reduce the impact of disasters significantly (see box 2.9).

Step 4: Finding the right mix of regulations and incentives can increase the effectiveness of a risk-based land use plan. It is common for municipalities to favor land use tools that once gained political acceptance; often these end up negating each other's gains. There is no magic bullet: risk will be reduced by using tools that do not work at cross-purposes; for example, if coastal zone regulations are imposed but land is not acquired for resettlement in keeping with a comprehensive plan, residents will probably not move, or will move to other locations that are also hazard-prone (see box 2.10).

Regulation alone does not work; it needs to be balanced with incentives. The choice of tools will depend upon institutional capacity, the availability of risk information, socioeconomic benefits to the community, compatibility with land use policies and practice, and cultural orientation to risk. Evaluation of the costs and benefits of reducing risks requires comprehensive probabilistic assessments that are not available in most countries. It may be cost-effective to concentrate on retrofitting the most vulnerable and critical facilities rather than spreading around investments to protect many risk-prone assets. In Mexico, for instance, the cost-benefit ratio for retrofitting the most vulnerable 20 percent of risk-prone public buildings was considered appropriate (UNISDR 2011).

Implementation

Institutional capacity is necessary to disseminate risk information, communicate with local stakeholders, update management strategies, and recommend modernization of regulations. Establishing institutional and legislative enabling frameworks for coordinating land use planning measures is the most important step (see box 2.11).

Coordination is needed between, among others, the agencies concerned with environmental protection, land cadastres, public works, transportation, water and

Box 2.8 Spatial Development Framework for Risk Reduction in Kaduna, Nigeria

Kaduna drafted a spatial development framework after analysis of natural assets and the risks associated with the Kaduna River, which is periodically subject to major flooding. The plan promotes development along corridors of new planned infrastructure while preventing development in the flood plain by zoning riverside areas for agricultural and amenity use only and also zoning as green corridors multiple tributaries and streams that serve as natural drainage channels to accommodate phased expansion of the city. Investment in infrastructure is limited to short-term demand in accordance with the overall planning vision; this protects investment in redundant infrastructure that may later be subject to hazards.

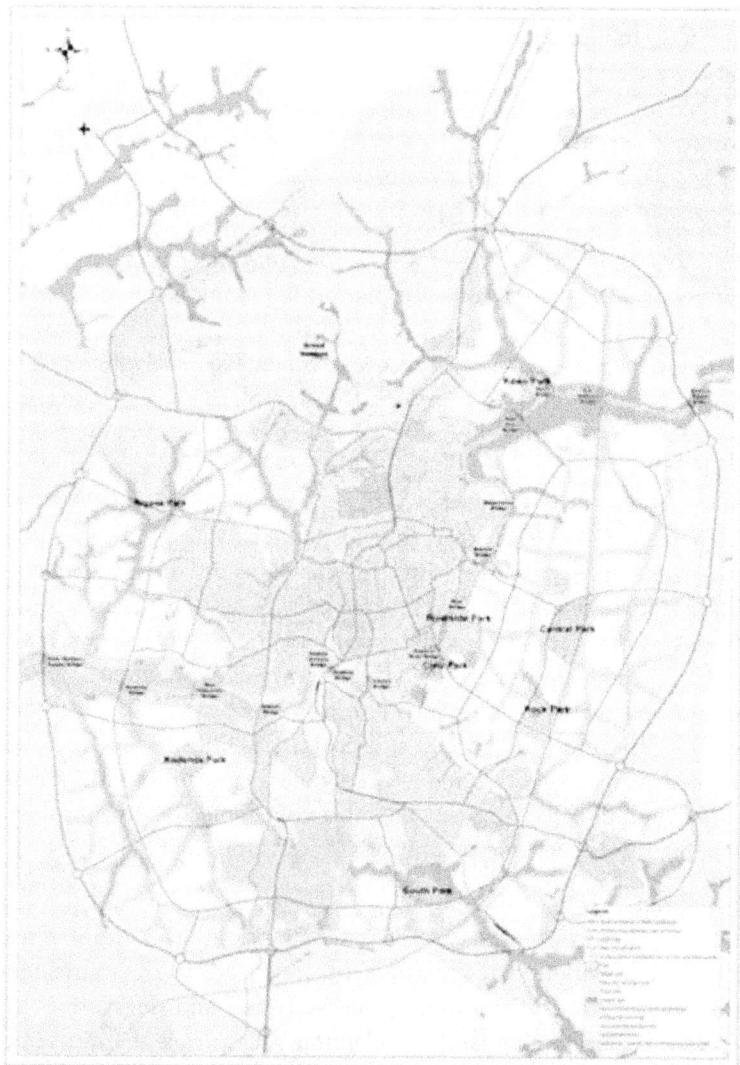

Source: Max Lock Consultancy 2010.

Box 2.9 Master Plan for Risk Reduction in Constitución, Chile

After the 2010 earthquake and tsunami, the government of Chile used the master plan for recovery and reconstruction efforts as an opportunity to incorporate risk assessment and mitigation into planning for future coastal settlements. The master plan calls for a system of streets for evacuation that are perpendicular to the sea and river on both sides of the settlement, allowing access to a safe point at 35 m above sea level on the seacoast side and 10 m above sea level on the river side. These corridors have been designed as pedestrian routes that end up in safe areas planned as community open spaces.

Source: Government of Chile 2012.

Box 2.10 Checklist for Land Use Risk Management Strategy

- Should risk concerns be incorporated into a comprehensive plan, a site-specific plan, or a hazard-specific plan?
- Is there a need for a hazard-specific regional plan on which multiple jurisdictions would have to cooperate?
- Is there adequate information and resources for conducting cost-benefit analyses of land use tools?
- Which tools are appropriate given the spatial distribution of risk, existing urban forms, the availability of open space, the condition of infrastructure, regulations already in place, and community socioeconomic conditions?
- Which regulations and incentives can support enforcement of the risk reduction plan? What is the right balance?

Box 2.11 Institutional Capacity for Risk Reduction

The Earthquake Mitigation Plan for Istanbul evaluates current legal structures, institutional responsibilities, and the financing needed for implementation. It stresses that risk management mostly relates to legal, social, and political issues. It covers assessment of the seismic vulnerability of buildings, developing seismic retrofitting methods, and identifying needed technical, social, administrative, legal, and financial measures. The Disaster Management Center of Istanbul City (AKOM) was built and equipped to collect, process, and disseminate disaster information.

In Kaduna, Nigeria, the Spatial Development Framework is based on a land use survey of the entire urbanized area and a sample household survey; the results are stored along with satellite imagery and topographical and hazard data in linked databases that will function as operational geodata infrastructure for urban management.

Sources: Ergenc, Ilkisik, and Murat n.d.; Max Lock Consultancy 2010.

sanitation, housing, and cultural heritage. Institutional partnerships between city agencies and building up agency capacity are needed to address redundancies and gaps. How can the efforts of municipal agencies be coordinated? Many cities opt to set up a separate disaster risk management (DRM) institution to facilitate coordination.

Ensuring multi-stakeholder cooperation through incentives for private sector and community engagement is critical to compliance with the risk-based land use plan. In the Philippines, the private sector is active in mobilizing resources to support risk reduction and reconstruction (UNISDR 2011). The communication strategy needs to ensure that the intent and implications of the plan reach all stakeholders (see table 2.4).

It may be necessary both to train technical staff in preparing land use plans based on risk assessment and to recruit technical experts. The UNISDR Education and Training Institute for Urban Risk Reduction, established in 2009, targets

Table 2.4 The Risk-Based Planning Process: Actors and Roles

Actors	Roles
Central or national government	• Apply federal/national law where the situation warrants. • Mobilize government agencies to undertake, commission, and supervise planning. • Provide funding or support for accessing international funding. • Provide any necessary specialized technical expertise. • Ensure that public investments conform to plans and codes.
State or provincial government	• Provide a legal mandate for the plans. • Create the policy environment in which the plans are prepared. • Mobilize government agencies, including regional entities, to guide and support the planning process. • Provide technical expertise as required. • Provide funding or support for accessing funding. • If regional planning is required, carry out the planning process.
Local government	• Carry out the planning process at the local level. • Create structures to enable meaningful community participation. • Be committed to implementing plans prepared with community participation. • Approve plans and issue the regulations to support implementation. • Carry out communications campaigns and training programs to ensure compliance with plans and codes. • Review and approve building plans, enforce building codes and land use regulations, carry out inspections, and apply sanctions.
Community (people directly affected as well as the larger community)	• Participate in the land use, physical, and strategic planning processes. • Formulate a collective vision for the future of the community. • Arrive at consensus on policy issues that cut across communities. • Where relevant, prepare detailed community plans that conform with larger policies.
Project facilitators (planners, nongovernmental organizations, and other intermediaries)	• Interpret government policies to set out the agenda for planning. • Educate the community on planning imperatives and the policy framework. • Interpret technical information and offer viable choices to government and communities to enable informed decision making. • Design and carry out projects that comply with plans and codes.
Technical experts	• Carry out technical investigations, data collection, and analysis to support planning. • Draft technical recommendations and options. • Assist with implementation of plans and codes.

Source: World Bank 2010b.

professional planners other than city managers and local disaster risk reduction officials; the Asia Regional Task Force on Urban Risks Reduction aims to build up networks of urban planners, architects, and engineers to ensure that risk reduction is incorporated into planning for urban development (UNISDR 2011).

Monitoring

While monitoring is desirable, municipalities usually do not have the capacity to enforce land use plans. Although an array of incentives can certainly elicit better compliance, it is still necessary to monitor performance in order to adapt the land use plan as needed and identify and address new risks as they emerge. Is there capacity to continuously monitor risk? What resources are needed? Monitoring can be effective if municipalities can set up open reporting on land use programs and the risks addressed; similarly, a system of community report cards can ensure that land use measures are indeed implemented and that the community appreciates that the risks are being offset.

The HFA sets out indicators for risk reduction at the national level, but work on local levels is limited (UNISDR 2011). Metrics for risk-based land use planning might include, for example, criteria for transportation infrastructure based on, e.g., total vehicle hours travelled pre- and post-earthquake (congestion); total vehicle km travelled post- and pre-earthquake (detour length); time delay between critical origin/destination pairs (e.g., from damaged areas to hospitals); and time to restore, say, 80 percent of pre-earthquake capacity. Other criteria might be observed land use changes; percentage of households that continue to occupy resettlement areas; and building code violations.

Concluding Remarks

The process of preparing a risk-based land use plan accomplishes many objectives:

- Communities have the opportunity to give comprehensive and practical consideration to critical risk issues in terms of community goals and priorities.
- Highlighting potential damage if development is permitted in high-risk areas provides the basis for related political and legal defenses.
- Community residents, developers, property owners, and elected officials, especially those at high risk, are more aware of the risks and feasible options to address them.
- The plan is a reference for elected and appointed officials making decisions about ordinances, allocating finances for capital improvements, or granting permits for new developments.

While risk-based land use planning can inform urban spatial development plans, comprehensive risk reduction requires social and economic policies and programs that increase the capacity of the urban population to adapt to disaster risks. For example, hazard maps can improve the quality of zoning, but a good zoning map and related regulations may not be enforceable if the people affected cannot afford to retrofit or relocate to avoid the mapped disaster risks.

Urban Ecosystem Management

Infrastructural   Social

Key Points

- Ecosystem management approaches make use of natural infrastructure and can decrease the cost of urban infrastructure projects.
- Ecosystem management requires an understanding of ecosystem services and local environments.
- Integrating ecosystem services into urban resilience planning requires that planners raise awareness of ecological approaches, generate useful information, turn knowledge into action, and effectively monitor and evaluate project implementation.

Summary

Ecosystem management approaches for resilience in urban areas make use of natural infrastructure and can significantly decrease the cost of urban infrastructure projects. This approach, discussed in chapter 1, assumes that nonengineered infrastructure can help reduce the vulnerability of a city to disasters. A holistic urban resilience program should, therefore, integrate ecosystem management with conventional, long-standing strategies for disaster reduction. A number of ecosystem management strategies are relevant to urban resilience and, more broadly, disaster risk reduction, such as

- Watershed management (see boxes 2.12 and 2.15);
- Coastal zone management;
- Urban landscape design;
- Green and blue infrastructure (see boxes 2.13 and 2.14);
- Environmental buffers (see box 2.12).

Urban ecosystem management projects often incorporate a combination of strategies and tools to mitigate disaster. The rehabilitation of the Maasin Watershed Reserve in the Philippines (box 2.12) provides an example of a combination of multiple measures.

Ecosystem management requires an understanding of ecosystem services and the local environment; there are methodological tools that can help to integrate ecology into urban resilience. This section will highlight how ecosystem management can contribute to urban resilience and also, in many cases, provide other benefits, such as helping to alleviate poverty.

These strategies should aim for well-planned, long-term, and labor-intensive interventions in which the community is continuously involved, rather than one-off construction projects. Healthy ecosystems highlight the synergies between disaster risk reduction and adaptation to climate change. This section also presents a methodology for incorporating ecosystem management into urban infrastructure projects in order to enhance resilience.

Box 2.12 Rehabilitation of the Maasin Watershed Reserve in the Philippines

The primary objective of the Maasin watershed rehabilitation program was to regulate flow within the watershed and in downstream urban areas like Iloilo City. Increasing the flow-regulation capacity of the watershed would prevent flooding during the rainy season and decrease water scarcity during the summer. Reforestation would also decrease surface runoff and soil erosion, help stabilize while contributing to slopes stability, and decrease the number of mudslides. In the course of the project, rehabilitation of the watershed to provide these ecosystem services involved the following:

- Improvements in agroforestry and management practices were introduced. When the project began in 1986, farmers and other residents were hired as tree planters and trained to plant only particular species between trees rather than as a substitute for the rice, corn, tobacco, and other crops that they had been planting.
- Commercial plantations were reforested with the fast-growing mahogany and *gmelina* species.
- Natural regeneration was allowed and promoting other vegetative measures promoted.

As the providers of the ecosystem services, the communities living within the watershed were trained in the various technical and organizational aspects of forest management. Existing community organizations and residents were brought together in the Maasin People's Organization Federation (KAPAWA). The communities organized were contracted to undertake comprehensive site development using reforestation, assisted natural regeneration, timber stand improvement, and agroforestry. Associated with the program were a total of 17 livelihood projects to benefit residents of the watershed.

The Metro Iloilo Water District (MIWD) is a semi-private utility that supplies water to Iloilo City, Maasin, and three other towns and supplies irrigation to 2,900 ha. of land. It is considered the user of the ecosystem service of water production. Since 1998 MIWD has been paying 1 percent of its gross income for the utilization and extraction of water, as mandated in the Philippines Local Government Code, which is the legal basis for local governance of the country's natural resources like watersheds. User fees are built into the water bills of MIWD customers, the beneficiaries of the service. Payment is distributed to the following government units where the water is located, as provided for in the Allocation of Share section of the Code:

- Iloilo province (20 percent);
- Municipality of Maasin (45 percent), which goes to the general fund for use in the acquisition of equipment for maintenance and protection of the watershed; and
- *Barangays* (35 percent), which is distributed to the 51 barangays that fall under the municipality of Maasin.

The Tigum-Aganan Watershed Management Board is composed of representatives from the local governments of Iloilo City and eight other towns, the irrigators' association, the water district, business groups, nongovernmental organizations, community organizations, and academia. This institutional mechanism for watershed management galvanized efforts to deal with issues faced by both upstream and downstream stakeholders.

box continues next page

Box 2.12 Rehabilitation of the Maasin Watershed Reserve in the Philippines *(continued)*

Results

As of 2004 the project had accomplished the following:

- 30 percent of the reserve was still cultivated by upstream/upland farmers (agroforestry).
- 40 percent of the area was covered by stable tree plantations (mahogany, gmelina, and other forest species).
- 20 percent was covered by fruit trees.
- 10 percent was old growth.
- 330 hectares of riverbank were stabilized.
- Vegetative erosion control measures were in place on 20,000 sq.m.

Key implementation lessons

1. Increased institutional capacity is necessary to ensure the long-term integrated management of a watershed after external funding has been used up. A mechanism that involves local governments both upstream and downstream is essential.
2. Community organizations of the providers of the ecosystem services, supported by the necessary laws, are instrumental in supporting payments for ecosystem services.
3. There is a need to raise awareness of, and thus willingness to pay for, ecosystem services. Concerned local government units initiated an information, education, and communication campaign in print, radio, and television to generate public awareness and support for the program. This brought in donations from civil society groups and engendered support for the cross-municipal management board.
4. Requiring downstream urban beneficiaries to pay for watershed services is good practice and can generate funding to help assist subsistence farmers and other landowners in upper watersheds to adopt more sustainable natural resource management practices and protect upland ecosystems. Although in this case user fees were associated with the provision of water supply, the arrangement also delivered urban resilience benefits.

Ecosystem Management and Risk-Based Land Use Planning

As part of their resilience interventions, local jurisdictions should incorporate ecosystem management projects into their comprehensive development and land use plans. Ecosystem approaches to disaster risk management usually need to consider spatial scales that go beyond individual municipalities. However, factors causing the decline of ecosystem services, such as rapid urban development and environmental degradation, occur locally and are often generated by local land use decisions. Actions to incorporate ecosystem management projects into risk-based land use planning are summarized in table 2.5. In general, risk-based land use plans should state clear and concise goals for effective resilience programs.

During the project cycle, it is important to facilitate a proactive approach to ecosystem management within land use plans, rather than changing policies after disasters have occurred or ecosystem integrity has been irreparably degraded by human impacts. Land use plans should provide a bottom-up and spatial

Table 2.5 Incorporating Ecosystem Management into Land Use Planning

1. *Inventory resources and determine the effects of urban development:* The basis for designing an ecosystem management project is an assessment of resilience issues (see section "Risk Assessment"). This assessment should include a determination of current and potential ecosystem services that might mitigate risk. Identifying the extent and root causes of the degradation of natural resources provides a baseline for projects to restore ecosystem services.

   To identify new land for use as an environmental buffer, for example, planners must first identify areas that may already be providing the service and who owns them. This inventory then becomes the basis for generating plans that incorporate green infrastructure projects.

2. *Set goals and objectives:* Goals and objectives articulate specific, measurable targets for reducing disaster risk, such as percent reduction in surface runoff to reduce flooding. Measurable objectives ensure clear indicators of increased resilience. Goals should also be spatially specific so as to be more effectively integrated into land use plans.

3. *Ensure coordination:* Cooperation by municipalities, landowners, and other stakeholders is necessary to effectively integrate ecosystem management into the land use plans of different jurisdictions.

   Ecosystem management approaches for urban resilience are often implemented over watersheds that extend upstream of cities, across large wetland areas, beyond a single planning area, or across organizations. Poorly coordinated local land use decisions can have unintended negative impacts on urban resilience; collaboration across jurisdictional boundaries is thus necessary for many types of ecosystem management projects.

4. *Assign responsibilities:* Successful ecosystem management approaches to reducing disaster risk depend on whether comprehensive plans designate responsibility for implementation and enforcing standards. There must also be a focus on monitoring ecological conditions so that a community project can be adapted to changing conditions.

Land use plans are not simply documents that articulate ecosystem management projects. They are also the starting point for the ordinances, land development codes, and environmental policies that enable the projects.

---

perspective for protecting the regulatory processes of ecological systems so that they can increase urban resilience over the long term.

Incorporating ecosystem *resource inventories* into local land use plans can help communities to understand which ecosystem services are available to support urban resilience and which are being degraded by poorly planned urban growth. Adaptive risk management needs to monitor the change of ecological conditions and the impact of human activity over time. With inputs from monitoring and evaluation, municipalities can adjust the targets and procedures of ecosystem management projects to better fit the circumstances on the ground.

Traditionally, the policies, tools, and mechanisms for implementing land use planning have tended to be regulatory rather than incentive-based. A shift in focus toward incentive-based tools can help produce significantly more effective programs by taking into account the potential of stakeholder engagement, employment creation, and community-based management opportunities, all of which are inherent in ecosystem management for urban resilience. *Incentives* encourage stakeholders to safeguard the integrity of ecosystem services voluntarily; for instance, *preferential tax treatments* can be granted in exchange for providing environmental buffers within a development. Table 2.6 lists common ecosystem management interventions. Box 2.13 provides further information on one of these interventions, green and blue infrastructure.

Table 2.6 Common Ecosystem Management Interventions

• Bio-retention	• Nitrogen-fixing plants
• Constructed wetlands	• Permeable pavement
• Coral/shellfish reefs	• Public parks/gardens
• Coastal wetlands	• Rain gardens
• Repair/protection	• Retention ponds
• Flood zone restoration	• Sand dunes/berms
• Forest repair/protection	• Tree planting
• Green roofs	• Vegetation planting for landslides
• Mangroves	• Watershed/wetland repair/protection

Box 2.13 Green and Blue Infrastructure

The term green infrastructure generally refers to a network of green spaces providing various ecosystem services (Benedict and McMahon 2002). Urban forests, tree stands, and parks, for example, protect against landslides, erosion, floods, and drought. Forest restoration in the hinterlands also protects urban communities, their livelihoods, and economic infrastructure, such as roads, ports, and hydroelectric dams. Blue infrastructure refers to green spaces that include water for regulating hydrological flows.

In most urban areas, rainwater flows into combined storm water and sewer drainage systems. Extreme precipitation can exceed the capacity of these combined systems, leading to flooding, backed-up sewage, and public health hazards. Green infrastructure is increasingly being used for storm water management, mimicking the natural infiltration and runoff reduction functions of natural ecosystems. Green roofs, bioswales, retention ponds, and permeable pavements are a few examples. When compared with rehabilitating or even replacing an entire network of combined storm water/sewer systems, green infrastructure is a cost-effective way to manage storm water.

This recognition of natural areas as functional infrastructure or environmental buffers necessitates their preservation and integration into comprehensive land use plans. This can be managed through urban projects that involve

• Integrated watershed management, including management of upstream forests;
• Management of natural freshwater wetlands; and
• Design of landscaping interventions and engineered measures to complement and emulate the resilience effects produced by existing ecosystems.

Methodology for Ecosystem Management

The United Nations Environment Programme (UNEP) has taken steps to apply ecosystem approaches in post-conflict environments; this requires rapid assessment and implementation of ecosystem management. The goal is to establish an integrated approach to sectors that deliver ecosystem services, identify ecosystem priorities, and finance those priorities. This methodology, which should be incorporated into all projects, implicitly requires that urban planners work with their communities to develop these strategies.

Step 1: Making the Case

To engage their communities, planners can do the following:

- Conduct awareness-raising workshops on the concept of place-based ecosystem management and on ecosystem services and the relationship between the ecology and human well-being.
- Create accessible guides on the ecosystem approach for local government units, local communities, and other stakeholders.
- Disseminate key messages as widely as possible, particularly about the links between ecosystem services and human well-being and about what drives ecosystem degradation.
- Facilitate assessment of ecosystem services that are linked to regional and national systems.

Step 2: Generating Knowledge

Ecosystem management, as noted, requires a deep understanding of the local urban environment. In this handbook it is not possible to account for every specific situation but it is likely that all will require data collection and analysis (see section "Data Gathering, Analysis, and Application" for more on collecting and managing data). To generate ecosystem information, it will be necessary to

- Establish networks for exchange of information on ecosystem services.
- Undertake or facilitate ecosystem assessments.
- Identify how specific ecosystem services relate to human well-being.
- Identify direct and indirect drivers of ecosystem change.
- Formulate plausible scenarios based on the impacts of direct and indirect drivers.
- Build capacity to undertake economic evaluation of ecosystem services. An example of a cost evaluation is illustrated in box 2.14.

Box 2.14 Gray and Green Infrastructure Costs Compared

To facilitate the integration of green infrastructure into land use plans, there needs to be a standardized method for evaluating the cost-effectiveness of "green" versus conventional "gray" infrastructure. The World Resources Institute (WRI) has devised a "Green-Gray Analysis" approach that in many cases shows that green infrastructure is more cost-effective (see figures that follow).

Green infrastructure alternatives are stream buffers, aquifer protection, bioswales, green roofs, reforestation, wetlands, mangrove coastal protection, etc. The costs associated with these options can be determined from, e.g., on-site consultations, publicly available data, and geospatial analysis. At present, WRI's Green-Gray Analysis is conservative: it does not yet include estimates of other benefits of green infrastructure, such as increased carbon

box continues next page

Building Urban Resilience • http://dx.doi.org/10.1596/978-0-8213-8865-5

Box 2.14 Gray and Green Infrastructure Costs Compared *(continued)*

Figure B2.14.1 Green vs. Gray Infrastructure Costs

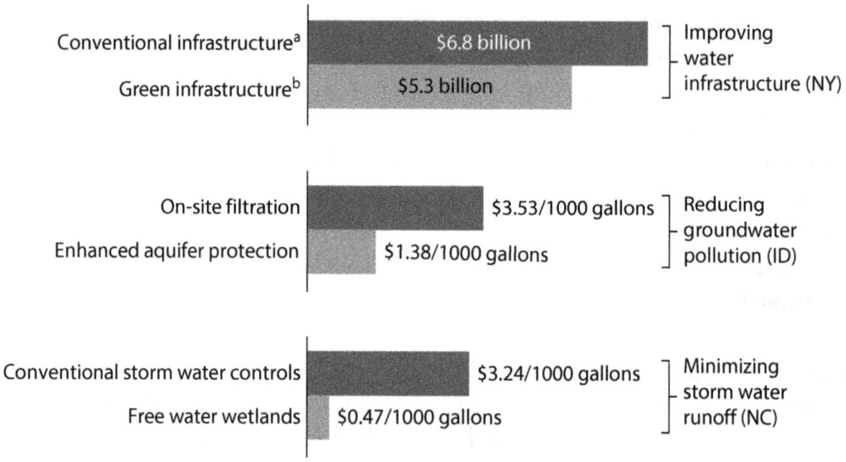

Source: Talberth and Hanson 2012, based on City of New York PlaNYC 2010 and other information sources.
a. Tunnels, diversion structures, and other approaches.
b. Restored stream buffers, bioswales, green roofs, and other approaches.

Figure B2.14.2 Green vs. Gray Infrastructure Costs for Securing Clean Drinking Water (Portland, Maine)
present value cost of investments over 20 years, US$ millions

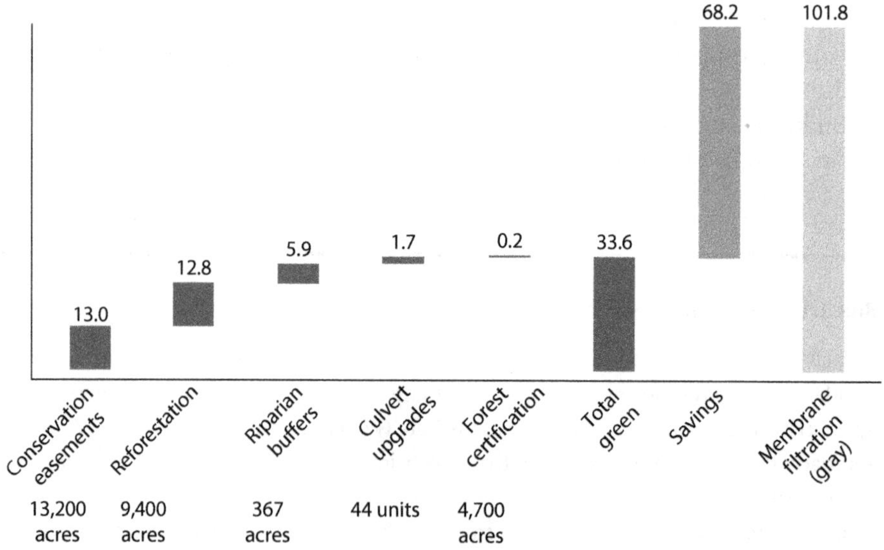

Source: Talberth et al. 2012.

sequestration, recreation opportunities, and higher property values. Including these benefits would tip the scales even further toward green alternatives.

Source: Talberth and Hanson 2012.

Step 3: Turning Knowledge to Action

Careful planning and long-term approaches to ecosystem services are necessary because the natural services most likely have far-reaching effects throughout and beyond the urban environment. A comprehensive ecosystem management strategy requires the participation of both the local community and regional and national stakeholders who might benefit downstream. Ecosystem management strategies should

- Determine which services have priority. See box 2.15 for an example of a phased approach.
- Decide on effective intervention strategies.
- Ensure that access and use of ecosystem services are equitable for all stakeholders.

Box 2.15 Lake Matthews: Watershed for Urban Development

In cooperation with representatives of the county, the Flood Control and Conservation District, landowners, and a residential developer, the Metropolitan Water District of Southern California designed a drainage management plan to mitigate the impacts of watershed development on reservoir water quality. Although the Lake Matthews Watershed and the Colorado River Basin are sparsely populated, they lie in the path of expanding growth. Urbanization of the watershed is expected to increase loadings of heavy metals, pathogens, sediments, oil, and grease.

The first phase of the drainage management plan focused on the Lake Matthews reservoir. Lake Matthews is a 180,000-acre terminal reservoir for imported Colorado River water. The 39-square-mile watershed is drained by Cajalco Creek, which feeds into Lake Matthews. One key element of the Lake Matthews management strategy is to use a series of wetlands to help cleanse water from first-flush and nuisance flows and also to provide wildlife habitat. Next, as first-flush diversion the water would flow into a constructed water quality pond and then into a sediment basin to capture bed load sediment before it enters Lake Matthews. Lastly, there are plans to construct a dam and detention basin designed to regulate 100-year peak flood flows from Cajalco Creek.

Source: U.S. Environmental Protection Agency n.d.

Step 4: Monitoring and Evaluation

To ensure optimal delivery of ecosystem services, planners need to

- Offer technical support for the development and review of indicators of ecosystem service delivery.
- Facilitate review of ecosystem service delivery against established baselines.
- Facilitate and build capacity to develop and implement feedback mechanisms into steps 1–3.

Building Urban Resilience • http://dx.doi.org/10.1596/978-0-8213-8865-5

Concluding Remarks

Ecosystem management approaches are gaining in popularity because they offer holistic approaches to issues previously treated separately. The gains from utilizing, enhancing, and repairing ecosystem services can be far greater than from creating new infrastructure. But urban planners also need to recognize the unintended impacts that altering natural ecosystems can have on an environment in and around an urban area. Ecosystem approaches are a key element of urban resilience, but they do require a nuanced understanding of the local environment. Box 2.16 provides an example of London's greening efforts.

Box 2.16 London's Green Grid

London has a wealth of green spaces and vegetation in public parks, private gardens, woodlands, street trees, wetlands, and river and transport corridors. Improving the quality, quantity, connectivity, and diversity of London's green spaces will increase the city's resilience and capacity to adapt to a changing climate.

Actions:

- As part of the regeneration of the East London subregion, a Green Grid is being delivered through projects designed to connect, add to, and enhance the potential of green spaces to absorb and store water, cool the vicinity, and provide amenity space and diverse habitats for wildlife. Projects worth more than £20 million have already been delivered. Planning guidance published by the Mayor of London enables borough-level and subregional implementation of the Green Grid.
- A London-wide Green Grid is also planned.
- Property owners are beginning to green roofs and walls. These green areas perform a range of ecosystem services essential to quality of life and ensure a high level of resilience, such as
    - supporting biodiversity;
    - reducing flood risk by absorbing and temporarily retaining rainfall;
    - moderating the temperature by offsetting the urban heat island effect;
    - reducing energy demand by providing shade and reducing wind speeds;
    - damping noise and air pollution; and
    - providing places for recreational and leisure activities that improve health.

Ecosystem service	Green roofs/ walls	Street trees	Wetlands	River corridors	Woodlands	Grasslands
Reduce flood risk	✓✓	✓	✓✓✓	✓✓✓	✓✓	✓✓
Offset urban heat island	✓✓	✓✓	✓✓	✓✓	✓✓✓	✓
Reduce energy demand	✓✓	✓✓			✓	
Reduce noise/air pollution		✓✓			✓✓	
Support biodiversity	✓✓	✓	✓✓✓		✓✓✓	✓✓✓
Recreation/leisure	✓		✓	✓✓	✓✓✓	✓✓✓

Source: Mayor of London 2010.

Urban Upgrading

Institutional   Infrastructural

Key Points
- Urban upgrading prioritizes investments in infrastructure, housing, livelihoods, and social networks for the vulnerable urban poor.
- In rapidly growing cities, inadequate planning for low-income households creates slum conditions that transfer a disproportionate burden of disaster risk to the poor.
- Urban upgrading is usually sector-based and piecemeal; risk reduction is challenged by the minimal documentation on slums and a lack of institutional coordination and municipal finance.
- Comprehensive urban upgrading reduces risks through slum upgrading and prevents new slum formation and risks by using incentives for private sector and community engagement to increase the supply of low-income housing.
- Risk resilience through urban upgrading should be incorporated into all phases of the project cycle.

Summary
Urban upgrading prioritizes investments in infrastructure, housing, livelihoods, and social networks for the vulnerable urban poor. Strategic urban upgrading can manage risks by (a) regulating slum development in hazard-prone areas through planned resettlement and building codes; (b) reducing losses by prioritizing critical infrastructure, escape routes, and community refuges in slums; and (c) promoting safe and socioeconomically viable low-income neighborhoods in accordance with a city-wide plan. This section discusses the need to mainstream urban upgrading to reduce risk in cities and barriers to implementation, and how project managers can integrate into the project cycle risk reduction through urban upgrading.

Mainstreaming Urban Upgrading
The phenomenal growth of slums in recent decades exposes far more urban poor to disaster risks. However, variations in slum conditions create different degrees of risk (Weber 2008). The occurrence of frequent everyday hazards due to climate change can turn into disasters for the urban poor who lack safe and serviced housing (Bull-Kamanga et al. 2003). Urban projects need to mainstream risk reduction through strategic urban upgrading. There are increasing examples of low-income communities negotiating safer and better-located land, rigid zoning and building standards being adapted to local needs, and vulnerable settlements being upgraded to reduce risks and participate in planning and budgeting (UNISDR 2011). Dar es Salaam, Jakarta, Mexico City, and São Paulo have all successfully addressed local risk through slum upgrading in addition to early warning systems and adaptation planning (World Bank 2011a).

Building Urban Resilience · http://dx.doi.org/10.1596/978-0-8213-8865-5

Implementation Challenges

Building risk resilience for the urban poor can be challenging because the notion that different communities face different degrees of vulnerability is generally not well understood. Although slums are growing faster than other urban areas, most governments do not report on slum conditions and trends. Slums are invisible parts of the city—"zones of silence" in terms of public knowledge (UN-HABITAT 2003b). Since slum enumeration is not entirely reliable, it is difficult to estimate the scale and scope of the target population for slum upgrading projects (WBI 2009).

Urban upgrading programs are usually sector-based, piecemeal, and politically driven by election cycles. Often, there is little coordination between different agencies involved in sector-specific upgrading, such as provision of sanitation or organizing solid waste management. Central policies for slum upgrading often conflict with both state priorities and local municipal capacities. For most municipalities, which struggle to finance urban services, upgrading slums is not a priority. Poor planning and even poorer implementation of upgrading programs at times results in substandard housing and poor environmental conditions that can create new risks. For example, a plan for paving streets that does not take into account drainage patterns and the plinth levels of houses can create new flood risks. The impact of disasters is greater in urban centers where authorities both are lax and have limited resources to ensure compliance with building codes, basic services, and social amenities (IFRC 2010).

The central challenge in slum upgrading is scale: upgrading has so far benefitted only a small percentage of slum residents (IDB 2010); piecemeal upgrading in a handful of slums can create new risks in other parts of the city. It is necessary to look beyond neighborhoods and take a comprehensive city-wide approach that addresses the root causes of slum formation and increases the supply of low-income housing throughout the city. This requires reconciling land tenure issues and urban management for a multi-sector and city-wide integrated approach that incorporates socioeconomic development so that slum residents can afford the increased expenses of formalized city services once the slum is upgraded (IDB 2010).

Integrating Urban Upgrading into the Project Cycle

An appreciation that disaster risks for the urban poor may vary widely enables project managers to prioritize upgrading projects in local government proposals for infrastructure investment. Poverty reduction programs designed to provide safe environmental conditions through improved housing structures and basic services can significantly reduce disaster risk; for such programs risk management should be a mandatory component at all stages of the project cycle (see table 2.7).

Projects targeting slums need to be customized given that slums form for many different reasons, in vastly different locations, and may have just sprung up or have been in place for decades, if not longer (World Bank 2011c). Urban upgrading programs have four objectives: (1) improve environmental and

Table 2.7 Risk Management in Urban Upgrading Projects

Stage of project cycle	Incorporating risk management in urban upgrading
Identification	Defining scale and scope of slum upgrading/new low-income housing. Political sensitization. Stakeholder consultation to identify priority projects.
Preparation/appraisal	Risk assessment for the urban poor. Preparing a strategic urban upgrading program. Institutional audit and stakeholder appraisal to ensure buy-in.
Implementation	Institutional strengthening and capacity building. Communication of plan intent and implications.
Monitoring, evaluation, and knowledge-sharing	Monitoring indicators. Institutional monitoring capacity and community participation.

socioeconomic conditions; (2) ensure that benefits reach the target population; (3) build organizational and technical capacity within slum households and the community; and (4) be affordable to the local government and community (WBI 2009). Local governments need to work with informed and engaged communities throughout the project cycle (see section "Community and Stakeholder Participation").

Project Identification
Defining the scale and scope of urban upgrading is necessary to identify priority sites for slum improvement and new low-income housing developments. The total number of households, geographical distribution, rate of growth, shortfall in low-income housing, and the driving forces for slum formation determine how much institutional capacity is required and the schedule. The severity of slum conditions—their exposure to disaster risk due to location characteristics, density (Nallathiga 2003), housing condition, tenure status, and community readiness—will determine the interventions required. The complications of tenure status can affect the feasibility of undertaking upgrading; sites may have single, multiple, or disputed ownership; occupied public lands are simpler to upgrade than private sites (WBI 2009).

It is important to sensitize city managers to the importance of using urban upgrading to reduce risk. Municipalities tend to ignore the existence of slums and what they contribute to the urban economy. Many governments still demolish slums as part of city beautification plans, which merely relocates slums to other parts of the city. The political attitude to slums can determine the feasibility of urban upgrading. Political bias needs to be influenced to recognize the contribution the informal economy makes to the urban economy: in Latin America and the Caribbean, in the past decade two out of three urban jobs were generated by the informal sector (IDB 2010).

Project Preparation and Appraisal
It is necessary to assess risks to the urban poor through surveys to determine infrastructure, environmental, and socioeconomic conditions and determine what

services to plan for. Constraints on land ownership should be assessed to identify land acquisition needs and alternatives. A strategic urban upgrading program to manage risks will include measures to mitigate current risks—such as planned resettlement, provision of secure tenure, and improvements in housing and basic services—as well as proactive measures to prevent new risks by increasing the supply of low-income housing. An institutional audit of all agencies engaged in urban upgrading projects will determine gaps and areas to be reinforced. Community appraisal is essential to gauge the commitment of the community and ensure that new risk reduction measures are affordable. In Rio de Janeiro, Brazil, the community was involved in the project preparation stage through workshops, door-to-door visits from community leaders, and events in which the community debated and approved settlement development projects (IDB 2010).

Risk Assessment for Slums: Although significant progress has been made, urban risk assessments still do not adequately address the vulnerabilities and capacities of the people (UNISDR 2011). Risk assessment for urban upgrading (see section "Risk Assessment") should identify the slum population and their locations and assess sector-specific risks (e.g., housing and tenure, basic services, critical infrastructure, transportation, social and economic vulnerabilities, community readiness, institutional capacity, and access to data and finances) as well as city-wide risks for integration with comprehensive urban planning goals. Both the complexity and the cost of a risk assessment must be considered in undertaking an urban upgrade.

Many local governments have no mechanisms for systematically monitoring formal urban growth, let alone informal, which makes it difficult to assess risks for informal settlements. The UN-HABITAT Urban Indicators Programme in 2005 reported that 80 of 120 cities had no monitoring systems to track changes in the spatial spread of the city. Moreover, different cities follow different measurement standards and are often influenced by current politics (Sliuzas, Mboup, and de Sherbinin 2008a). City-wide statistics on urban poverty based on slum definition parameters used by the Global Urban Observatory (GUO) mask the heterogeneity; they do not differentiate between magnitude (percentage of slum dwellers) and severity[2] (degree of deprivation); and the durability of housing is analyzed solely in terms of building materials. They do not consider compliance with building standards; hazardous location, such as steep slopes, floodplains, and toxic sites; and settlement characteristics, such as condition of roads, drainage, management of solid waste, and air pollution (Sliuzas, Mboup, and de Sherbinin 2008a).

For targeted risk reduction measures in urban upgrading, disaggregated information on neighborhood poverty indicators is needed. An initiative led by GUO, CIESIN, and ITC[3] identified methods using very high resolution (VHR) remote sensing with census data that take into account exposure to natural hazards apart from building construction characteristics (size, materials, shape); roads and open space; access to social amenities; site conditions (location within the urban area, slope, natural vegetation, hazards); and the slum formation process itself. An increasing number of community-based organizations and NGOs are using VHR for slum surveys (Sliuzas, Mboup, and de Sherbinin 2008a). In Pune, India, an NGO has successfully mapped slums using satellite imagery to better target provision of basic services (see box 2.17). However, access to satellite imagery can be expensive.

Box 2.17 Slum Mapping in Pune and Sangli-Miraj-Kupwad, India

The NGO Shelter Associates is working with slum communities to use satellite imagery and field surveys together to negotiate for slum improvement. Very High Resolution (VHR) images from Google Earth are used to digitize slum boundaries and attach information on households, dwellings, and site characteristics from field surveys collected by slum residents. Settlements are mapped by professional agencies using plane table methods that show plot boundaries. Spatial and socioeconomic data are entered into a GIS database and accessed by the community to prepare upgrading plans.

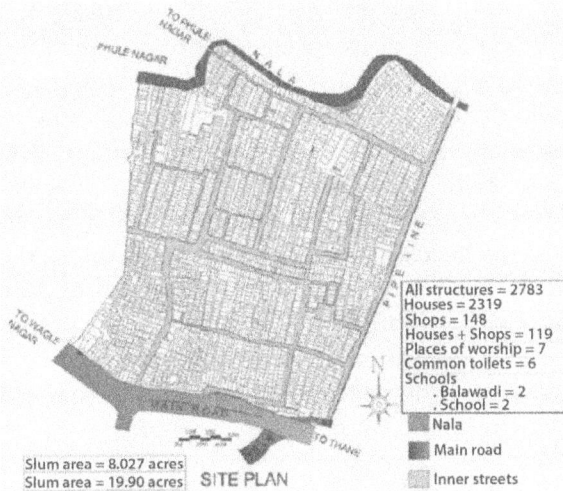

All structures = 2783
Houses = 2319
Shops = 148
Houses + Shops = 119
Places of worship = 7
Common toilets = 6
Schools
  . Balawadi = 2
  . School = 2

Nala
Main road
Inner streets

Slum area = 8.027 acres
Slum area = 19.90 acres   SITE PLAN

box continues next page

Box 2.17 Slum Mapping in Pune and Sangli-Miraj-Kupwad, India *(continued)*

In Pune, satellite images were used to provide evidence that individual slums were not growing but that to prevent formation of new slums in-migration needed to be planned for. Working with slum residents, Shelter Associates compelled the local government to legitimize migrants and initiate city planning to improve slum settlements by widening roads, installing flood protection, and building new infrastructure. The Pune slum census covered over 100,000 households in over 200 pockets throughout the city. The residents gained skills in data collection, a better understanding of their collective community problems, and opportunities to negotiate with the local government in the planning process.

In Sangli-Miraj-Kupwad, slum mapping by the community initiated a comprehensive approach with the local administration and its elected members to improve all slum pockets. Many slums have been mapped and improvement plans produced cost-effectively.

Source: Sliuzas, Mboup, and de Sherbinin 2008b. For more details, see also http://www.shelter-associates.org/.

Local governments need to work with national bodies, universities, and research institutes as well as private firms to access the latest techniques. Data and technology should also be simple enough for slum residents to use with minimum investment in training (Sliuzas, Mboup, and de Sherbinin 2008a). In Jakarta, Indonesia, an assessment of disaster risks to the poor found that data created by a number of agencies—multi- and bilateral organizations, NGOs, and private consultants—were extremely scarce, inconsistent, or very difficult to access because some agencies were reluctant to release information. Among the missing data were poverty maps, subsidence maps, socioeconomic and housing data for the very poor, definitions of slums and urban settlements, information on land tenure, updated census data, census data on the very poor, immigration and emigration rates, plans for resettlement of vulnerable areas, and financing and long-term plans for flood protection (World Bank 2011a).

Urban Upgrades: Ineffective urban planning and governance, lack of investment in infrastructure, and little community engagement explain differences in how the urban poor in different countries are affected by the same hazards (World Bank 2011a). Strategic urban upgrades used in combination can address numerous risk-reduction goals, such as regulating slum development in hazard-prone areas through planned resettlement and building codes; reducing losses by preparing the community for emergency response and prioritizing critical infrastructure, community refuges, and escape routes in slums; and promoting safe and socioeconomically viable low-income neighborhoods in accordance with a city-wide plan. Urban upgrades to reduce disaster risk, as already noted, include planned resettlement, slum upgrading through secure tenure, controls on development, provision of basic services, pedestrian road networks and open space planning, ensuring the safety of critical community facilities, and comprehensive city-wide urban upgrading that includes socioeconomic development.

Planned Resettlement: When slums are located on hazard-prone sites, planned resettlement of those communities, though politically sensitive, may be the only option. However, finding suitable sites on which to resettle communities is not easy; often the resettlement sites have not been planned, or have been planned without good access to employment opportunities (WBI 2009). Moreover, most households want to stay where they are because of reliable and known access to livelihoods and social networks (IFRC 2010). In São Paulo, Brazil, the municipality uses maps of precarious settlements to selectively relocate the fewest possible number of families from unsafe sites. For successful planned relocation of slums, community and private sector engagement is critical (see sections "Risk-Based Land Use Planning" and "Urban Upgrading").

Security of Tenure: Even where environmental conditions are reasonable, lack of secure tenure and livelihood options in slums and threats of forced evictions prevent households from investing in upgrading their homes, which increases their vulnerability to disasters (IIED n.d.; Lall and Deichmann 2009). Several tenure systems are viable, such as temporary occupation rights, lease agreements, community land trusts, adverse possession rights, and anti-eviction rights. In Dar es Salaam, Tanzania, the government is identifying all properties in informal settlements and issuing land, property licenses, and right of occupancy licenses, which may be used as collateral (World Bank 2011a). Programs for tenure security, however, often exclude minority communities, new migrants, women, the elderly, and tenants. Cooperative ownership can be an effective arrangement to accommodate the lowest-income households while discouraging premature sale of plots after ownership or occupancy rights are secured.

Controlling Development: Since squatters always live with the threat of eviction, their structures are small and mostly made of temporary materials, especially in new and very small slums. A census of slums in six cities in Bangladesh found that 56 percent of the structures were of very poor quality (Center for Urban Studies 2006). The collapse of one fragile structure built on unstable soil can trigger the collapse of others like dominoes; collapsing structures threaten safety and damage infrastructure; and accumulation of debris can block access to relief. For example, poorly constructed houses compounded the severity of the impacts of the Great Hanshim-Awaji Earthquake in Japan; rubble blocked transportation networks, obstructed firefighters, and made recovery difficult (Nakagawa, Saito, and Yamaga 2007).

Risk-based development controls and building codes tend to be based on standards that are not realistic for slum neighborhoods and call for construction and retrofitting that exceed the financial capacity of low-income families; risk-resilient standards are therefore often ignored (UNISDR 2011). For example, in Caracas, República Bolivariana de Venezuela, although various groups are working to repair and rebuild housing in safer locations, because of poor planning and seismic code enforcement in barrios where homes are constructed with unreinforced masonry, squatters have returned to highly vulnerable sites (Dilley et al. 2005). Disaster-resilient building standards need to be affordable and flexible to allow incremental building. In Windhoek, Namibia, standards and regulations for plot size and infrastructure development were revised to be more affordable, and a community loan fund was set up for service improvements; about 1,000 groups have taken advantage of it (IFRC 2010). Site and housing retrofits should be performed using energy-efficient and affordable building technologies that reduce GHG emissions. Dense low-income areas can be models of environmental efficiency because high densities combined with better management can reduce energy delivery costs.

Planning and building regulations that influence the entire housing stock, such as plot size, road reservations, building setbacks, and floor area ration (FAR) need to be reviewed to encourage private investment in low-income housing in safe parts of the city, but there must be a corresponding increase in infrastructure capacity to keep new risks from arising. In China, with house prices surging, at least 70 percent of the land on which urban housing is constructed is to be allocated to low-rent units and smaller units of less than 90 sq.m. to better house the urban poor (WBI 2011). Development regulations, such as those allowing for mixed land use, can safely support the informal economic activities common to slum dwellers. Streamlining administrative procedures that are complex, time-consuming, and expensive and discourage compliance can heighten compliance with building safety requirements. Regulatory reform can be the single most effective tool for reducing future slums (WBI 2009).

Slum redevelopment that captures urban land values for redistributive purposes and makes urban land affordable to the poor through site-specific development controls has been effective in some cities (see box 2.18), with durable housing for slum dwellers subsidized by higher-income or commercial development on the same site to attract developers (WBI 2009). With additional density of development, it is important to ensure that there is off-site infrastructure.

Basic Services: Enhancing provision of sector-specific services can improve environmental conditions and reduce the vulnerability of slum residents to disaster risks; for example, installing drains to cope with heavy rainfall reduces their vulnerability to flood hazards. Providing basic infrastructure is relatively simple and can be done quickly; it costs less and can be financed by tax and user charges (WBI 2009). Illegal subdivisions in peri-urban areas are increasingly laid out systematically to accommodate later installation of services (UN-HABITAT 2003a).

Trunk infrastructure is expensive. For risk resilience, the use of small-scale distributed green infrastructure in patches that can be connected to existing trunk infrastructure can ensure basic services to a large number of slum residents at relatively little cost. Small-scale distributed infrastructure takes less space, can be accommodated within irregular layouts, and can function as a neighborhood network. Since such projects are designed to restore the ecosystem services of land that has been developed, they may reduce the number of climate change events (UN-HABITAT 2009).

Box 2.18 Incentive-Based Regulations for Low-Income Housing in Jakarta, Indonesia

In 2007 major floods in Jakarta prompted the provincial government to undertake flood mitigation by relocating 350,000 people living along the river bank and improving infrastructure, community preparedness, and early warning systems. The government provides rental flats for low-income households and ownership flats for lower middle-income families (costing about US$12,000–$13,000 for a 36 sq.m. unit); but of an estimated 70,000 housing units needed, the Jakarta government was able to provide only 2,000 a year through its own housing program— and for many slum inhabitants who live on government land, rehousing was considered too expensive, partly because it would negatively impact their informal livelihood activities.

In response to a presidential mass house-building initiative, Jakarta is now working with 28 private developers through the Real Estate Indonesia Association in Jakarta to deliver within a few years up to 20,000 high-rise units in 250 blocks. Developers rely on cross-subsidizing low-income units with middle-income apartments; however, the loss of floor space increases the high-rise unit cost to $21,000. As a result, the developers are shifting to target the middle-income market. The provincial government may withdraw legislation that requires commercial developers to contribute 20 percent of the developable land for low-income housing. The rule was being circumvented by developers who instead pay money into a central fund to provide alternative low-cost accommodation in cheaper, more remote locations.

Sources: Case study courtesy of Budhi Mulyawan. Berita Indonesia 2009; Koran Jakarta 2010; Kristanti 2011; Priliawito and Maryadie 2011; Mirah Sakethi Team 2010; Sawarendro 2010.

Pedestrian Road Networks and Open Spaces: How mobile the urban poor are determines their income opportunities and their integration into society (Baker et al. 2005). Mobility is affected by road safety, the existence of internal road networks, and proximity to major transportation networks. Poor and expensive public transportation to peri-urban slums limits the opportunities of their residents. Haphazard layouts and inadequate open space in slums block ventilation and increase ambient temperatures. Irregular layouts and narrow streets originally planned for pedestrian traffic limit the number of possible locations for water supply, sanitation services, and solid waste collection. Irregular streets can impede relief efforts, especially in large slums; in Port au Prince, Haiti, where 70 percent of the population lives in slums, unplanned growth slowed rescue efforts immediately after the 2010 earthquake because there were no access roads between streets, just a patchwork of unmarked corridors (IFRC 2010). Developing a pedestrian network and planning community open spaces in slums ensures access to livelihoods, escape routes, and community refuges in hazardous areas.

Critical Infrastructure: Slums usually lack adequate health care and educational facilities. The capacity of a slum community to contain losses and recover quickly after a disaster will be greatly enhanced by adequate critical amenities and retrofitting to align with hazard-specific building codes.

Comprehensive Citywide Urban Upgrading: Scaling up strategic slum upgrading and planning for spatial expansion by low-income families in a city-wide urban upgrading program may be complex, time-consuming, and expensive, but it offers a disaster-risk-proof approach (see box 2.19). Physical upgrading can be accomplished with tenure security, basic infrastructure, and socioeconomic development through health services, education, support for employment opportunities, assistance to micro and small businesses, and financial policies for cost allocation, cost recovery, and affordability. If an urban upgrading program is to be realistic, it is necessary to consider the level of services to be provided, building standards, land acquisition, infrastructure, employment generation, and increasing incomes through training and support for small businesses, microfinance, and loans for housing and building materials (WBI 2009). Sites for new housing development, especially in peri-urban areas, must be well connected to employment opportunities and social amenities. Comprehensive urban upgrading requires a legal, institutional, and financial framework to supply land, buildings, services, and credit. Demand for housing and land requires a budget to acquire safe land that has access to transportation and livelihoods. Common approaches to providing low-income housing are "sites and services," land pooling, and land readjustment (WBI 2009). Linking sites with services for housing development has been successful in Lima, Peru. Land readjustment pools plots of strategically located underutilized land and replots them for higher densities; it is being used Indonesia, Malaysia, Nepal, and Thailand (WBI 2011).

Supplying more low-income housing can be facilitated by supporting development finance as well as focusing on consumer access to low-cost housing loans. Apart from conventional economic development programs targeted at reducing poverty, the livelihoods of slum residents can be diversified by engaging them directly in disaster preparedness, early warning and emergency response, and urban upgrading. In Accra, Ghana, street paving, sanitation, and reliable electricity supply in the Suzame Magazine, an area known for informal employment in the automobile mechanical sector, boosted local economic development; the area became a training zone for automobile mechanics, and the projects generated direct employment based on small-scale contracts (IDB 2010).

Project Implementation

For comprehensive risk reduction, it is important to recognize that since all infrastructure is provided in the same space, it should be coordinated in a city-wide spatial plan that maps urban poverty. Conventionally, cities treat urban upgrading as a provision of infrastructure by separate sector-specific agencies. However, slum mapping enhances capacity to upscale slums with benefits across sectors. In Jakarta, Indonesia, despite the city's commitment to the Mayor's Taskforce on Climate Change, Disaster Risks, and the Urban Poor, the idea of integrating projects and programs that increase resilience, improve spatial planning, and decrease poverty into one systematized application is new for the government, which needs institutional reinforcement (World Bank 2011a). Relationships between the local government, line agencies, financial institutions, collection

Box 2.19 Strategic Upgrading of Precarious Settlements in São Paulo, Brazil

In São Paulo, 32.27 percent of the population lives in precarious settlements. Gathering data about the residents of *favelas*, informal subdivisions, slum tenements, and hazardous areas as well as government housing projects for entry into a geo-referenced managerial information system, the Information System for Social Housing in the City of São Paulo (HABISP), made it possible to understand and classify these settlements and set prioritization criteria for interventions. The HABISP identified settlements in the potable water reservoir areas as most precarious.

Table B2.19.1 Characterization of Precarious Settlements for Strategic Intervention

Information needed	Areas unsuited for occupation	Characterization
General description	By approach ramps	Not upgradable
Condition unsuited for	Under bridges or viaducts	↑
occupation	In traffic circles or traffic islands	Total
Legal status	On sanitary landfill or other dumps	Partial
Existing infrastructure	Under high-tension lines	↓
Community organization	On unbuildable areas and riverbeds	Upgradable
Existing programs	In areas at risk of cave-ins or landslides	
	In contaminated areas	
	In nonbuildable areas of the active highway system	
	In nonbuildable areas of the active railway system	

In the Breho Area, flood-prone areas were upgraded; at least 180 households were estimated as needing relocation in resettlement housing and 308 were redistributed on-site.

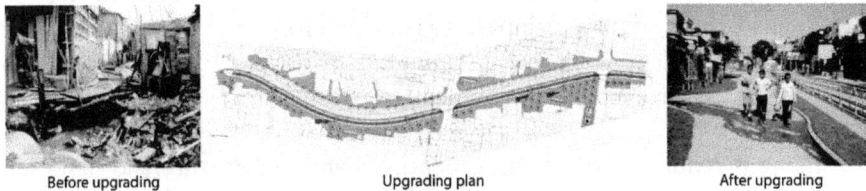

Before upgrading   Upgrading plan   After upgrading

Grotinho Risk Area: Flood-prone area upgraded with relocation of at least 182 families

Before upgrading   During upgrading   After upgrading

Source: Diniz 2010.

The HABISP allowed the Housing Secretariat of the Municipality of São Paulo (SEHAB) to strategically develop numerous community-specific areas through land tenure, slum upgrades, sanitation improvement in environmentally fragile water supply areas, and

box continues next page

Box 2.19 Strategic Upgrading of Precarious Settlements in São Paulo, Brazil *(continued)*

regularization of informal subdivisions. Technical criteria based on indicators of infrastructure, health, social vulnerability, and risk were established to prioritize interventions in each program so as to better allocate funds. A key feature has been integration of public spaces. New housing units that include rental properties are being built. In 2005–08, 2,330 dwelling units were upgraded, 268 affordable rental units constructed, and 2,111 units built by Companhia Metropolitana de Habitação de São Paulo (Cohab-SP). The partnership, which has survived changes in city government and leadership changes within Cities Alliance, demonstrates the importance of long-term planning.

SEHAB's managerial information system, the HABISP, provides data that is geo-referenced to cartographic and photographic databases and has user-friendly data design and entry tools. Data entry was standardized and information from dispersed databases merged so that the extent of slums could be evident. Structure boundaries were determined using aerial photography and field inspections of dwelling units. Data on the water and sewer mains network were crosschecked against geo-referenced data to identify the extent of coverage in each settlement. It is now possible to identify the degree of environmental precariousness in each of the 103 city sub-basins. Continuous updating of the database automatically produces a new chart of precarious conditions, making it possible to evaluate housing assistance in real time. Since March 2008 all content has been open to the public and can thus be monitored.

Source: Cities Alliance 2009. For more information see http://www.habisp.inf.br.

---

agencies, maintenance organizations, the private sector, and civil society need to be tightened through partnerships based on relative advantages of scale and proximity. Being able to work with communities on design and building of physical works and on livelihood development for small businesses and residents is critical (WBI 2009).

Funding is required for risk assessments, urban infrastructure and basic services, and capacity building. Cities currently rely on national and local tax revenues, the private sector, public-private partnerships, and loans and concessional sources through multilateral development banks and donors. The financial structure for cost recovery depends on the financing available, the effectiveness of local taxation, and private sector and community engagement. In the Latin America and Caribbean region, most urban upgrading programs have successfully used cost-benefit analysis to determine financing requirements and allocate funds to the areas most in need (IDB 2010).

Project Monitoring

Indicators to monitor risk reduction through urban upgrading can be linked to the Millennium Development Goals. Several cities have successfully engaged the community in maintenance arrangements and monitoring of slum upgrades. In Rio de Janeiro responsibility for waste management was transferred to community associations; the associations contract with and manage the teams in charge of collecting waste, and the municipal corporation provided training and supervision (IDB 2010).

Concluding Remarks

In essence, urban upgrading is a tool urban planners can use to prioritize risk resilience for the most vulnerable. Apart from building up institutions and engaging the private sector and the community, the key to successfully implementing an urban upgrade program is to maintain an open information system on slum conditions and upgrade programs.

Key Resource

- *Approaches to Urban Slums: Adaptive and Proactive Strategies*, World Bank Institute 2009.

Community and Stakeholder Participation

Social   Institutional

Key Points

- Participation of communities and other stakeholders in urban programming initiatives is a way to build social resilience, which in turn helps to build overall urban resilience.
- Community-driven programming is essential to the success of urban planning and infrastructure projects.
- Bringing neighborhood, community, and municipal men and women into urban programming initiatives and into all phases of the project cycle is a priority.
- Multisector and multilevel partnerships with government and civil society, including community-based organizations, the private sector, and academia, are an effective way to build social resilience, given the diverse range of factors that contribute to disaster and climate-related risk.
- It is vital to ensure that vulnerable and marginalized populations are full and meaningful participants in all processes.

Summary

The limitations of local government capacity to address the disaster risk reduction and climate change adaptation needs of the urban poor has led to recognition of the importance of supporting direct action by low-income individuals, households, and communities. This work has centered on initiatives to protect and increase or diversify their livelihoods and to build community-based disaster risk management capabilities. It includes building the ability of local communities to make demands on local governments and, where possible, to work in partnership with them.

Urban investment planners can help at-risk communities to protect and improve their asset base and build social capital by incorporating actions into urban upgrading, resettlement, and development projects that support household- and community-based responses. Table 2.8 gives examples of asset-based activities that can build resilience to extreme weather events. (Specific sector-level actions are identified in chapter 3.)

Community-Level Programming

Community-based disaster risk management (CBDRM) is an established methodology for building local resilience that has its roots in the good practices developed over several decades of community-focused development and programming to reduce poverty. It takes a holistic approach to disaster risk management that recognizes the links between vulnerability, poverty, and socioeconomic development. Thus, the programming can target combinations of livelihood, infrastructure, and disaster preparedness activities (see table 2.8). The CBDRM approach seeks to understand and build on community coping and adaptation capacities; in recent years, a number of organizations have incorporated a climate change focus (e.g., the Red Cross/Red Crescent Climate Centre).

While a CBDRM approach may not be appropriate to all types of urban investment projects, elements of it should be incorporated into most urban planning, upgrading, and sectoral initiatives that are expected to bring changes to the lives and livelihoods of citizens. For example, in Metro Manila, Philippines, the AusAID-supported pilot program Building the Resilience and Awareness of Metro Manila Communities to Natural Disaster and Climate Change Impacts (BRACE) incorporates a CBDRM component that complements other components for housing and infrastructure, livelihoods, urban planning, and scientific hazards analysis (AusAID 2011).

Many of the World Bank's Social Fund/Community-Driven Development (CDD) projects and subprojects have in recent years also been incorporating activities to build community resilience and local institutional capacity to mitigate the impacts of hazard events as one of the mutually reinforcing components of social protection. The on-site managers of these projects are able to give invaluable local advice from their experiences of working with community and civil society organizations.

Scaling Up: Because undertaking CBDRM processes takes time and resources and can generate expectations, replicating individual local initiatives at scale can be challenging. International CBDRM experience has shown, for instance, that poor communities are unlikely to have the means to reduce many facets of the risks they face without some kind of incentive (IFRC 2010). Box 2.20 provides an example from Bangladesh.

Community-Driven Approaches

Urban investment planners can act as catalysts to encourage and support municipal disaster risk reduction and climate change activities. Urban investment projects can support NGOs and civil society organizations (CSOs), particularly those formed by the urban poor, in collaborating with local

Table 2.8 Examples of Asset-Based Actions to Build Resilience to Extreme Weather

Areas of intervention	Household and neighborhood	Municipal	Regional or national
Protection	Take household and community-based actions to improve housing and infrastructure. Conduct community-based negotiation for safer sites in locations that serve low-income households. Take community-based measures to build disaster-proof assets (such as savings) or protect assets (e.g., insurance).	Work with low-income communities to support slum and squatter upgrades, informed by hazard mapping and vulnerability analysis. Support increased supply and reduced costs of safe sites for housing.	Make government plans to support household, neighborhood, and municipal action. Make risk-reducing investments and take any actions needed beyond urban boundaries.
Pre-disaster damage limitation	Draft community-based disaster preparedness and response plans, covering early warning systems that reach everyone, measures to protect houses, identified safe evacuation sites if needed, and help for those less able to move quickly.	Install early warning systems that reach and serve groups most at risk. Prepare safe sites with services, and organize transportation to them. Protect evacuated areas from looting.	Establish national weather monitoring systems capable of providing early warning. Support community and municipal actions.
Immediate post-disaster response	Support immediate household and community responses to reduce risks in affected areas. Support recovery of assets. Formulate and implement responses.	Encourage and support active engagement of survivors in decisions and responses. Draw on resources, skills, and social capital of local communities. Rapidly restore infrastructure and services.	Fund and provide institutional support for household, community, and municipal responses.
Rebuilding	Provide support for households and community organizations to get back to their homes and communities. Plan to rebuild with greater resilience. Provide support for household and local economic recovery.	Ensure that the reconstruction process supports household and community actions, including addressing the priorities of women, children, and youth. Build or rebuild infrastructure to more resilient standards.	Fund and provide institutional support for household, community, and municipal action. Address deficiencies in regional infrastructure.

Source: Moser and Satterthwaite 2010.

Box 2.20 Scaling Up and Integrating CBDRM into Local Planning Processes

The Comprehensive Disaster Management Programme (CDMP) is a whole-of-government strategy led by the Bangladesh government's Ministry of Food and Disaster Management and implemented by a range of government and private organizations. The community intervention component aims to increase community resilience and strengthen local government capacity to manage risk reduction as part of its development responsibilities.

The program has devised a standardized community risk assessment tool and helped draft local action plans for mainstreaming disaster risk reduction into the work of government authorities. Most important, the program provides a structure to provide local funding for priority actions, motivating local authorities and communities to take part.

More than 400 NGO staff members have been trained to carry out community risk assessments. These are participatory processes that combine scientific data and predictions with discussion of local knowledge. The assessments are done from an all-hazards, all-risks, and all-sectors perspective. As of 2010, assessments had been completed in 622 *parishads* (local governments just below the subdistrict) within 16 districts. About 550 community projects prioritized in the risk reduction action plans had been funded.

The World Bank's Local Government Support Program has begun to use risk reduction action plans drafted using the CDMP to guide its development funding. The program is also training local officials to use this risk assessment guideline to assess vulnerabilities across all sectors, devise strategies to mitigate risk, and facilitate local mainstreaming of disaster risk reduction.

Source: UNISDR/ILO/UNDP 2010, 2–4.

---

and national governments to undertake or scale up demand-driven pro-poor activities that build resilience. Many poverty reduction activities are already closely linked to environmental hazard reduction. Slum upgrading programs are a good example of initiatives that address "everyday" hazards and greatly reduce the vulnerability of the urban poor (see D'Cruz and Satterthwaite 2005).

The International Institute for Environment and Development (IIED) has documented many of the innovative government-CSO urban resilience-building initiatives now under way. Among these are many partnerships between local governments and federations of slum and shack dwellers. In some nations these programs receive considerable support from the national government, as in the *Baan Mankong* (secure tenure) program in Thailand, supported by the government's Community Organizations Development Institute. The Baan Mankong program is a relatively rare example of such programs being undertaken at scale without external financing.

Urban investment projects can help local governments to ensure a pro-poor policy environment and the skills for taking participatory approaches to projects from start to finish.

Support to Public-Private Partnerships

Donor-assisted urban investment projects can help local governments to effectively engage local businesses in project planning and implementation. Local businesspeople, too, must be stakeholders in building urban resilience. Private actors can make real contributions to building resilient economies, infrastructure, and communities by actively participating in such activities as

- assessments of hazard, risk, and coping/adaptive capacity;
- generating hazard and climate change awareness;
- disaster preparedness training and drills;
- improving the logistical efficiency of rescue and relief operations;
- provision of engineers, architects, and building artisans trained in hazard-resilient construction;
- developing and applying cost-effective hazard-resistant technologies;
- developing all-hazard warning and monitoring systems; and
- developing risk financing, transfer, and social safety net instruments.

Local, and sometimes national, government support is crucial for enabling the private sector to do its part. In addition to identifying resource-sharing opportunities, planners of urban projects can facilitate information exchange and dialogue between local government and private sector representatives about areas of potential risk and joint mutual interest and the options available for private sector participation to achieve shared objectives. If the government has a department promoting business and industry, it should be active in this process (Shaw and Matsuoka 2010).

Possible Areas for Collaboration

Business and economic continuity: Small and local businesses need to identify ways to protect themselves from the effects of disasters. Local chambers of commerce and business associations can educate formal or informal businesses about the risks from disaster and climate change and identify methods to better protect small businesses from these risks.

Built environment: Private sector involvement in formulating and improving technical and legal procedures for construction and maintenance of hazard-resilient infrastructure is critical to their acceptance and success. Outreach to small-scale local providers of construction-related services can be particularly important, since much of the building work in informal settlements and urban slums takes place beyond formal government regulatory systems. If resettlement or settlement upgrades are planned, the impact on small businesses should be fully assessed.

Disaster preparedness and early warning systems: Provision of urban lifeline utilities, such as communications, energy, transport, water, and wastewater systems, are often contracted out to private firms. The public-private interdependencies must be understood and planned for in order to protect productive enterprises. Local governments in at-risk locations may enter into a mutual aid agreement with such firms to formalize support that may be needed in a disaster. The local and international private sector has traditionally taken on a major role in post-disaster relief and recovery and should be involved in formulating local disaster risk and hazard risk management systems.

Human and social capacity: Local NGOs and CSOs can help private firms to attain corporate social responsibility goals; for example they might collaborate with finance and insurance companies on risk transfer mechanisms for poor urban communities.

Participation of Vulnerable and Marginalized Populations

It is essential at all levels of the project cycle that urban planners identify the poor and marginalized populations, such as minorities, women, the disabled, or the elderly, that are at greatest risk from future disasters. While the benefits of coordination between these groups and different community stakeholders may be clear, there are many issues that require that strategies be well-thought-out beforehand.

Competing priorities: The residents of poor and informal settlements may see few benefits for them in such partnerships. Survival needs and economic priorities often conflict with risk reduction and climate change adaptation objectives.

Legitimacy and trust: Another major obstacle can be the inability or unwillingness of local government units within a city to work with residents of informal settlements. Many see them as problems rather than contributors to the urban economy (Moser and Satterthwaite 2010).

History of collective organization: Established neighborhoods are usually more resilient due to a dense fabric of social networks that builds up over time; these networks can even transcend sociocultural differences within the community.

Discrimination within communities: Within any urban setting there are likely to be groups who are marginalized or otherwise disadvantaged. The disabled, the elderly, and the very poor—including tenants and informal settlers in urban settings—are often the least resilient populations within a community.

Gender equality: It is often mistakenly assumed that all members of a household experience disaster and climate-related risks in the same way and hence will benefit from the same resilience-building approaches and activities. Because men and women have different roles and responsibilities in their households and communities, however, they face different forms of risk and vulnerability; they will also have different needs and perceptions of what is required to reduce risk. Power differentials due to cultural and sociopolitical constructs of acceptable roles for men and women can mute the voices of women in the project planning process (World Bank 2011b). Therefore, gender analysis of all proposed urban interventions is essential for assessing and identifying specific actions to promote the full and active participation of both genders in project decision making and activities.

Building Urban Resilience • http://dx.doi.org/10.1596/978-0-8213-8865-5

Integrating Community and Stakeholder Participation

To the extent possible projects should promote and enhance community/stakeholder participation, regardless of whether the proposed investment focuses on the neighborhood or the municipal level. Generic steps and actions to accomplish this are outlined in table 2.9.

Project Identification

Project options and scenarios can identify approaches or entry points to incorporate social resilience-building and the time and resources required for stakeholder engagement in detailing the design. For World Bank projects, the Project Concept Note (PCN) and Project Information Document (PID) should summarize the opportunities for, and possible risks associated with, community and stakeholder participation. These may include:

- Conduct initial preparatory work.
- Analyze the sociopolitical context and identify advocates for change.
- Choose effective local partners and form effective partnerships.
- Educate stakeholders (see box 2.21).
- Form stakeholder working groups.
- Encourage stakeholders to share risk information.

Analyze the sociopolitical context: An initial challenge in planning for the mainstreaming of resilience in urban investment projects can be a lack of

Table 2.9 Opportunities for Community and Stakeholder Participation in Urban Investment Projects

Stage of project cycle	Opportunities for community/stakeholder participation
Identification	Conduct initial preparatory work. Analyze the sociopolitical context for participatory approaches and building disaster/climate resilience. Choose effective local, regional, and national partners. Educate and build the support of stakeholders. Form stakeholder working groups.
Preparation/appraisal	Recruit technical experts in sociology and community development. Conduct risk, vulnerability, and coping/adaptive capacity analysis (VCA) and draft participatory scenarios. Undertake multi-stakeholder planning. Draw up a community participation and communications strategy that is social- and gender-inclusive, with performance indicators.
Implementation	Form neighborhood associations. Carry out resilience education with participating communities. Conduct local VCAs or community hazard/spatial mapping and draw action plans for CBDRM subprojects.
Monitoring, evaluation, and knowledge-sharing	Develop a system for monitoring and evaluating participatory community projects. Put in place community-centered complaints handling and grievance procedures. Support community and local government peer-to-peer exchanges. Encourage sharing of risk information in sustainable ways.

Box 2.21 Stakeholder Collaboration in Indonesia

The Merapi Forum is a multi-stakeholder forum that manages the risks and resources of Mt. Merapi, an active volcano on the island of Java. The entire population of the four surrounding districts is vulnerable to Merapi's eruptions, and more than 320,000 people live in the most hazardous areas. The Forum targets stakeholders from three surrounding districts under the authority of Central Java Province and one under the Special Region of Yogyakarta Province. Among the members are community groups; four district and two provincial governments; BPPTK (the Office for the Study and Development of Volcanic Technology, National Ministry for Energy and Mineral Resources); universities; media; an NGO; the Indonesian Red Cross; and a number of donors.

The Forum was initiated in 2006 by local government authorities, although groundwork for the collaboration stretched back several years. The secretariat is hosted by BPPTK, the national institution with the highest authority over geological hazards. This has been effective because BPPTK is perceived as more or less free from vested interests and can be accepted by local participants as a neutral arbiter. The initiative has substantially built the capacity of local communities and local governments through a range of practical joint activities on disaster risk reduction, such as disaster simulations, contingency planning exercises, and participatory risk mapping. It has fostered mutual understanding among the stakeholders and established cross-border and cross-sector collaboration in risk reduction.

The participatory process gives communities space to take the lead in their areas of responsibility for reducing disaster risk, and the local governments have appreciated their work. Ownership has been fostered, particularly among local governments and community members directly at risk from the volcano. Different stakeholders have shown substantial willingness to contribute resources to programs and activities, with practical support provided by central and provincial governments.

Source: Government of Bangladesh, Ministry of Disaster Management and Relief n.d.

awareness, interest, or capacity for disaster risk reduction and climate change adaptation within city/municipal governments; nor are civil servants necessarily comfortable with community-centered approaches. The early stages of discussion of a potential urban investment project between donor and partner government may need to be preceded by, or to incorporate, activities with local government partners to raise awareness, build political support, and identify capacity gaps.

The first step in this process is a preliminary situation analysis of the sociopolitical and institutional context in order to assess opportunities (e.g., existing consultative mechanisms, effective advocates for inclusive decision making, potential project partners) and constraints (e.g., weak, disinterested, or oppositional authorities; history of conflict) on effective stakeholder participation or disaster risk reduction and climate change adaptation. A stakeholder analysis should be part of this process to identify supportive individuals in positions of influence who can act as champions for disaster/climate resilience and a participatory decision making process—an approach that has proven effective (Center for Science in the Earth System 2007). These can come from inside or outside government. However, if such leadership is lacking, a champion may need to be cultivated.

Form effective partnerships: Experienced, locally respected, and politically independent implementing partners can act as a bridge between communities and local authorities. Some international NGOs have observed that there is usually not a large pool of CSOs or NGOs in urban areas with a specific focus on, or competencies in, disaster risk reduction or climate change adaptation. Often local partners have been involved in other areas of resilience-building support to local communities (Pelling 2010). For example, many local government-community partnerships in Africa and Asia have been initiated through federations of slum dwellers (World Bank 2011a, 21). Multilevel partnerships are also important for bringing communities together with their local, regional, and national governments. For instance, advocacy by national agencies has sometimes been central in changing the attitudes of local governments toward their citizens, and thus their practices. National disaster risk reduction and climate change adaptation policies, legislation, and coordination mechanisms have also helped leverage resources for local activities (Pelling 2010).

Educate and build the support of key stakeholders: Local champions and partner organizations can guide and support early work to sensitize stakeholders to disaster and climate change risks, e.g., through discussion, peer learning exchanges with other municipalities, and formal training. Because local governments have to make decisions about many competing priorities, there is a natural tendency to give priority to addressing immediate and visible risks rather than avoiding future negative outcomes. It is therefore usually preferable for awareness-raising activities to draw from real-life examples and evidence of the costs of inaction and link the benefits of potential courses of action to achievement of broader urban development priorities (Center for Science in the Earth System 2007). The information should be adjusted to reflect the interests of different stakeholder groups, e.g., explaining to the housing authorities how consultation with women can result in safer and more practical housing and settlement designs (Pasteur 2011).

In some cases, building on momentum created by a recent disaster can be an effective entry point to engage local governments and communities with long-term resilience building efforts. For example, the Asian Cities Climate Change Resilience Network (ACCCRN) found that cooperative action by diverse city actors in Surat, India, was triggered by the memory of the 2006 floods and other disasters (ACCCRN 2011).

Project Preparation/Appraisal

For World Bank–supported projects, the detailed design and the Project Appraisal Document (PAD) should specify the nature and extent of social resilience and serve as a foundational document during this stage. It may also be necessary at this point to consult with experts in community development.

Conduct risk, vulnerability, and coping/adaptive capacity analysis: The Vulnerability and Capacity Assessment (VCA) methodology is generally used in CBDRM projects to involve local government and business leaders and identify resource needs (Pelling 2010). The analysis can be used as a basis for municipal planning for a wide range of resilience-building measures, not just those related to disasters. In recent years, climate change and hazard trends have been increasingly incorporated into VCA methodologies. The World Bank has used participatory scenario development to identify risk from future climate change, which can be adapted to VCA.

Multi-stakeholder planning: Collated technical and community data, including programming options, should be analyzed and discussed with a range of stakeholders. Public meetings and structured dialogues with the affected communities are effective. A good example of multi-stakeholder planning is explored in box 2.22.

Box 2.22 Stakeholder Participation in Climate Resilience Awareness-Raising and Planning

The City of New York decided that multi-stakeholder, multilevel decision making on urban development and climate change was essential to build policy and programming mixes that were robust enough to deal with most possible future scenarios and ensure that policy choices did not have unacceptable consequences for stakeholders. In 2006 Mayor Michael R. Bloomberg created the Office of Long-Term Planning and Sustainability and charged it with drafting a comprehensive sustainability plan for the city's future. The result, the PlaNYC, was a plan to prepare the city for one million more residents by 2030, strengthen the economy, combat climate change, and enhance the quality of life for all New Yorkers. As part of the office's mandate to address housing, transportation, and other infrastructure needs over the next 25 years, it coordinated formulation of a climate adaptation strategy. A Climate Change Adaptation Task Force was convened to draw up a coordinated plan for critical infrastructure. It consisted of over 40 public and private sector stakeholders and was supported by a panel of scientists, academics, and private sector experts.

The planning office, in coordination with the relevant city departments, met with more than 100 advocacy organizations, conducted community meetings in each borough, and collected thousands of e-mails through its website. A "stakeholder interactive approach" was exercised by building contacts with national, regional, and municipal agencies involved in areas like urban planning, transport, environmental management, and disaster response. The city-wide adaptation plan and the more comprehensive PlaNYC sustainability plan were released in 2007. The plans bring together more than 25 city agencies to work toward the vision of a greener, greater New York. Rather than guiding outward urban expansion it gives priority to improving current buildings and building codes and to strategic placement of public facilities. PlaNYC also calls for a community-based approach to deal with the situation of the most vulnerable communities: the city has been working on site-specific adaptation plans through a community planning process with stakeholder groups.

---

box continues next page

Box 2.22 Stakeholder Participation in Climate Resilience Awareness-Raising and Planning
(continued)

Significant progress has been reported toward achievement of the long-term PlaNYC goals. As of 2011, hundreds of acres of new parkland have been built and existing parks improved. More than 64,000 units of housing have been created or improved, along with entire new neighborhoods with access to transit. The city government has also enacted ambitious laws to make buildings more energy-efficient and has reduced greenhouse gas emissions 13 percent below 2005 levels. Overall, more than 97 percent of the 127 initiatives in PlaNYC were launched within a year of its release and almost two-thirds of its 2009 milestones were achieved completely or almost completely.

Sources: City of New York 2011; Rosenzweig and Solecki 2010; World Bank 2008, 67, 68; World Bank 2011a, 16.

Community participation and communication strategy: Throughout the project the consultative process should produce information about appropriate approaches to community/stakeholder participation and communication, taking into account social and gender inclusiveness.

Implementation

Form neighborhood associations: Established urban neighborhoods in poor communities and informal settlements, along with their neighborhood associations, can be a good entry point for working with communities on building social resilience; this is especially the case where communities lack cohesiveness or do not trust outsiders. Where there are no associations, they may need to be formed and given sufficient time to build their legitimacy and capacity. Some strategies for effective use of neighborhood associations are

- Engaging a network of community promoters to deliver and reinforce project messages to new households in the community;
- Community-led training of new committee members; and
- Continuing opportunities for peer learning and support.

Educational activities: Where disasters do not recur regularly or have not been previously experienced, building and maintaining community participation in projects can be challenging. Innovative approaches to education about disaster/climate change risks may be required, combined with hands-on demonstrations of cost-effective methods to reduce risk. For example, in Senegal the city of St. Louis has set up climate change observation centers, put in place special training programs, and enlisted teachers to explain climate change (UNISDR 2011). Examples of public awareness and social marketing tools that have been effective include the following:

- Commissioned scripts adapted for street performance, radio, and TV;
- Curricula for schools;

- Training community members to conduct outreach to households; and
- Community events, such as dances, competitions, and sports meets (ADPC 2005).

Nepal incorporated these elements in its approach to education about earthquakes (see box 2.23).

Monitoring, Evaluation, and Knowledge-Sharing

Monitoring: There are many proven methods of involving community groups or members in a participatory monitoring system, such as public posting of project information and public meetings, adopting complaints handling and grievance procedures, monitoring by CSOs, and social audits. Box 2.24 provides an example from Indonesia.

Evaluation: Where possible, representatives of community-based organizations, NGOs, CSOs, and local businesses should be invited to play specific roles in any program/project evaluation.

Knowledge-sharing: Developing a community of practice with different stakeholders can also be useful for building effective partnerships. As data are

---

Box 2.23 Building Earthquake Risk Awareness and Safety in Nepal

Nepal has a long history of destructive earthquakes, with seismic studies suggesting that major earthquakes occur about every 75 years. Since the last major earthquake of 1934, the risk for the Kathmandu valley has increased significantly because of uncontrolled development, failure to incorporate earthquake safety into construction, and lack of awareness among the authorities as well as the general population. The Kathmandu Valley Earthquake Risk Management Project (KVERMP) sought to address this situation—a challenging task when there had been no earthquake for many years.

The project used a variety of means to increase community and government understanding and action to reduce earthquake risk. There was a symposium, an awareness rally, and an art exhibition and competition, and posters, booklets, and leaflets were distributed. Much of this activity was centered on Nepal's annual Earthquake Safety Day. The ability of 10 schools to withstand earthquakes was assessed, and 4 were selected for retrofitting. In each municipality local stakeholders were consulted. It was agreed that the project would contribute technical assistance and train local masons and carpenters on earthquake-resistant construction, and the communities would provide material and labor.

The low-tech approach adopted for school seismic safety screening and the use of simulations and loss estimates from the 1934 earthquake for educational activities had a significant impact on the community without causing undue panic. Ordinary people started taking interest in earthquake issues and raising questions. In two wards of the Kathmandu municipality, residents took action on their own initiative to assess and decrease risk to their neighborhoods.

Source: Adapted from ADPC 2006.

Box 2.24 Monitoring the National Program for Community Empowerment in Indonesia

The National Program for Community Empowerment (PNPM) urban program in Indonesia won a World Bank innovation award in 2009 and continues to set a high standard for community/stakeholder participation and community-friendly features like these:

- *Community participatory monitoring* involves community groups or their members in monitoring and overseeing program activities. In addition to assessing progress and identifying ways to improve the program, these activities facilitate community learning.
- *Information accessibility and transparency*: Project information must be accessible for community members to check and verify. Information about project activities and budgets should be posted on information boards and project sites.
- *Open public meetings:* As a general principle for community participation and transparency and accountability, all project meetings should be open to the public and community members should be allowed to participate. As works in progress, projects should also hold accountability meetings to report on project status and finances.
- *Complaints handling and grievance procedures:* Community members and the general public can channel complaints or inquiries via P.O. box, short message service (SMS) (since cell phones reach most urban areas) or communication with local government officials and facilitators. There are activities to build the awareness of residents about their rights and the complaint mechanisms.
- *Management information systems (MIS) and website-project MIS*: The public website contains basic project information and updates, including reports on the status of complaints.
- *NGO monitoring*: CSOs and NGOs have been invited to monitor the program independently. They are seen as playing a critical role in ensuring that communities, especially marginalized groups, the poor, and women, have the opportunity to participate in PNPM urban activities.

Source: World Bank 2010c.

collected, it is important to encourage that the information be shared in sustainable ways.

Concluding Remarks

Community and stakeholder participation is at the very center of development, yet the reality is that such programs are very difficult because the priorities of communities and stakeholders are often different from those of urban planners. It may be easy to think that there is no reason for community participation in infrastructure development because infrastructure will be a universal good, but in fact such programs are the actual connections between communities and governance structures. This handbook takes a long-term view of resilience because establishing good governance takes generations. There is no minimum standard for community and stakeholder participation to be met in an urban project; rather, there should always be enough flexibility to do what is reasonable in a given context. The practical application of resilience theory is to always be building better systems so that communities are better equipped for the future.

Disaster Management Systems

Infrastructural   Institutional   Economic

Key Points
- Providing accurate and timely information to decision makers and response units is crucial for saving lives and property.
- Recognition of residual risk implies that cities need to continuously improve risk communication, early warning systems, and emergency contingency, evacuation, and recovery planning.
- Disaster management systems depend on effective assignment of responsibilities and communication and collaboration between the government, local stakeholders, and the community affected.

Summary
Disaster management systems are part of an operational mitigation approach that addresses preparedness and temporary measures to reduce the immediate impacts of disasters. Although locational and structural approaches can reduce the potential for damage from a natural disaster, it is often not possible to eliminate these risks. Given residual risks, there must be operational capability for responding to disasters. While technological advances have made it easier to prepare for and manage disasters, at the heart of any disaster management system is effective cooperation between government, local stakeholders, and the community. Crowd-sourcing and modern applications like Twitter have greatly enhanced response capacity in urban areas; however, authorities must still clearly delineate and communicate responsibilities before a disaster (Acar and Muraki 2011). This type of collaboration requires a robust institutional framework, day-to-day work, and training.

Institutional and Legal Frameworks
Urban-focused disaster management should be seen as an extension of local networks, national systems, and even international regional disaster networks. As complex systems exposed to natural disasters, urban areas need to have in place an emergency response framework that aligns with regional and national disaster management systems. The objective is to create systems that are complementary and encourage collaboration between different levels of authority and affected communities.

Whether disaster management systems will be effective depends on *legislation* that delineates rules and responsibilities for preparing for and responding to disasters. Responsibility for geographic and hazard-related areas should be specified clearly and communicated across government, the private sector, NGOs, and civil society. An early entry point for cities is to fully review existing capacity to prepare for and respond to natural disasters so that planners can determine what is still needed. Consultations will not only identify gaps but also help stakeholders to understand their roles and ensure their participation in the process.

Public Awareness

Understanding natural and technological hazards and communicating needed information is vital. Public authorities have a responsibility to protect their citizens, which includes giving them information about risks. Public awareness strategies include dissemination of response *information materials* (e.g., hazard and evacuation maps) through a variety of channels (radio, TV, press, public information centers, mailing lists). Age-differentiated student education on natural hazards, prevention, preparedness, and response is effective; it saved many lives in Japan after the 2011 earthquake and tsunami. *Educational programs* can be general or tailored to a region or a certain type of disaster. Targeted school curricula, educational materials, and teacher training can transmit a scientific understanding of natural hazards.

Local Resilience Action Plans

Effective upstream planning for short- and long-term hazards offers a unique opportunity for planners to rethink past practices, improve the sustainability of human settlements, and effectively prepare communities to deal with threats and risks. Cities might consider an LRAP or similar tool based on the potential impacts of climate change and natural disasters at least for highly vulnerable areas and where possible for the entire city. The plan is preparation for protecting citizens, infrastructure, and such assets as the city's historical and cultural heritage. Ideally the action plan would deal with both hard (infrastructure and physical investments) and soft (governance, education, and awareness) measures to reduce risk, and would define institutional responsibilities and a preferred sequencing of action. The National Association for Voluntary and Community Action (NAVCA) in the United Kingdom has published guidance notes on creating an LRAP on its website (www.navca.org.uk).

Emergency Response Planning

An emergency response plan should identify patterns for stakeholder coordination, both horizontally with local actors and vertically with regional and national authorities. Typically, emergency response plans have both *operational and logistical components*, including procedures for damage and needs assessment after a disaster. National response plans often specify procedures on how to request international assistance; local plans pay more attention to evacuation and shelter. Stakeholder consultations should inform the drafting of these plans (see box 2.25) to ensure effective coordination during and after a disaster.

Building Urban Resilience • http://dx.doi.org/10.1596/978-0-8213-8865-5

Box 2.25 Case Study: Lincolnshire Mapping of Critical Assets

In 2010 in the United Kingdom, Lincolnshire's Critical Infrastructure and Essential Services Group held a series of workshops to analyze critical infrastructure along the coast. They were attended by local representatives and asset owners, including Anglian Water, CE Electric, British Telecom, and five local drainage boards. The results fed into local Multi-Agency Flood Plan community impact assessments.

The agenda for the workshops covered four issues: identifying assets, assessing their ability to continue to provide services during a flood, highlighting interdependencies between asset owners, and how long it would take to restore services. The workshops were an opportunity to review and update Lincolnshire's GIS system, which already contains such sites as telephone exchanges, electricity substations, water and waste assets, and such vulnerable community assets as blue light services, rest centers, and schools. Highlighted were locations where the impact of community flooding would be significantly worsened by infrastructure failure.

Source: U.K. Cabinet Office 2011.

Emergency Operations Center

Establishing an emergency operations center (EOC) is crucial to coordinate emergency services. The EOC activates staff to respond to emergencies; requests resources, such as equipment and rescue teams; coordinates response and recovery activities; tracks resources; and collects damage and needs assessments and other information from the field. Its effectiveness relies on the country's legislative and institutional disaster risk management (DRM) platform, which clearly identifies stakeholder responsibilities and institutionalizes coordination. In Turkey, World Bank projects helped establish the national emergency operations center in Ankara and the center for Istanbul province, which has full technical information and communication capacities to manage emergencies and disasters.

Early Warning Systems

Monitoring, alert, and early warning systems communicate hazard forecasts to the public. An early warning system comprises a regularly tested process to receive data and disseminate warnings 24 hours a day, 7 days a week and a back-up system to ensure that communications can continue if the primary system fails. Communications are hazard-specific, and emergency directions are clear.

Alert and warning systems are designed for specific hazards. For instance, flood, heavy rain, and strong wind warning systems combine meteorological data (rainfall, snowmelt, storms) with river and reservoir water-level measurements to provide data for warnings. The early warning system should establish data sharing and functional linkages between hydrometeorological service organizations, emergency response units, and the authorities to allow sufficient time to inform the public of what can be done, such as evacuations, and launch rescue operations. With regard to flood early warning, cooperation between administrative entities sharing river basins is particularly important.

Earthquakes have been the one major natural hazard that traditionally has not had a near real-time warning. Conceptually, instruments sited close to known earthquake faults can detect initial waves and send a radio or landline signal to a city a few seconds before the damaging ground motions. This basic concept underlies the recent development of Earthquake Early Warning Systems (EEWS) in Japan; Taiwan, China; Mexico; and Turkey: The Urgent Earthquake Detection and Alarm System (UrEDAS) has been used widely in the Japanese railway system since the 1980s. Mexico City established an EEWS in 1991 after the disastrous 1985 earthquake; as of May 2005 the system had generated 57 warning signals with an average of 60 seconds in advance of earthquake effects, with 11 of the warnings broadcast to the public.

Post-Disaster Services
First-response services consist of firefighting, medical, public safety, and search and rescue services. Typically firefighters not only manage fires but also respond to vehicle accidents and hazardous material emergencies, such as explosions. Search and rescue, swift water rescue, and other specialized teams usually fall under civil protection or firefighting services. Provision of equipment and tools like personal protection equipment or emergency medical units can strengthen first response. Planning for location of emergency response equipment should consider accessibility and storage safety. *Continuous training* and exercises strengthen first responders. An essential element of emergency response is mass care for the public, such as temporary shelters and stations to provide medical assistance, food, and water. Effective public care takes into account shelter services, sanitation, emergency power, safety of emergency supplies, and prevention of infectious outbreaks.

Training Exercises
Once plans are drafted, relevant groups need training and exercises to test for gaps and shortfalls. National, regional, and local levels should test coordination, response, and readiness and modify emergency response plans as needed.

Logistics
The backbone of emergency response is logistics, which covers facility management, resource management, and transportation. Facility management encompasses the identification, acquisition, and set-up of response facilities, such as staging areas. Resource management refers to the identification, acquisition, storage, maintenance, distribution, accounting, and disposal of emergency resources. Transportation prepares for movement of resources into the affected area. Logistics requires close coordination of all emergency functions. Box 2.26 gives examples of emergency standards for businesses and infrastructure

Building Urban Resilience · http://dx.doi.org/10.1596/978-0-8213-8865-5

Box 2.26 Risk Management and Business Continuity Standards

ISO 31000:2009

ISO 31000 is a family of standards relating to risk management codified by the International Organization for Standardization. The purpose of ISO 31000:2009 is to provide principles and generic guidelines; it seeks to provide a universal paradigm for practitioners and companies employing risk management processes to replace the myriad of standards, methodologies, and paradigms that differ by industry, subject matter, and regions. ISO offers three publications on ISO 31000 to help organizations address risk in a standardized way:

- ISO 31000: Principles and Guidelines on Implementation;
- IEC 31010: Risk Management—Risk Assessment Techniques; and
- ISO/IEC 73: Risk Management—Vocabulary.

Source: ISO n.d.

British Standard 25999 for Business Continuity Management

In the United Kingdom, as part of their organizational resilience strategy, infrastructure owners and operators may adopt plans based on British Standard 25999 for Business Continuity Management. This benchmark standard for corporate resilience enables organizations to change business processes and decisions to improve their ability to manage disruption from natural hazards.

The U.K. Cabinet Office notes that

> Meeting the requirements of BS 25999 certification may be disproportionate. For example, infrastructure owners may already be legally obligated to maintain high-quality business continuity plans or, for smaller firms in particular, the cost may be too high. However, organizations may find it valuable to review BS 25999 to assess whether following the principles and process within the British standard would strengthen their current business continuity arrangements. Many small businesses may not find it cost-effective to comply fully with BS 25999. But the government will encourage organizations to adopt and embed improved business continuity management within their operations.

As follow-up, the U.K. Cabinet Office has sponsored development of a Publically Available Specification in Crisis Management (PAS 200). The premise for the PAS is that crisis management is much more than simply the ability to respond to crises as they occur.

Source: U.K. Cabinet Office 2011.

---

operators, highlighting both advantages and limitations. Effective use of standards relies on close stakeholder coordination.

Communications

Delivery of accurate and timely information to decision makers and response units is crucial for saving lives and property. In damaging infrastructure, disasters can immediately change the way citizens communicate. It is the role of the disaster management system to prepare for such failures and ensure that affected communities receive the information they need through, e.g., interoperable communication systems for both voice and data across emergency management agencies, such as fire brigades and medical units. Emergency management information systems collect, analyze, and share real-time data across national, regional, and local levels. The system should allow for two-way processing of information and support daily agency operations as well as extending information all the way to individual and family levels.

Crowd Sourcing, Social Media, and New Technologies

Because decentralized social systems have proved vital in recent natural disasters, they should be recognized in disaster management communication strategies. Information essential to victims needs to be communicated repeatedly through multiple media to ensure that it has reached and been understood by all who need it. Online information and social conversations need to be part of the mix of tools for recovery (see box 2.27).

Retention of information can be challenging for people affected by disasters. Internet and cell phone networks can be essential because of the huge population displacements after disasters. Social media tools *Twitter* and *Ushahidi* have proved useful in disasters. Box 2.28 gives an example of how social media were applied in the Horn of Africa crisis.

Box 2.27 Uses of Social Media in Disasters

People use social and online media to get real-time information. With the recent expansion of cell phone networks, in disaster situations mobile phones are often the major means of two-way communication available. While radio is a universal source of emergency information, the increasing use of smart phones means that those caught in these circumstances are searching the web or using tools like Twitter to get location-based information.

Disaster information is one of the most highly forwarded information in social media. Many users, though often removed from the situation, forward information to ensure it reaches as wide an audience as possible. This has its advantages—but also its dangers.

Incorrect information can spread like wildfire. Information is placed on social media sites on the good-faith understanding that the poster has the correct information. In disaster situations, however, the information can sometimes be incorrect because emergency situations often change faster than the speed of social media, or the heightened state of pressure during a crisis can lead to a misreading of the situation.

Social media can help monitor and address disaster and recovery issues. The immediacy of social media makes it invaluable for monitoring situations. Victims of natural disasters, taken out of their comfort zones and regular modes of interaction with services, will often vent frustration through many outlets. Monitoring online media can help identify issues that may not be obvious on the ground.

Source: Micallef 2011.

Box 2.28 Sharing Data to Rebuild a Region

The 2011 hunger crisis in the Horn of Africa is an intense reminder that development and humanitarian actors need to work together closely in monitoring and engaging early in slow-onset disasters.

The World Bank/GFDRR has now developed the Horn of Africa Mapping Project, an initiative for sharing all the data collected by humanitarian and development agencies working on the Horn of Africa response. The Mapping Project's objectives are to

- Systematize the collection of data by organizations working in the region into a single open-source mapping platform to support decision making and build resilience.
- Build capacity within the region to host and share the data collected on the mapping platform.
- Collect further critical data.
- Create maps of the region to aid in planning and recovery.
- Create tools to enable offline usage of the data.

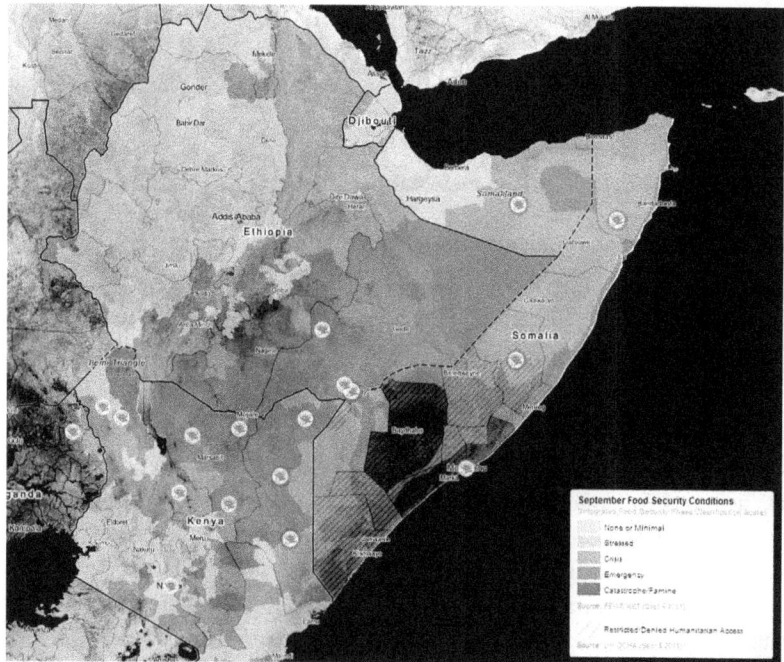

A data-sharing platform based on GeoNode is being hosted by a regional mapping agency in Nairobi and populated with data provided by teams at the Global Facility for Disaster Reduction and Recovery (GFDRR), the World Food Programme (WFP), the United Nations Office for Coordination of Humanitarian Affairs (UNOCHA), the Famine Early Warning System Network (FEWS), the U.S. State Department's Humanitarian Information Unit (HIU), the Regional Center for Mapping of Resources for Development (RCMRD), and a number of other

box continues next page

leading technical or mapping agencies. Regular meetings further institutionalize the partnership; the partners jointly invest in developing offline and low-bandwidth tools to make the project more useful; and there is a strong commitment to focus on supporting Bank programming in the countries affected. The conversation will continue as the teams elaborate a joint work program for this initiative.

Source: http://horn.rcmrd.org. See also: http://www.gfdrr.org/gfdrr/node/1035.

Integration of *Twitter* into simple mobile phones has helped with near real-time hazard monitoring and post-disaster impact assessments. While disaster management authorities can create accounts where users can send direct messages, it is probably users who will control how topics are presented. Communication strategies should incorporate capacity to monitor Twitter and transmit key information to first responders and other authorities. Even though there are improvements needed for the use of Twitter in disaster response, such as a robust way of semantic analysis related to the disaster, it can still be used to communicate directly with users who tweet from disaster areas and open dialogue between victims and responders.

Ushahidi, another crowd-sourcing tool, uses volunteer technical communities (VTCs) brought together through the Internet and mobile telephones. Ushahidi is a nonprofit that works with local governments to use the tool on open-source platforms, but it also can be used and managed without local government. Ushahidi does require management for gathering data from disaster zones, verifying it, and transmitting the information to authorities. It helps disaster management systems to gather information from citizens in near-real-time and display that information in maps. So far, Ushahidi has primarily been used for disaster assessments and impacts.

Concluding Remarks

Response systems are central to mitigating the impacts of a disaster. Capacity to respond to disasters and quickly recover is vital to resilience and operational mitigation. Given residual risk and future uncertainties, continuous investments in the institutional, operational, logistical, and communication components of emergency and response systems are crucial for any disaster risk management system.

Data Gathering, Analysis, and Application

Institutional   Infrastructural

Key Points
- Data systems and risk analysis are the basis for well-informed decision making to effectively mitigate disaster impact.

- Urban planners should have a strategy that brings local government units, communities, and stakeholders into the process of gathering, analyzing, and managing data.
- Tools for creating, managing, and sharing GIS data are instrumental in all steps of resilient disaster risk management.
- GeoNode is an open-source platform for analysis, management, and the web-based publication of geospatial data.

Summary

Reaching decisions on how to prioritize resilience efforts depends on a spatial and temporal understanding of risk. GIS tools are important for spatially understanding resilience in an urban area, especially if operated in a dynamic and sustainable way. Risk data should be used to understand the current state of resilience and set goals rather than being used as a predictive tool (Cutter, Burton, and Emrich 2010).

Being able to quantify the impacts of planned or proposed investments is critical to reducing risk. Sustainable risk information systems and analytical tools allow for systematic and evidence-based understanding and communication of risk. National, local, and city governments need to both invest in geospatial risk information and make it available in a sustainable and user-friendly format so that the whole community can actively participate in reducing and preventing disaster risk. Providing credible and reliable information, such as the geographic distribution of hazards and the vulnerability of structures, can be seen as both a public good and a critical element of urban hazard management (Lall and Deichmann 2009).

Data Gathering

Urban planners view data gathering as a way to increase the capacity of institutions to build and maintain disaster-related information and inform long-term decision making. Data gathering may be global or local—both are important for understanding resilience, even though the information extracted depends on the scale. Global data provide a general picture of resilience. Local case studies provide a nuanced understanding of a given territory or community; though they may explore resilience to a single hazard, the data resolution is very high. In all cases, the goal of data gathering is to encourage efforts to collect and maintain data in a form that governments, international organizations, and other stakeholders can easily use.

GIS Platforms and Tools

With the explosion of new technology in recent years, integration of GIS into development projects has increased dramatically. GIS platforms and tools are a sustainable and smart way to manage geospatial information. Geographic data make it possible to collect local indicators, such as population density or infrastructure locations, that can be used to build resilience. Generally speaking, projects and studies that gather localized data require a good deal of resources and because of funding issues the data are often not kept current. The Hazus standard and software created by the U.S. Federal Emergency Management Agency is a good example of a well-managed stand-alone database, although web-based applications and platforms are increasing (see box 2.29).

Box 2.29 Hazus

Hazus is a standardized methodology and software application for the United States that contains models for estimating potential losses from earthquakes, hurricanes, and floods. Hazus uses geographic information system (GIS) technology to estimate the likely physical, economic, and social impacts of disasters. It graphically illustrates the limits of locations identified as at high risk. Users can then visualize the spatial relationships between populations and permanently fixed geographic assets or resources for the specific hazard being modeled. Potential loss estimates analyzed in Hazus include

- Physical damage to residential and commercial buildings, schools, critical facilities, and infrastructure;
- Economic loss, including lost jobs, business interruptions, and repair and reconstruction costs; and
- Social impacts, including estimates of shelter requirements, displaced households, and populations exposed to scenario floods, earthquakes, and hurricanes.

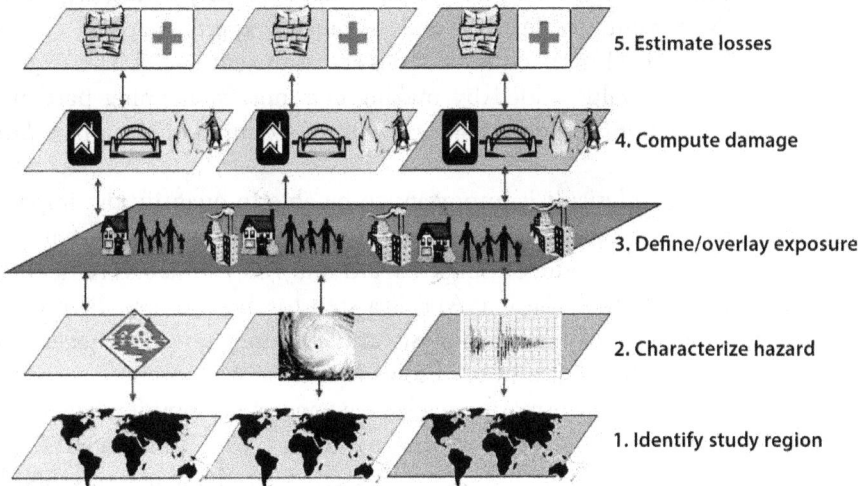

Source: FEMA, Hazus, website: http://www.fema.gov/hazus/.

OpenStreetMap (OSM) is an innovative approach to collecting primary and field data pre- and post-disaster. It makes use of new 2.0 technology and VTCs (World Bank/GFDRR Labs 2011). Since it is web-based it can create a free and open map of the entire world, built entirely by volunteers surveying with GPS, digitizing aerial imagery, and collecting and liberating public sources of geographic data. Information from OSM can fill in base map data gaps to support disaster and crisis response. Just as OSM data bridges missing information, the Humanitarian OpenStreetMap Team (HOT) acts as a bridge between traditional humanitarian responders and the OSM community. HOT works both remotely and physically to help countries collect and use geographic data and train communities in using OSM tools.

The Community Mapping for Preparedness initiative in Indonesia started in 2011 as a partnership led by the Australia-Indonesia Facility for Disaster Reduction (AIFDR), Indonesia's National Disaster Management Agency (*Badan Nasional Penanggulangan Bencana* [BNPB]), and HOT with support from the World Bank/GFDRR. The main goal was to use OSM tools to collect building-level exposure data for risk assessment applications, such as a post-disaster needs analysis (PDNA), and preparedness and contingency planning exercises. Among particularly useful OSM features are open source tools for online or offline mapping, a common platform for uploading and hosting data with free and open access, and an active global community of users.

In a little over a year, more than 200,000 buildings were mapped and new partners—five of Indonesia's largest universities, local government agencies, international development agencies, and CSOs—were trained and are now using the platform in Jakarta. Most recently the OSM tools were part of the data preparedness and flood contingency planning activity led by the Province of Jakarta's disaster management agency. Teams of university students, government officials, community leaders, and technical experts mapped critical infrastructure and neighborhood boundaries across the entire city. This experience highlights the value added by making community mapping part of a disaster risk reduction program. Figure 2.3 is an example of the maps produced by OSM.

InaSAFE data analysis: It is important to be able to quantify the impacts of planned or proposed investments, but it is also critical to invest in the underlying science to produce robust hazard and risk estimates. A flexible, dynamic, and simple tool like InaSAFE is a step toward more resilient decisions by making state-of-the-art analysis available to disaster managers for their daily work. InaSAFE is a suite of tools that close the loop between sharing data and actionable information, including concrete recommendations for actions, to support resilient decision making. Since early 2011 InaSAFE has been under development in Indonesia through a partnership with BNPB, AIFDR, World Bank/GFDRR Labs, and the World Bank Building Urban Resilience in East Asia Initiative. InaSAFE is being developed dynamically through deep technical engagement with government of Indonesia stakeholders.

InaSAFE is designed to work as a web-based tool on top of the GeoNode, an open source geospatial data management platform, or as a desktop system using QuantumGIS open source software. It combines critical elements of GIS analysis

Figure 2.3 Illustration of OpenStreetMap Use: Critical Infrastructure in Kelurahan Tomang in Jakarta, Indonesia

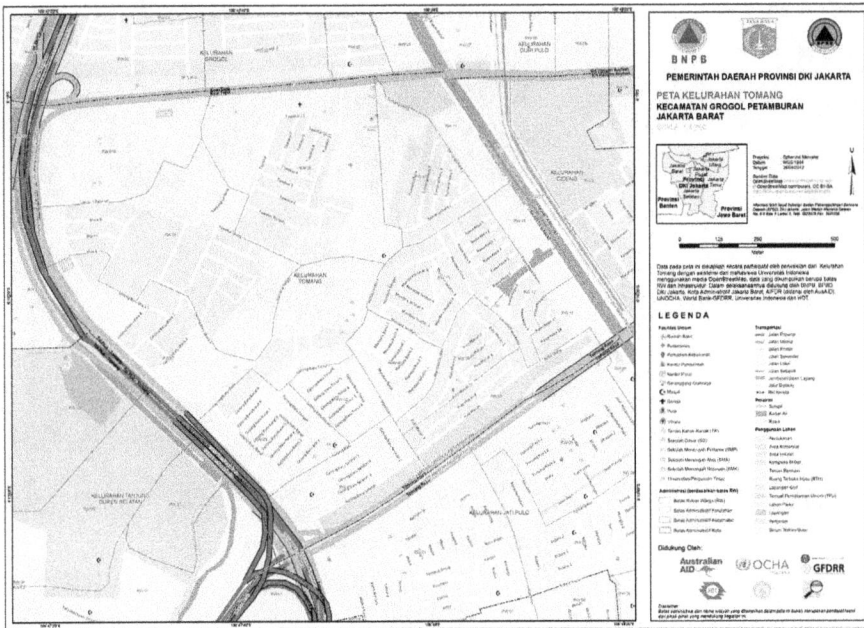

Source: InaSAFE.

with the ability to quantify impact metrics for informed decision making. In a pilot engagement in Jakarta, stakeholders were exposed to the beta functionality of InaSAFE; future work will produce applications for infrastructure investment decisions. Figure 2.4 is an example of an InaSAFE map.

GeoNode is a web-based platform for analysis, management, and publication of geospatial data. It brings together mature and stable open-source software projects in a consistent, easy-to-use interface allowing users with little training to quickly and easily share data and create interactive maps. Its new approach to spatial data infrastructure focuses on user needs and collaboration, allowing them to

- Edit metadata in one place;
- Set up privacy controls to restrict access as needed;
- Download data in a variety of formats;
- Use data in the system to create maps; and
- Export maps to other web applications or in PDF format.

Box 2.30 provides a recent example of GeoNode use.

Communicating Risk Information

Global approaches tend to quantify resilience to multiple hazard types and then draw up an index of a country's resilience relative to other countries.

Figure 2.4 Illustration of InaSAFE Output: Historical Flood in Kelurahan Tomang in Jakarta, Indonesia

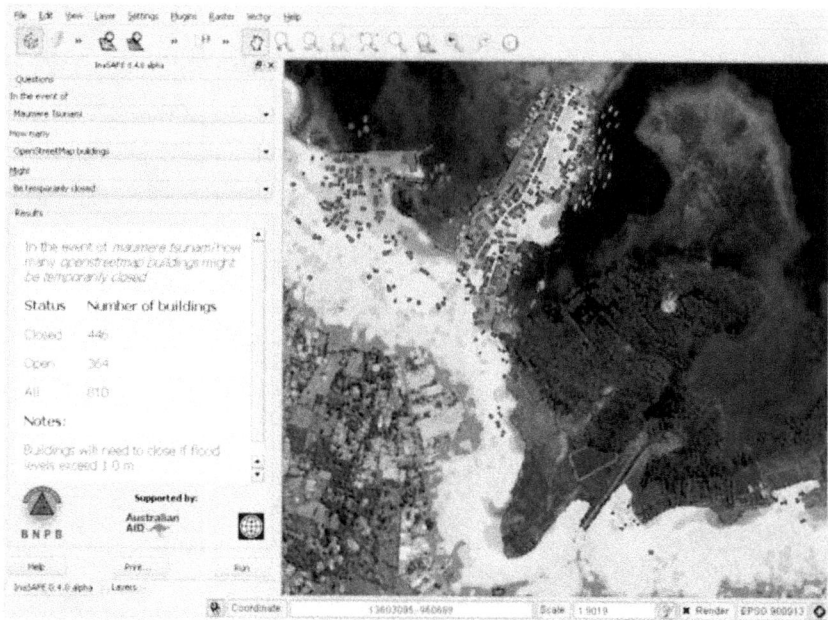

Source: InaSAFE.

Box 2.30 The Pacific Risk Information System

The Pacific Risk Information System is a web-based GeoNode application to enhance management and sharing of geospatial data within the Pacific DRM community. It makes it possible to create a dynamic online risk data community by piloting the integration of social web features with geospatial data management. It is the first deployment at this scale of a web-based data-sharing platform in combination with a risk assessment initiative.

Adequate preparation based on credible information and risk assessments can substantially mitigate the devastation of natural disasters. The Pacific Risk Information System is part of the Pacific Catastrophe Risk Assessment and Financing Initiative (PCRAFI), which is a joint program of the Secretariat of the Pacific Community (SPC/SOPAC), the World Bank/GFDRR Labs team, and the Asian Development Bank, with financial support from the government of Japan. The question at the heart of the initiative was how to efficiently share with the region's DRM community terabytes of risk data for 15 Pacific Island countries to improve best practices.

The Pacific Risk Information System incorporates a regional geospatial database and country-specific catastrophe risk models. It draws from one of the most comprehensive GIS data sets ever compiled for the Pacific, containing comprehensive information on population; land use and land cover; topography; bathymetry; soils and their engineering properties; assets such as infrastructure and buildings; satellite images; historical catalogues; information on cyclones, earthquakes, and tsunamis; and general risk models and risk profiles for participating

box continues next page

Box 2.30 The Pacific Risk Information System *(continued)*

countries. The database provides full coverage of a country's entire landmass. Compiling the database involved intensive field visits to 11 countries to survey more than 80,000 buildings; digitizing from satellite imagery the footprints of 450,000 buildings; and inferring from satellite imagery 2,900,000 buildings and other assets. The participating countries are Cook Islands, Federated States of Micronesia, Fiji, Kiribati, Palau, Papua New Guinea, Marshall Islands, Nauru, Niue, Samoa, Solomon Islands, Timor-Leste, Tonga, Tuvalu, and Vanuatu.

Impact: Exposure, hazard, and risk maps (illustrated in the figures that follow) produced as part of PCRAFI and accessible through this platform are powerful visual tools for informing decision makers and facilitating communication and education on disaster risk management. Shared by all users, the risk information captured is the foundation for future steps by the PCRAFI and any government and donor projects related to macro-economic planning and disaster risk financing, urban investments and infrastructure planning, and rapid post-disaster damage estimation.

Figure B2.30.1 Field-Surveyed Bridge in Fiji with Photo Validation

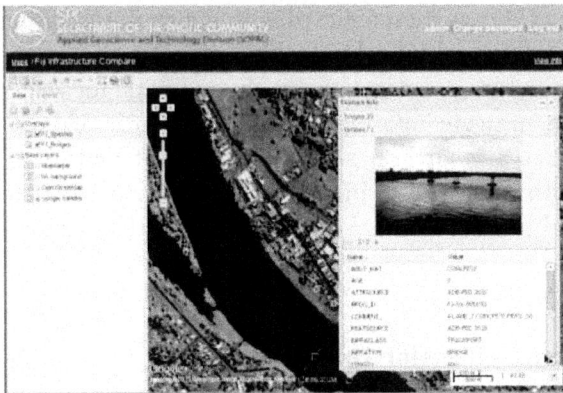

Figure B2.30.2 Cyclone Wind Hazard Map for the Solomon Islands

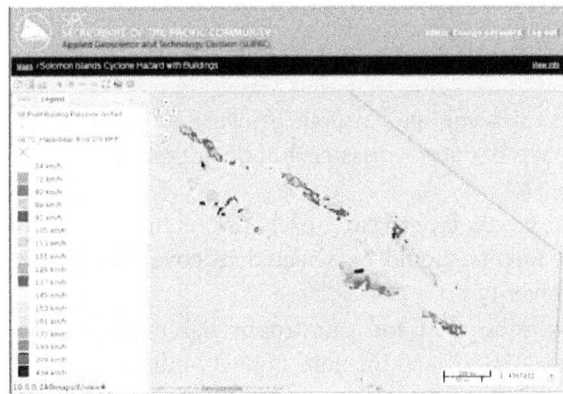

Source: Pacific Risk Information Systems website: http://paris.sopac.org/.

While some of the data are gathered through remote sensing, most come from national surveys and censuses, which often do not provide data for urban and suburban levels. Indicators like GDP, population density, or sheltering needs are not granular enough to be applied to a given urban area. While there have been efforts to collect data for urban areas, most notably the Resilience Capacity Index, they are not widespread and have not been applied in the developing world, though similar efforts include the UNDP Disaster Risk Index, the Human Development Index, and the Global Adaptation Index. Data like these are helpful in identifying and planning project stages to give a sense of the relative resilience of an urban area and identify other areas that have faced similar issues.

Concluding Remarks

It is critical to be able to quantify the impacts of planned or proposed investments to reduce risk. Having a flexible, dynamic, and simple tool like InaSAFE at hand is a step toward more resilient decisions. However, it is still imperative to invest in the underlying science to produce robust hazard and risk information that can be integrated within a chosen decision support tool. Data systems and risk analysis deserve the attention of governments, donors, and the private and civic sectors because they are vital for well-informed decision making to mitigate disaster impacts effectively. Urban planners thus need a clear strategy that brings local government units, communities, and stakeholders into the process of gathering, analyzing, and managing data. The goal should be a governance system that sees the value of data and uses it effectively.

Risk Financing and Transfer Approaches

Economic   Social

Key Points

- Financial resilience is central to a comprehensive disaster risk management strategy.
- Disaster risk financing and insurance instruments can protect against the financial impacts of natural disasters but do not reduce the amount of damage and loss.
- According to the risk layering approach, risk retention, risk financing, and risk transfer instruments should be selected to cover disasters of different frequency and severity.
- Financial risk assessment and catastrophe risk modeling tools are useful in assessing the economic and financial impact of disasters.
- A standardized exposure database of public and private assets at risk is particularly important for fiscal risk management strategies, such as development of private catastrophe insurance markets.

Summary

Financial approaches to urban disaster resilience aim to reduce the impact of disasters on individuals, communities, and the private and public sectors. With high concentrations of people and assets, in addition to their socioeconomic, business and trade, and political and institutional roles, cities need to build up their financial resilience. After a disaster, financial strategies can help increase the financial response capacity of governments at all levels while protecting their long-term fiscal balances. Ensuring quick access and disbursement of funding for repair and recovery can help minimize the disruption caused by a disaster and reduce the economic and fiscal burden by transferring losses through a range of mechanisms, including private capital and insurance markets. In the continuous effort to expand the suite of instruments and services available to local governments and cities, there are lessons that can be learned from current disaster risk financing and insurance interventions available at the national level. This section reviews certain risk financing and transfer mechanisms (see box 2.31 for the definition of related terms).

Box 2.31 Key Terms Related to Risk Financing

Risk financing refers to the process of managing risk and the consequences of residual risk through products like insurance contracts, catastrophe bonds, reinsurance, or options.

Risk layering is the process of separating risk into tiers for more efficient management and financing of risks.

Risk pooling is the aggregation of individual risks to manage the consequences of independent risks.

Risk retention refers to the process in which a party retains the financial responsibility for loss if there is a shock.

Risk transfer is the process of shifting the burden of financial loss or responsibility for risk financing to another party through insurance, reinsurance, legislation, or other means.

Source: Cummins and Mahul 2009.

Cities and Risk Financing

With people and assets increasingly concentrated in high-risk zones, cities are becoming more vulnerable (Cummins and Mahul 2009). The combination of rapid and unplanned urbanization, poorly constructed settlements, and degraded ecosystems—often in already hazardous areas along the coast, in floodplains, or along seismic rifts—puts at risk a growing number of urban dwellers and businesses, as well as public and private infrastructure. This has serious implications both for economic growth and sustainable development and for regional and global trade patterns.

Development of disaster risk instruments for cities and local governments is challenging. Often, due to the localized nature of hazards in cities, such as flooding, limited scale for efficient risk pooling, and the high vulnerability of city dwellers and assets, risk financing and transfer mechanisms are unaffordable or unviable. Cities and local governments also face constraints because of limited financial resources, capacity, or availability of risk information.

In overcoming these challenges, it is crucial to invest in the development of and capacity to use robust risk information to inform disaster risk financing, and more broadly disaster risk management strategies; and to explore ways for cities and local governments to benefit from financing and insurance mechanisms already available. Some institutions, such as the Asian Development Bank (ADB), have begun to offer local and provincial governments a suite of products suited to the needs of urban areas (see box 2.32).

Box 2.32 Financial Instruments for Cities and Provinces

The Asian Development Bank (ADB) is currently assembling an Integrated Disaster Risk Management (IDRM) framework that incorporates elements of disaster risk reduction (DRR), climate change adaptation (CCA), and disaster risk financing (DRF) (ADB 2009, 2010). The purpose is to recognize DRM linkages and synergies and to leverage these synergies to craft risk management solutions for member countries, with particular attention to the disaster management needs of urban areas. A combination of factors, such as urban migration, concentrated economic development, expanded infrastructure, and climate change, has given rise to the need for urban-specific IDRM strategies and instruments.

With support from the Japan Fund for Poverty Reduction (JFPR), ADB is working with the governments of the Philippines, Indonesia, and Vietnam to launch DRF programs for two cities in each country. The programs will profile urban risk, which will support the development of city selection criteria through collaboration between government agencies and development partners. Once the cities are selected, DRF options will be tested through consultations and workshops to assess feasibility and market acceptance; the options might include disaster liquidity mechanisms, critical asset and infrastructure insurance, and social protection programs for households and small businesses involving micro-insurance or micro-finance. The projects are scheduled for completion in 2014.

Source: World Bank/GFDRR 2012.

Risk Information

The development of a strategy for risk financing and insurance depends on the availability of robust data and models to assess key elements of risk. Risk assessment provides detailed analysis of hazard, exposure, and vulnerability; it feeds into urban development plans and investment strategies as well as financial mechanisms. Advances in risk mapping and hazard forecasting bring considerable benefits for all levels of government, local authorities, households, and businesses. For instance, better flood risk information allows for better predictions of the risk to public and individual assets, which helps with planning for protection against flooding.

Probabilistic risk modelling, initially developed by the insurance industry, can help decision makers to deal with uncertainty about current as well as future risks. In urban areas, probabilistic risk assessments can guide urban planning, ensuring that buildings, schools, hospitals, and other assets are located in safe areas. More recently, such models have been coupled with climate change models to account for future changes in hazards and over time (Ranger et al. 2011; Way 2012). Among the many uses of probabilistic risk assessments are insurance premium calculations based on accurate information about annual expected loss and probable maximum loss for a given location. For example, the government of Mexico designed the disaster risk assessment tool R-FONDEN to assess the contingent liability of the National Disaster Fund (FONDEN) with respect to natural disasters and to devise a disaster risk financing strategy (FONDEN 2012, see box 2.33 for more information about FONDEN; World Bank 2012b).

Investing in reliable risk information data, financial risk assessments, and catastrophe risk modelling tools can help decision makers assess the economic and budgetary impact of disasters. A standardized exposure database of public and private assets can help guide fiscal risk management strategies, such as development of private catastrophe risk insurance markets. Putting together risk data sets can be expensive, especially for cities and small governmental entities. The Pacific Catastrophe Risk Assessment and Financing Initiative (PCRAFI) helps small island countries overcome the burden of the initial investment and

---

Box 2.33 Mexican Natural Disaster Fund (FONDEN)

To address its vulnerability to natural disasters, over the years Mexico has put together a comprehensive financial protection strategy that relies on both risk retention and such transfer mechanisms as reserve funds, indemnity-based reinsurance, parametric insurance, and catastrophe (cat) bonds.

Founded in 1996, the Fund for Natural Disasters (FONDEN) was originally established as a budgetary tool through which federal funds were annually allocated for post-disaster response. It has since evolved significantly. In 1999 it established a catastrophe reserve fund—the FONDEN Trust Fund—to enable it to accumulate the unspent portion of annual budgetary appropriations. In 2005 the government of Mexico empowered FONDEN to put in place a catastrophe risk financing strategy to leverage its resources, relying on a layered combination of risk retention and risk transfer instruments. In 2006 FONDEN issued the world's first government cat bond, which was renewed in 2009. Currently FONDEN consists of two complementary budget and financial accounts, the FONDEN Program for Reconstruction and the FOPREDEN Program for Prevention. Fiduciary responsibility for the financial accounts lies with BANOBRAS, Mexico's state-owned development bank.

- The FONDEN Program for Reconstruction is FONDEN's primary budget account.
- The FOPREDEN Program for Prevention supports disaster prevention by funding activities related to risk assessment, risk reduction, and capacity building.
- The FONDEN Trust provides resources for the activities of the FONDEN Program and acts as the contracting authority for risk transfer mechanisms, such as insurance and cat bonds.

box continues next page

Box 2.33 Mexican Natural Disaster Fund (FONDEN) *(continued)*

Figure B2.33.1 The Role of FONDEN's Instruments in Mexico's System of Civil Protection

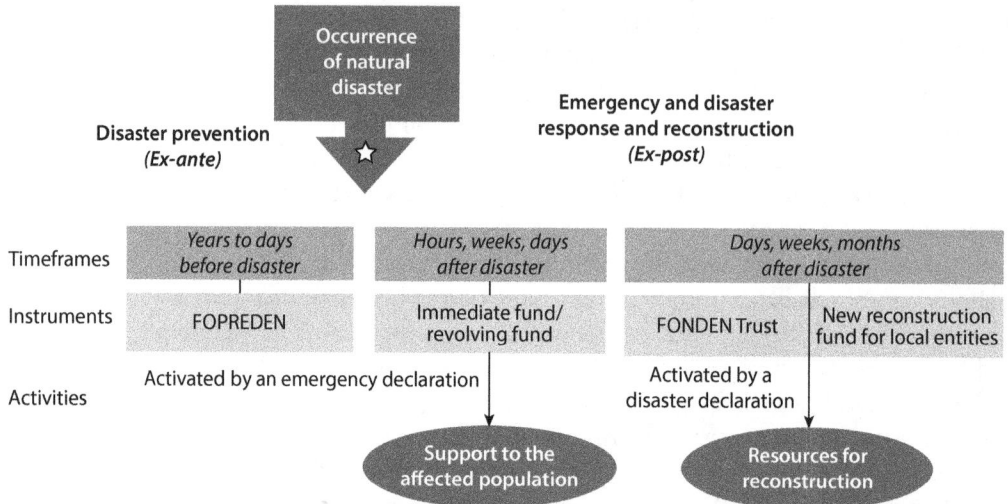

☆ *All federal plans and programs are activated for disaster response.*

Market-based risk transfer instruments: To manage the volatility of demand on its resources, FONDEN is allowed to transfer risks through insurance and other mechanisms, such as cat bonds. However, it is not allowed to contract debt. FONDEN first transferred disaster risk to the international capital market in 2006, buying a three-year US$160 million parametric cat bond to insure against earthquake risks in three zones. It also secured a three-year policy for US$290 million of parametric reinsurance coverage for the same three zones, bringing its total protection to US$450 million. When the cat bond expired in 2009, FONDEN increased its cover by issuing a three-year US$290 million multi-peril parametric earthquake and hurricane cat bond. Most recently, in 2011 and 2012 it secured US$400 million in excess-of-loss reinsurance coverage for losses from damages to government assets and low-income housing that exceed US$1 billion in a single fiscal year.

Source: FONDEN 2012.

reap the benefits of sharing robust risk information among stakeholders in future projects and applications (see section "Data Gathering, Analysis, and Application" on Communicating Risk Information). In January 2012 PCRAFI started a next phase to develop regional and country-level disaster risk financing solutions as part of the Pacific Disaster Risk Financing and Insurance Program. This program provides institutional capacity building on disaster risk financing and insurance for the Pacific island countries and is piloting sovereign parametric catastrophe risk insurance. The pilot, launched in the fall of 2012 with five countries (Marshall Islands, Samoa, Solomon Islands, Tonga, and Vanuatu), will be the first-ever transfer of catastrophe risk from the Pacific to the international reinsurance markets. Implemented over two years, the pilot will test the feasibility of a catastrophe risk pooling and transfer approach for the Pacific.

Disaster Risk Financing and Insurance

Risk financing is important to a comprehensive disaster risk management strategy that depends on continuous effort at all stages, from risk identification and assessment through institutional capacity building. The primary objective of the World Bank Disaster Risk Financing and Insurance (DRFI) program is to increase financial resilience to disasters through sovereign disaster risk financing and development of a catastrophe risk market to increase coverage for residents, businesses, and agricultural producers (see figure 2.5). The approach is primarily through interventions at the national level. While many of the general principles apply widely, more needs to be done to understand and design appropriate interventions at the urban level.

Sovereign Disaster Risk Financing

Sovereign disaster risk financing is based on strategies to increase the financial response capacity of governments after natural disasters while protecting their long-term fiscal balances. Delays in accessing and disbursing funding after a disaster can have serious socioeconomic consequences from the macroeconomic to the household level (World Bank/GFDRR 2012). A government has a variety of options for ex ante or ex post fiscal and market-based instruments to finance disasters. Figure 2.6 lists the most common sources of post-disaster funding and indicates their use.

Ex ante financing gives the government immediate access to liquidity in the relief and early recovery phases. It may consist of *budget reserves, contingent*

Figure 2.5 World Bank Approach to Disaster Risk Financing and Insurance

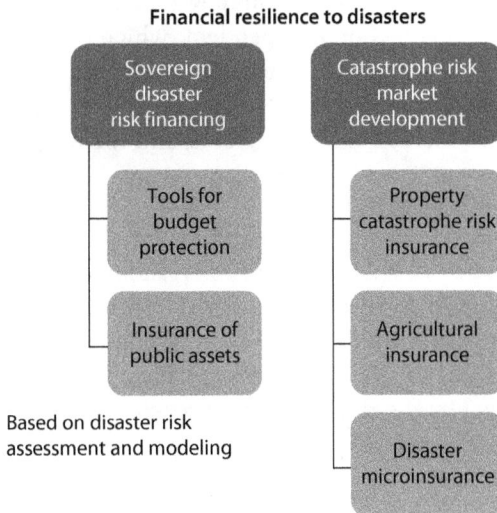

Source: World Bank/GFDRR DRFI Program.

Figure 2.6 Sources of Post-Disaster Funding

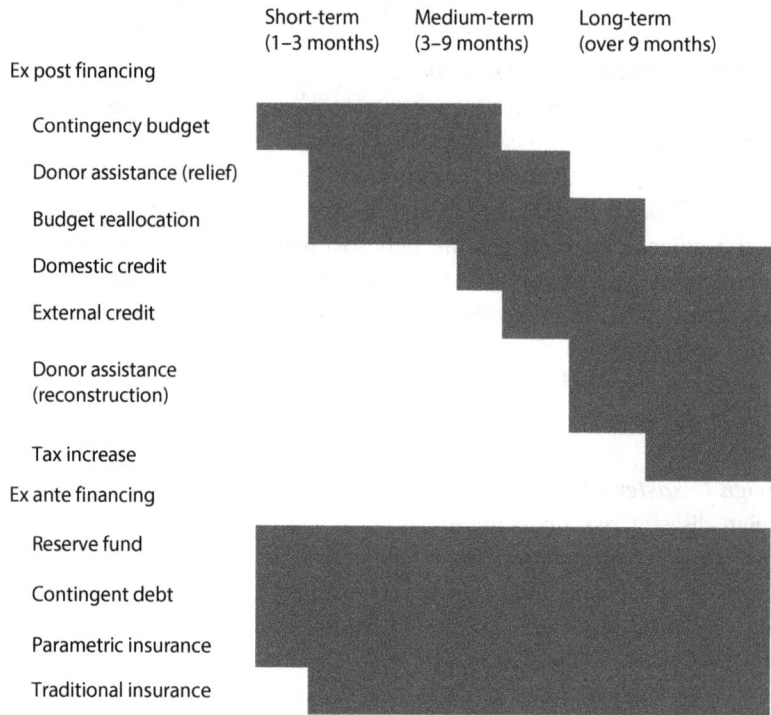

	Short-term (1–3 months)	Medium-term (3–9 months)	Long-term (over 9 months)

Ex post financing

  Contingency budget

  Donor assistance (relief)

  Budget reallocation

  Domestic credit

  External credit

  Donor assistance (reconstruction)

  Tax increase

Ex ante financing

  Reserve fund

  Contingent debt

  Parametric insurance

  Traditional insurance

Source: Ghesquiere and Mahul 2007.

credit lines, or *transfer mechanisms*, such as *catastrophic risk insurance, risk pools, weather derivatives*, and *catastrophe (cat) bonds*. Ex post funding mechanisms include *budget reallocation, domestic credit, external credit, tax increases*, and *donor assistance*. While post-disaster funding may be available, disbursements are not assured and may be donor-dependent, which can have severe negative impacts after a large-scale disaster. For the recovery and reconstruction phases, governments typically mobilize funds through such ex post instruments as deficit spending, tax increases, spending cuts, and recovery loans.

Selecting Risk Financing and Transfer Options

The choice of financial instruments depends on the specific funding needs and the time constraints linked to a disaster and the phase (relief, recovery, or reconstruction). Once needs and constraints are identified, appropriate instruments can be chosen. An optimal national approach to financing disasters generally combines ex ante and ex post instruments. The consequent risk financing strategy is guided by the risk layering approach.

Risk layering is the process of separating risk into tiers for more efficient financing and risk management (Cummins and Mahul 2009). The frequency and severity of disasters guide the selection among *risk retention, risk pooling and financing*, and *risk transfer mechanisms*. Different layers of risk are addressed by different instruments. Typically, low-severity and high-frequency risks, such as annual floods or drought, can be self-financed through annual budget disaster reserves. Medium-severity and medium-frequency risks are addressed using contingent lines of credit. Low-frequency but high-severity risks that cause extensive damage, such as earthquakes or tsunamis, should be transferred to the risk market through catastrophic insurance, risk pools, or cat bonds. Figure 2.7 lists products available for increasing fiscal and economic resilience.

A country's fiscal risk profile, its socioeconomic situation, and the cost and availability of products on national and international markets shape the selection of the mix of risk instruments. Country liquidity, procedural arrangements for disbursement, reserve budget allocations, regulations on international donor assistance, and the borrowing capacity of a country also influence the timing for accessing funds and consequently the selection of instruments. The availability of instruments in local and international markets, as well as the client group (households, communities, businesses, or national, regional, or international entities) will determine the choice of risk financing methods. Box 2.33 described Mexico's approach to developing a comprehensive disaster risk financing strategy.

Risk Retention

The risk of damages from high-frequency/low-severity events can be covered by such mechanisms as budget reserves, contingent financing, reserve funds, and pooled reserves. Budget mechanisms are the most cost-effective option for retaining the risk of annual or highly recurrent events. However, there are often political and budget barriers to maintaining large disaster reserves. The World Bank provides support to IBRD and IDA countries with ex ante contingent credit, grant agreements, and emergency response mechanisms; Table 2.10 gives an overview of the main contingent and emergency crisis response instruments.

Figure 2.7 Types of Risk and Possible Sources of Funding

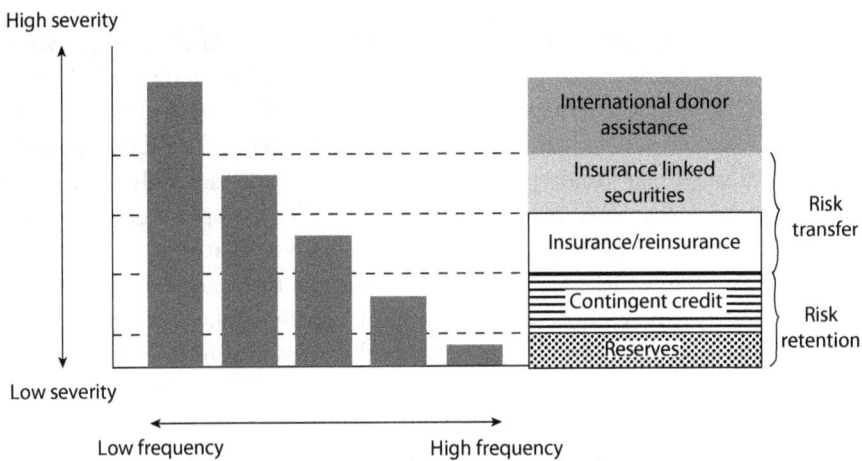

Source: Cummins and Mahul 2009.

Table 2.10 World Bank Contingent and Emergency Crisis Response Instruments

Mechanism	Eligibility	Instrument	Comments
Contingent emergency response components	IDA, IBRD	Investment Lending (IL), Development Policy Loan (DPL)	Preparation consists of allocating a specific sum or a "zero" component into a standard loan. For IDA countries, ex ante funding of contingent components comes from their IDA allocations.
Catastrophe deferred draw down option	IBRD	DPL	Preparation follows standard DPL procedures. Access is up to US$500 million or 0.25 percent of GDP, whichever is less. Once IBRD receives a request to draw down Cat-DDO funds after a disaster, funds are typically transferred within five business days.
Immediate responses mechanism	All current IDA beneficiaries	IL	Allows for use of 5 percent (US$5 million) of an undisbursed IL portfolio (restructuring). Preparation is done before a crisis; the request is approved within one week, and the first disbursement is possible within 1 week of approval.
Crisis response window	IDA only	IL, DPL	Provides limited additional financing. Average time from concept to approval is 6.8 months; average time from approval to effectiveness is 4 months.
Emergency recovery loans	IDA, IBRD	IL	This is a post-disaster lending instrument that follows standard procedures.

Source: World Bank 2011c.

Contingent financing can take the form of self-standing contingent loans or ex ante emergency components of standard investment operations. *Contingent components* as part of investment lending (IL) projects have been put in place in, e.g., Bangladesh, Grenada, India, Indonesia, the Lao People's Democratic Republic, and St. Vincent and the Grenadines (World Bank 2011c). In Lao PDR after Typhoons Haima and Nok Ten in 2011, the contingent component was used to meet immediate emergency road repairs.[4] The Development Policy Loan (DPL) with a Catastrophe Deferred Drawdown Option (Cat-DDO) is an example of a self-standing contingent financing provision for budget support for IBRD countries (see box 2.34).

Emergency instruments, such as the *Immediate Response Mechanism (IRM)*, or the *Crisis Response Window* (CRW) can provide rapid or additional finances. Putting the IRM in place requires an operations manual and up-front agreements with countries on detailed implementation arrangements. The CRW provides limited additional post-disaster financing that can be accessed only after severe exogenous shocks. An *Emergency Recovery Loan* (ERL) supports economic and social recovery immediately after an extraordinary event that seriously disrupts a borrower's economy. ERLs are also used to reinforce the management of reconstruction and recovery efforts and to develop disaster-resilient technology and early warning systems to prevent or mitigate the impact of future emergencies.

Risk Transfer

When expected losses are beyond their ability to self-finance, countries may opt for risk transfer mechanisms, which transfer the financial risk of disaster loss to

Box 2.34 Development Policy Loan with a Catastrophe Deferred Drawdown Option

Launched in 2008, the World Bank Development Policy Loan (DPL) with catastrophe deferred drawdown option (Cat-DDO) offers immediate post-disaster liquidity to cover urgent financing needs while other resources, such as national reserves, bilateral aid, or reconstruction loans, are mobilized. The Cat-DDO has a soft rather than a parametric trigger; funds can be drawn down when a natural disaster occurs that results in declaration of a state of emergency. Borrowers are required to have in place an integrated disaster risk management program, which is periodically reviewed by the World Bank.

Six countries in the Latin America and the Caribbean region have made use of this instrument. In mid-2011 the Philippines became the first country in the East Asia Pacific region to sign a contingent credit (amounting to US$500 million) for natural disasters with the World Bank; the credit was drawn down on December 29, 2011, to relieve the devastating impacts of Tropical Storm Sendong (Washi).

Further information: World Bank/GFDRR DRFI Program.

a third party that provides coverage for a given type of disaster. Risk transfer mechanisms make it possible to mobilize funds without additional post-disaster impact on budgets. The examples listed are mechanisms developed for use at the national level.

Catastrophe Risk Insurance

Public and private risk insurance can help reduce the contingent liability of governments and increase the resilience of a society as a whole (World Bank 2012b). Traditional catastrophe risk insurance is indemnity-based: payouts are based on damages the insured incurs. This type of catastrophe insurance is appropriate for governments concerned about extreme aggregate or cumulative losses but may not address immediate budgetary needs after a catastrophic event and may be difficult to find in countries without insurance markets. For budget insurance, governments are increasingly using innovative parametric insurance products.[5]

Insuring critical public infrastructure (hospitals, schools, bridges, etc.) can help reduce the state's contingent liability. Some countries, among them Costa Rica, Mexico, and Colombia, require that public assets have coverage against natural disasters. In practice, however, most public assets are under- or completely uninsured, in part due to limitations of risk information as well as resources (World Bank 2012b). Some subnational governments, including some cities, are proactively insuring critical assets. In Indonesia, the municipality of Yogyakarta has insured its government buildings, schools, hospitals, traditional marketplaces, and motor vehicles since 2003. After a 2006 earthquake, it received a payout of IDR 3.4 billion, which was 14 times the annual premium (World Bank/GFDRR 2011).

Catastrophe Risk Market Development

Private catastrophe insurance can help homeowners, small and medium enterprises, and governments shift the burden of disasters. In developing countries, where private insurance markets are often underdeveloped, catastrophe losses are primarily borne by the people and the government. Developing these markets increases the share of insurers in disaster losses. Particularly in middle-income countries, where asset bases at risk are rapidly expanding, functioning catastrophe risk insurance markets are important for mitigating the financial and fiscal impacts of a disaster (Cummins and Mahul 2009).

Often government intervention is required to support development of catastrophe insurance markets. Governments can, for instance, put in place enabling laws and regulations (see also box 2.35). They can also provide "risk market infrastructure"—public goods that contribute to market growth, such as product development, catastrophe risk assessment and pricing methodology, and underwriting and loss procedures. Investing in a standardized database of public and private assets at risk is particularly important to development of private catastrophe insurance markets.

Catastrophe Insurance Programs

In many countries the government has entered into public-private partnerships (PPPs) to increase catastrophe insurance coverage (see OECD 2012). Often, these PPPs use risk pooling to reduce costs and increase financial resilience to catastrophes. Although catastrophe insurance programs are most common in high-income countries, in recent years middle-income countries like Turkey and Romania have signed on. The World Bank and other international organizations work with low- and middle-income countries to create programs to insure property against catastrophe. The Turkish Catastrophe Insurance Pool (TCIP) is a public company with distribution through Turkish insurers and with private sector reinsurance (see box 2.36).

Box 2.35 The Southeast Europe and Caucasus Catastrophe Risk Insurance Facility

The Southeast Europe and Caucasus Catastrophe Risk Insurance Facility (SEEC CRIF) is facilitating development of national catastrophe and weather risk markets by designing and introducing low-cost insurance products and insurance business production technologies, reforming regulation, educating consumers, and providing reinsurance. The project has created a new platform to provide low-cost insurance service infrastructure, including access to web-based insurance production and claims settlement. The platform supports sale of complex catastrophe and weather insurance products. The facility will also develop standardized weather insurance and reinsurance products; automate insurance underwriting, pricing, and claims settlement for these products; and increase public awareness of weather risk in participating countries.

Source: World Bank 2012b.

Tools for Building Urban Resilience

Box 2.36 Turkish Catastrophe Insurance Pool

The Turkish Catastrophe Insurance Pool (TCIP) was established in 2000 to overcome problems of market failure in Turkey, specifically the lack of local earthquake capacity and low demand for earthquake insurance. The facility was established by the Government of Turkey, in collaboration with the World Bank and other partners, to support a compulsory earthquake insurance scheme and create a pool for earthquake risk that would build the capacity of the domestic insurance market to underwrite the risk while isolating it from the risk of insolvency because of an extreme event. Domestic insurers underwrite catastrophe risk but pass the risk on to the pool, which is supported by risk capital from the international reinsurance community, the government, and donors. TCIP is a public company that is managed on commercial insurance principles. It purchases commercial reinsurance and the Government of Turkey acts as reinsurer of last resort for claims arising out of any earthquake that has a return period of more than 300 years.

Source: World Bank/GFDRR 2012.

For localized hazards, such as flooding, risk pooling might not be viable because the risk is systemic. One way to address the issue is for city dwellers to participate in a broader risk pooling mechanism (for instance, on a regional scale or also covering other hazards) that would spread the risk. However, decision makers are then faced with the problem of supporting accumulation of assets in hazardous areas. This is an issue common to regional and national schemes (see box 2.37). Insurance companies also point out that while some insurers have the advantage of providing products to low-risk customers, others also have to cover many high-risk properties. Some countries and insurance programs have put in place incentives for residents to take preparedness measures, which are rewarded by lower insurance premiums.

Regional insurance schemes can lower insurance costs by pooling risk. Parties to a regional collective pay an annual premium proportionate to their risk exposure and receive compensation as agreed in the coverage contract. A portion of the pooled risk is retained through a joint reserve mechanism, which reduces the insurance premiums. This can be particularly advantageous for smaller countries where premiums would be high. The Caribbean Catastrophe Risk Insurance Facility (CCRIF) is an example of a successful pool; it functions as a mutual insurance company controlled by participating governments. The facility was initially funded by the countries and donor partners, including the World Bank. Since becoming operational in 2007, CCRIF has disbursed more than US$30 million to participating countries affected by natural disasters to help them finance post-disaster expenditures. CCRIF relies on a parametric trigger.

Alternative Risk Transfer

Alternative risk transfer (ART) refers to any nontraditional form of insurance risk transfer (Cummins and Mahul 2009). ART primarily takes the form of risk-linked

Box 2.37 Flood Insurance in the United Kingdom

In the United Kingdom, private insurance enables individuals to mitigate their flood risk. Unlike in the United States, where flood insurance is sold as a separate policy, in the UK flood cover is bundled into standard policies. As a result, the majority of people who insure their property against fire and theft are also insured against flooding; an estimated 95 percent of domestic buildings are covered. This arrangement, also known as the "Statement of Principles" between the insurers and the U.K. government and developed administration, allows (private) flood risk to be transferred to the private market. The agreement, which runs until June 2013, is based on a division of responsibility whereby the government primarily funds flood defenses and insurers agree to pick up the residual risk for most properties. The government and the insurance industry are currently discussing a new agreement. The U.K. government is also working with local authorities and other partners to discern the extent to which communities, acting together, can help to manage the costs of flood insurance.

Commercial flood risk is also potentially insurable in the United Kingdom, and public infrastructure can be insured or self-insured by local authorities and infrastructure companies. This leaves the central government supporting local authorities only for the cost of emergency management—a fraction of the total cost of a flood. However, this system also leads to complacency and lack of preparedness among residents at risk of flood and can undermine any incentive for the government to invest fully in flood defense.

Sources: DEFRA 2012; Land et al. 2009 in World Bank 2012a, 340.

---

securities that transfer catastrophe risk to the capital markets, such as a cat bond. A "sponsor" transfers catastrophe risk to a *special purpose vehicle* (SPV) through a reinsurance contract. The SPV acts as an intermediary with the capital markets and issues notes to investors, the terms of which mirror those of the reinsurance contract. In other words, investors collect the premium paid by the sponsor, but they risk losing this premium and sometimes a portion or all of the funds they have spent on the bond if a triggering catastrophe occurs. The SPV collects the premium from the sponsor and manages the collateral account of investor funds. If no triggering events occur before the term ends, the SPV returns the principal to investors with the final interest payment. As noted, if a triggering event does occur, some or all of the principal is transferred to the sponsor and payments to the investors cease.

Countries with a solid risk financing strategy can make use of cat bonds. In 2009 the government of Mexico issued a multiperil, multiyear catastrophe bond (US$290 million) as part of the World Bank–sponsored MultiCat Program. The issuing SPV indirectly provides parametric insurance to the government's Natural Disaster Fund (FONDEN) against earthquake risk in three regions around Mexico City and against hurricanes on the Atlantic and Pacific coasts. The bond will repay the principal to investors unless an earthquake or hurricane triggers a transfer of the funds to the Mexican government (World Bank/GFDRR 2012).

Disaster Micro-Insurance

The poor generally have little access to formal sources of credit, private insurance against risk, or social insurance. Because of minimal if any income, unstable wages, or inability to meet interest or premium payments, the poor often rely instead on mechanisms like savings, informal insurance, and reciprocal arrangements like kinship ties, community self-help, and remittances. Many households use harmful coping options, such as reducing spending on food, health, and education, or attempt to increase incomes by sending children to work. People in these situations are often forced to take out high-interest loans, default on current loans, sell assets, or engage in low-risk, low-yield farming to lessen exposure to extreme events (Twigg 2004).

Microfinance institutions (MFIs) provide solid networks for delivering services to promote resilience and reduce vulnerability to disasters. In Bangladesh, El Salvador, India, and Nicaragua, MFIs have integrated loans for housing repair or reconstruction, in particular, into their portfolios for poor communities (O'Donnell and ProVention Consortium 2009).

Micro-insurance mechanisms are designed to facilitate access to disaster insurance to protect the livelihood of the poor against extreme weather. In recent years, a number of micro-insurance schemes have been developed or extended to cover disaster risks. These often promote reduction of disaster risk in conjunction with social programs like conditional cash transfer programs. There are also examples of bundling with savings programs, such as the micro-insurance program of the Self-Employed Women's Association (SEWA) in India, which allows its members to save for insurance through fixed deposits in savings accounts (SEWA 2001, see also Churchill et al. 2003). Box 2.38 provides an example of a micro-insurance initiative launched in 2004 in India. Index-based insurance is an approach tested in a number of countries that has helped poor farmers manage weather-related risks and herders manage risks related to livestock losses.

International reinsurers and brokers are also beginning to participate in the more developed micro-insurance markets (World Bank/GFDRR 2012). This can facilitate growth in the supply of more sophisticated products. For example, in Indonesia Allianz underwrites two group micro-insurance products that are distributed through MFIs and community-based organizations. In the Philippines, Munich Re reinsures parametric credit portfolio protection underwritten by an umbrella cooperative and licensed composite insurer, Cooperative Life Insurance and Mutual Benefit Services (CLIMBS). Zurich Financial is underwriting property catastrophe micro-insurance for Holcim Ltd. that will be available for purchasers of Holcim construction materials or fertilizers (World Bank/GFDRR 2012).

Women often face additional barriers to accessing credit or insurance due to higher poverty, eligibility criteria biased toward male heads of household,

---

Box 2.38 Insuring the Poor against Disasters

In 2004 the All India Disaster Mitigation Institute (AIDMI) and the ProVention Consortium introduced a micro-insurance project, Afat Vimo, under a Regional Risk Transfer Initiative (RRTI). RRTI partners included the World Bank Hazard Risk Management Unit and the International Federation of Red Cross and Red Crescent Societies. Afat Vimo aims to bring micro-insurance, micro-credit, and micro-mitigation into convergence for low-cost local risk transfer. It insures policyholders among the poor against 19 types of disasters (e.g., earthquake, cyclone, landslide). Damages to a policyholder's house, household assets, and trade stock and losses of wages and livelihood are covered up to Rs. 75,000. The life insurance component pays out Rs. 20,000 in case of death. The yearly premiums amount to Rs. 146 (about 3 days' wages).

The insurance product was unique in that it combined nonlife and life insurance from different companies into one policy. AIDMI acted as an intermediary between communities and companies. To ensure immediate coverage it pays policyholder premiums up front, collecting payment later; supports policyholders with claims settlement; and provides training in disaster preparedness and legal/procedural requirements. Within 20 months of its creation, Afat Vimo's membership increased by 675 percent, with renewal rates averaging about 88 percent, indicating the popularity of its unified policy design. This response suggested a high potential to scale up the operation while keeping operating and administrative costs feasible.

Source: O'Donnell and ProVention Consortium 2009, 58, based on Churchill et al. 2003.

---

and lack of access to information about their options. Collateral can be a particular problem because land and other assets are often legally in the name only of the male head of household. Because they mostly engage in lower-paid occupations and in the informal sector, many poor women find it difficult to save for investment in income-earning opportunities or to cover expenses when there is a major shock. Female-headed households are also averse to risking investment of their scarce resources for uncertain future benefits.

Social protection initiatives that help poor women to establish local savings groups have a demonstrated track record of helping women to improve their situation. Funding can also be channelled through MFIs and savings societies to meet women's credit and insurance needs. Investment in informal insurance mechanisms, such as health associations and burial societies, also offer accessible options to protect women and their families from post-disaster impacts.

Concluding Remarks
Risk financing and transfer approaches provide tools and strategies for increasing resilience to the impact of disasters. They must be part of a comprehensive approach to disaster risk management. Investing in robust risk

information on hazard, exposure, and vulnerability is vital for the use of risk financing instruments. Current disaster risk financing and insurance mechanisms provide options for national governments and small and medium businesses as well as families and individuals, but amassing a suite of instruments for cities and local governments is an area where further research is needed.

Further Reading

- *Populations at Risk of Disaster: A Resettlement Guide* (Correa 2011a).
- *World Bank Resettlement Handbook* (World Bank, forthcoming).
- *Sustainable Reconstruction in Urban Areas: A Handbook* (IFRC 2012).
- *Safer Homes, Stronger Communities: A Handbook for Reconstructing after Natural Disasters* (World Bank 2010b).
- CIESIN/Columbia University Global Slum Mapping (website).
- *Building Resilient Communities: Risk Management and Response to Natural Disasters through Social Funds and Community-Driven Development Operations* (World Bank 2009).
- *The Comprehensive Disaster Management Programme* (Government of Bangladesh n.d.).
- *Building Resilience to Natural Disasters: A Framework for Private Sector Engagement* (World Economic Forum/World Bank/UNISDR 2008).
- *A Guide for Implementing the Hyogo Framework for Action by Local Stakeholders* (Shaw and Matsuoka 2010). Asia Regional Task Force on Urban Risk Reduction/UNISDR/Kyoto University 2010).
- *Public Awareness and Social Marketing: Experiences from the AUDMP* (ADPC 2005).
- *Volunteer Technology Communities: Open Development* (World Bank/GFDRR Labs 2011).
- *Tools for Building Urban Resilience: Integrating Risk Information into Investment Decisions. Pilot Cities Report—Jakarta and Can Tho* (World Bank 2012).
- *Using High Resolution Data for Identification of Urban Natural Disaster Risk* (World Bank 2012).
- "Policy Options for Disaster Risk Financing and Transfer and Issues in Quantification of Disaster Losses and Exposures: An OECD Perspective" in *Improving the Assessment of Disaster Risks to Strengthen Financial Resilience* (World Bank 2012).
- *Advancing Disaster Risk Financing and Insurance in ASEAN Member States: Framework and Options for Implementation* (World Bank/GFDRR 2012).
- *2009 Global Assessment Report—Practice Review on Innovations in Finance for Disaster Risk Management* (O'Donnell and ProVention Consortium 2009).
- *How to Design and Implement Gender-sensitive Social Protection Programmes: Toolkit* (Overseas Development Institute 2010).
- *Resilience, Equity, and Opportunity: The World Bank's Social Protection and Labor Strategy 2012–2022* (World Bank 2012).

Notes

1. For a comparison of spatial plans, see Appendix C or UN-HABITAT's 2009 *Planning Sustainable Cities.*

2. All census enumeration areas (EAs) where >50 percent of population is deprived in at least one of the five indicators are counted as slums irrespective of any EAs that have multiple deprivations and thus poorer conditions.

3. The UN-HABITAT Global Urban Observatory/Monitoring Systems Branch; the International Institute for Geoinformation Science & Earth Observation (ITC), The Netherlands; and The Center for International Earth Science Information Network (CIESIN), Earth Institute, Columbia University, USA.

4. Damage to road transport accounted for more than 60 percent of the total damage caused by the typhoons. A disaster damage, loss, and needs assessment conducted in July estimated the total damage at US$44 million and losses at US$22 million.

5. Parametric insurance is a type of risk transfer where financial payouts are initiated according to a predetermined indicator related to, e.g., rainfall, soil moisture content, or wind speed.

References

Acar, A., and Y. Muraki. 2011. "Twitter for Crisis Communication: Lessons Learned from Japan's Tsunami Disaster." *International Journal of Web Based Communities* 7: 392–402.

ACCCRN (Asian Cities Climate Change Resilience Network). 2011. *Methodology for Multi-Directional and Inclusive Shared Learning Dialogues.* New York: Rockefeller Foundation.

ADB (Asian Development Bank). 2009. *Establishment of the Asia Pacific Disaster Response Fund.* Manila: ADB.

———. 2010. *Asian Development Outlook 2010: Macroeconomic Management beyond the Crisis.* Manila: ADB.

ADPC (Asian Disaster Preparedness Center). 2005. *Public Awareness and Social Marketing: Experiences from the Asian Urban Disaster Mitigation Program (AUDMP).* Safer Cities No 14, May. Bangkok: ADPC.

———. 2006. *Guidebook on Advocacy: Integrating CBDRM into Local Government Policy.* Bangkok: ADPC.

AusAID (Australian Agency for International Development). 2011. *Building the Resilience and Awareness of Metro Manila Communities to Natural Disasters and Climate Change Impacts (BRACE Program).* Project Design Document, Canberra.

Baker, J., R. Basu, M. Cropper, S. Lall, and A. Takeuchi. 2005. "Urban Poverty and Transport: The Case of Mumbai." Policy Research Working Paper 3693, World Bank, Washington, DC.

Benedict, M. A., and E. T. McMahon. 2002. "Green Infrastructure: Smart Conservation for the 21st Century." *Renewable Resources Journal* 20 (3): 12–17.

Berita Indonesia. 2009. Mendobrak Jalan, Membangun Kendala. http://www.beritaindonesia.co.id/metropolitan/mendobrak-jalan-membangun-kendala.

Bull-Kamanga, L., K. Diagne, A. Lavell, E. Leon, F. Lerise, H. MacGregor, A. Maskrey, M. Meshack, M. Pelling, H. Reid, D. Satterthwaite, J. Songsore, K. Westgate, A. Yitambe. 2003. "From Everyday Hazards to Disasters: The Accumulation of Risk in Urban Areas." *Environment & Urbanisation* 15 (1): 193–203.

Burby, R. J. 2006. "Hurricane Katrina and the Paradoxes of Government Disaster Policy: Bringing About Wise Governmental Decisions for Hazardous Areas." *Annals of the American Academy of Political and Social Science* 604: 171–91.

Center for Science in the Earth System. 2007. *Preparing for Climate Change: A Guidebook for Local, Regional, and State Governments.* Seattle, WA: University of Washington/ ICLEI.

Center for Urban Studies. 2006. "Slums of Urban Bangladesh—Mapping and Census, 2005." Dhaka.

Churchill C., D. Liber, M. J. Mccord, J. Roth. 2003. *Making Insurance Work for Microfinance Institutions: A Technical Guide to Developing and Delivering Microinsurance.* Geneva: International Labour Organisation (ILO).

Cities Alliance. 2009. *Social Housing in Sao Paulo: Challenges & New Management Tools.* Washington, DC: Cities Alliance.

City of New York. 2010. *NYC Green Infrastructure Plan: A Sustainable Strategy for Clean Waterways.* City of New York.

———. 2011. "PlaNYC: A Greener, Greater New York," Update April 2011. City of New York.

Correa, E. 2011a. *Populations at Risk of Disaster: A Resettlement Guide.* Washington, DC: Global Facility for Disaster Reduction and Recovery, World Bank.

———. 2011b. *Preventive Resettlement of Populations at Risk of Disaster—Experiences from Latin America.* Washington, DC: Global Facility for Disaster Reduction and Recovery, World Bank.

Cummins, J. D., and O. Mahul. 2009. *Catastrophe Risk Financing in Developing Countries: Principles for Public Intervention—Overview.* Washington, DC: World Bank.

Cutter, S. L., C. G. Burton, and C. T. Emrich. 2010. "Disaster Resilience Indicators for Benchmarking Baseline Conditions." *Journal of Homeland Security and Emergency Management* 7 (1): Article 51. http://regionalresiliency.org/library/Diaster_Resilience_ Indicators_Susan_Cutter_et_al_2010_1281451159.pdf.

D'Cruz, C., and D. Satterthwaite. 2005. "Building Homes, Changing Official Approaches." Poverty Reduction in Urban Areas Series Working Paper 16. International Institute for Environment and Development (IIED), London.

DEFRA (Department for Environment, Food and Rural Affairs). 2012. "Progress on Affordable Flood Insurance." http://www.defra.gov.uk/news/2012/07/11/ progress-on-affordable-flood-insurance/.

Dilley, M., R. S. Chen, U. Deichmann, A. L. Lerner-Lam, and M. Arnold, with J. Agwe, P. Buys, O. Kjekstad, B. Lyon, and G. Yetman. 2005. "Natural Disaster Hotspots: A Global Risk Analysis." Synthesis report, International Bank for Reconstruction and Development/The World Bank and Columbia University, Washington, DC.

Diniz, Maria Teresa. 2010. *Cross-Sectoral Cooperation and Citizen Engagement in Slum Upgrading.* Sao Paulo: SEHAB.

Ergenc, M. Nilay, O. M. Ilkisik, and M. T. Murat. n.d. *Earthquake Risk and Mitigation Studies in Istanbul.* Disaster Coordination Center, Istanbul Metropolitan Municipality, Istanbul.

FONDEN. 2012. "FONDEN: Mexico's Natural Disaster Fund—A Review." World Bank, Washington, DC. http://www.gfdrr.org/gfdrr/sites/gfdrr.org/files/documents/DRFI_FONDEN_Paper_June12.pdf.

Ghesquiere, F., and O. Mahul. 2007. "Sovereign Natural Disaster Insurance for Developing Countries: A Paradigm Shift in Catastrophe Risk Financing." Policy Research Working Paper 4345, World Bank, Washington, DC.

Government of Bangladesh, Ministry of Disaster Management and Relief. n.d. *The Comprehensive Disaster Management Programme*. http://www.cdmp.org.bd.

Government of Chile. 2012. "Building Resilience: Risk Models and Urban Planning." In *Improving the Assessment of Disaster Risks to Strengthen Financial Resilience: A Special Joint G20 Publication by the Government of Mexico and the World Bank*. pp. 92–118. Washington, DC: World Bank.

IDB (Inter-American Development Bank). 2010. *Building Cities: Neighborhood Upgrading and Urban Quality of Life*. Washington, DC: IDB.

IFRC (International Federation of Red Cross and Red Crescent Societies). 2010. *World Disasters Report 2010: Focus on Urban Risk*. Geneva: IFRC.

IIED (International Institute for Environment and Development). n.d. "Climate Change and the Urban Poor: Risk and Resilience in 15 of the World's Most Vulnerable Cities." London.

IOS (International Organization for Standardization). n.d. http://www.iso.org/iso/home.html.

Istanbul Metropolitan Municipality Disaster Coordination Center. n.d. *Istanbul Redevelopment for Earthquake Risk Reduction*. Istanbul.

Joyce, J. M., and M. S. Scott. 2005. *An Assessment of Maryland's Vulnerability to Flood Damage*. p. 87. Eastern Shore Regional GIS Cooperative, Salisbury University, Salisbury, MD.

Kinyanjui, M. 2010. "Development Context and the Millennium Agenda." In *The Challenge of Slums: Global Report on Human Settlements 2003*. Chapter 1. Revised and updated version (April 2010). Nairobi: UN-HABITAT.

Koran Jakarta, 2010. *Bantaran Kali Bebas dari Kekumuhan* (River Bank Free from Slums), January 21. http://www.koran-jakarta.com/berita-detail.php?id=43055.

Kristanti, A. 2011. "Hujan, Banjir di Muara Baru Makin Tinggi" (Rain, Flood in Muara Baru Is Higher), January 21 Tempo Interactif, Jakarta. http://www.tempointeraktif.com/hg/jakarta/2011/01/21/brk,20110121-307958,id.html.

Lall, S. V., and U. Deichmann. 2009. "Density & Disasters: Economics of Urban Hazard Risk." Policy Research Working Paper 5161, World Bank, Washington, DC.

Makau, J. 2011. "Solving the Land Information Gap through GIS." Slum Dwellers International, Cape Town. http://www.sdinet.org/blog/2011/02/21/solving-the-land-information-g/.

Max Lock Consultancy. 2010. "Kaduna Master Plan Draft." Unpublished report, Nigeria.

Mayor of London. 2010. *Draft London Climate Change Adaptation Strategy*. Public Consultation Draft, Greater London Authority, London.

Micallef, D. 2011. "The Role of Online and Social Media in Natural Disasters." *Social Media Today*. http://socialmediatoday.com/saysdavid/261898/role-online-and-social-media-natural-disasters.

Mirah Sakethi Team. 2010. *Mengapa Jakarta Banjir?* (Why Jakarta Flooded?), Jakarta: PT Mirah Sakethi.

Moser, C., and D. Satterthwaite. 2010. "Toward Pro-Poor Adaptation to Climate Change in the Urban Centers of Low- and Middle-Income Countries." In *Social Dimensions of Climate Change: Equity and Vulnerability in a Warming World*, edited by R. Mearns and A. Norton. Washington, DC: IBRD/World Bank, pp. 231–259.

Nakagawa, M., M. Saito, and H. Yamaga. 2007. "Earthquake Risk and Housing Rents: Evidence from the Tokyo Metropolitan Area." *Regional Science and Urban Economics* 37: 87–99.

Nallathiga, R. 2003. "The Impacts of Density Regulations on Cities & Markets: Evidence from Mumbai." *International Journal of Regulation & Governance* 5 (1): 13–39.

O'Donnell, I., and ProVention Consortium. 2009. "2009 Global Assessment Report— Practice Review on Innovations in Finance for Disaster Risk Management." A Contribution to the 2009 UN ISDR Global Assessment Report on Disaster. http://www.preventionweb.net/english/hyogo/gar/background-papers/documents/Chap6/ProVention-Risk-financing-practice-review.pdf.

OECD (Organisation for Economic Co-operation and Development). 2012. "Policy Options for Disaster Risk Financing and Transfer and Issues in Quantification of Disaster Losses and Exposures: An OECD Perspective." In *Improving the Assessment of Disaster Risks to Strengthen Financial Resilience: A Special Joint G20 Publication by the Government of Mexico and the World Bank*. Chapter 17, pp. 265–287. Washington, DC: World Bank.

Pasteur, K. 2011. *From Vulnerability to Resilience: A Framework for Analysis and Action to Build Community Resilience*. Rugby, U.K.: Practical Action Publishing, Ltd.

Pelling, P. 2010. *Review and Systematization of Disaster Preparedness Experiences in Urban Areas in the Caribbean Region*. Oxford, U.K.: Oxfam.

Priliawito, E. and Maryadie. 2011. "Atasi Banjir, Laut Jakarta Dibendung" (Overcoming Floods, Dam Built along Jakarta Coast), February 5. http://us.fokus.vivanews.com/news/read/202976-atasi-banjir--laut-jakarta-dibendung.

Ranger, N., S. Hallegatte, S. Bhattacharya, M. Bachu, S. Priya, K. Dhore, F. Rafique, P. Mathur, N. Naville, F. Henriet, C. Herweijer, S. Pohit, and J. Corfee-Morlot. 2011. "An Assessment of the Potential Impact of Climate Change on Flood Risk in Mumbai." *Climatic Change* 104 (1): 139–67.

Rosenzweig, C., and W. Solecki. 2010. Introduction to "Climate Change Adaptation in New York City: Building a Risk Management Response." *Ann. New York Acad. Sci.* 1196, 13–18.

Ruijgrok, E. C. M., R. Brouwer, and H. Verbruggen. 2004. "Waardering van Natuur, Water en Bodem in Maatschappelijke Kosten Baten Analyses." Een handreiking ter aanvulling op de leidraad OEI. Ministerie van Landbouw, Natuur en Voedselkwaliteit, in samenwerking met de ministeries van Verkeer en Waterstaat, Economische Zaken, Financiën en VROM.

Satterthwaite, D., S. Huq, M. Pelling, H. Reid, and P. R. Lankao. 2007. "Adapting to Climate Change in Urban Areas, The Possibilities and Constraints in Low- and Middle-Income Nations." Human Settlements Discussion Paper Series 1, International Institute for Environment and Development (IIED), London.

Sawarendro. 2010. *Sistem Polder & Tanggul Laut—Penanganan Banjir Secara Madani di Jakarta* (Polder System & Sea Dam—Community Based Floods Mitigation in Jakarta). Jakarta: Indonesian Land Reclamation & Water Management Institute.

SEWA (Self-Employed Women's Association). 2001. "Microinsurance: A Case Study of an Example of the Full Service Model of Microinsurance Provision," by Michael J. McCord, MicroSave; Jennifer Isern, CGAP; and Syed Hashemi, CGAP. Nairobi. http://www .microfinancegateway.org/gm/document-1.9.28248/2841_02841.pdf.

Shaw, R., and Y. Matsuoka. 2010. *A Guide for Implementing the Hyogo Framework for Action by Local Stakeholders*. Kobe, Japan: Asia Regional Task Force on Urban Risk Reduction/ UNISDR/Kyoto University.

Sliuzas, R., G. Mboup, and A. de Sherbinin. 2008a. "Background for the Expert Group Meeting on Slum Identification & Mapping using Geo-Information Technology." UN-HABITAT, Nairobi; CIESIN–Columbia University, NY; ITC, Enschede, Netherlands.

———. 2008b. "Report of the Expert Group Meeting on Slum Identification & Mapping." UN-HABITAT, Nairobi; CIESIN–Columbia University, NY; ITC, Enschede, Netherlands.

Talberth, J., E. Gray, E. Branosky, and T. Gartner. 2012. *Insights from the Field: Forests for Water*. WRI Issue Brief 9. Washington, DC: World Resources Institute. http://pdf. wri.org/insights_from_the_field_forests_for_water.pdf.

Talberth, J., and C. Hanson. 2012. "Green vs. Gray Infrastructure: When Nature Is Better than Concrete." *WRI Insights*. Washington, DC: World Resources Institute. http://www .wri.org/news/2012/06/green-vs-gray-infrastructure-when-nature-better-concrete.

Twigg, J. 2004. "Disaster Risk Reduction: Mitigation and Preparedness in Development and Emergency Programming." Good Practice Review 9, Overseas Development Institute/Humanitarian Practice Network, London.

U.K. Cabinet Office. 2011. *Keeping the Country Running: Natural Hazards and Infrastructure. A Guide to Improving the Resilience of Critical Infrastructure and Essential Service*. http://www.cabinetoffice.gov.uk/resource-library/ keeping-country-running-natural-hazards-and-infrastructure.

U.S. Environmental Protection Agency. n.d. http://www.epa.gov/.

UN-HABITAT. 2003a. "Slums of the World: The Face of Urban Poverty in the new Millennium? Monitoring the Millennium Development Goal, Target 11— World-Wide Slum Dweller Estimation." Working Paper, London.

———. 2003b. *The Challenge of Slums: Global Report on Human Settlements*. London: Earthscan Publications Ltd.

———. 2009. *Planning Sustainable Cities: Global Report on Human Settlements*. London: Earthscan Publications Ltd.

———. 2010. *Participatory Climate Change Assessments. A Toolkit Based on the Experience of Sorsogon City, Philippines*. Cities and Climate Change Initiative Discussion Paper No. 1. UN-HABITAT: Nairobi.

UNISDR (United Nations International Strategy for Disaster Reduction). 2011. *Global Assessment Report on Disaster Risk Reduction: Revealing Risk, Redefining Development*. Geneva.

UNISDR/ILO/UNDP (International Labour Organization/United Nations Development Programme). 2010. *Local Governments and Disaster Risk Reduction: Good Practices and Lessons Learned*. Geneva: UN-ISDR.

Wagemaker, J., J. K. Leenders, and J. Huizinga. 2008. "Economic Valuation of Flood Damage for Decision-Makers in the Netherlands and the Lower Mekong Basin." 6th Annual Mekong Flood Forum, May 27–28, Phnom Penh, Cambodia.

Way, M. 2012. *Spotlight: Innovative Insurance Solutions Help Ease Climate Change Impacts.* Published online through the Global Adaptation Institute. http://news.gain.org/post/25592752683/spotlight-innovative-insurance-solutions-help-ease.

WBI (World Bank Institute). 2009. *Risk Sensitive Land-Use Planning.* World Bank Institute Distance Learning Program—Natural Disaster Risk Management Program. Washington, DC: World Bank.

———. 2011. *Sustainable Urban Land Use Planning eLearning Course.* Washington, DC: World Bank.

Weber, C. 2008. "From Slum Detection to Slum Definition." Paper presented at Expert Group Meeting on Slum Mapping, UN-HABITAT, CIESIN–Columbia University, ITC.

World Bank. 2008. *Climate-Resilient Cities: A Primer to Reducing Vulnerabilities to Disasters.* Washington, DC: World Bank.

———. 2010a. "Mainstreaming Building Energy Efficiency Codes in Developing Countries." World Bank Working Paper 204, Washington, DC.

———. 2010b. *Safer Homes, Stronger Communities: Resources for Reconstructing Housing and Communities after Natural Disasters.* Washington, DC: World Bank.

———. 2010c. "World Bank National Program for Community Empowerment Urban Project Appraisal." March 4, Washington, DC.

———. 2011a. *Climate Change, Disaster Risk, and the Urban Poor—Cities Building Resilience for a Changing World.* Washington, DC: World Bank.

———. 2011b. "Guidance Note on Making Women's Voices Count: Addressing Gender Issues in Disaster Risk Management in East Asia and the Pacific." Gender and Disaster Risk Management Guidance Notes, Washington, DC.

———. 2011c. "Proposal for an IDA Immediate Response Mechanism." IRM, Washington, DC.

———. 2012a. *Cities and Flooding. A Guide to Integrated Urban Flood Risk Management for the 21st Century.* Chapters 1, 2, 4, 6. Washington, DC: World Bank.

———. 2012b. "Improving the Assessment of Disaster Risks to Strengthen Financial Resilience. Experience and Policy Lessons from the Work of the World Bank." In *Improving the Assessment of Disaster Risks to Strengthen Financial Resilience: A Special Joint G20 Publication by the Government of Mexico and the World Bank.* Chapter 1, pp. 10–35. Washington, DC: World Bank.

———. 2012c. *Building Urban Resilience: Tools for Building Urban Resilience: Integrating Risk Information into Investment Decisions.* Pilot Cities Report, Washington, DC: World Bank.

World Bank/GFDRR (Global Facility for Disaster Reduction and Recovery). 2011. *Indonesia: Advancing a National Disaster Risk Financing Strategy—Options for Consideration.* Washington, DC: World Bank.

———. 2012. *Advancing Disaster Risk Financing and Insurance in ASEAN Countries: Framework and Options for Implementation.* Vol. 1. Washington, DC: World Bank.

World Bank/GFDRR DRFI (Disaster Risk Financing and Insurance) Program. n.d. http://www.gfdrr.org/gfdrr/DRFI.

World Bank/GFDRR Labs. 2011. *Volunteer Technology Communities: Open Development.* Washington, DC: World Bank/GFDRR.

World Economic Forum. 2008. *Building Resilience to Natural Disasters: A Framework for Private Sector Engagement.* Washington, DC: World Economic Forum/World Bank/UNISDR.

CHAPTER 3

The Practice of Urban Resilience

Key Points

- *Resilience can be built into all urban sectors.* Water supply and wastewater systems, energy and communications, and transportation systems deserve particular attention because they are vital for the quick recovery of a community and the livelihoods of its members.
- *The complexity of the built and natural infrastructure, the level of risk, and an analysis of the costs and benefits* will determine specific strategies and concrete steps for enhancing urban resilience.
- *An understanding of current and future risks and uncertainties, the possibility of failure, and planning to respond to failure in a way that causes the least damage* need to be part of any measure taken within the environment, built or natural.
- *The four essential strategies for building resilience in urban sectors* relate to management of the locational, structural, operational, and financial aspects of risk. Most successful strategies will rely on a mixture of these.
- *Structural and locational measures should be aligned with building social and institutional resilience* by relying on stakeholder and community participation, good governance, livelihood improvement, and sustainable development and planning.
- *A locational approach is an effective long-term method* for addressing disaster risks; it is particularly suitable for infrastructure development and planning.
- *Avoidance, relocation, and redundancy* are locational options.
- *A structural approach,* a medium-term method for addressing risk, is most effective for existing infrastructure.
- *Green and grey infrastructure measures and legislative and sociocultural actions* can be part of the structural approach.
- *Operational mitigation addresses the possibility of system failure and plans what to do if a system fails.* Operational measures should always be considered even when the emphasis is on locational, structural, and fiscal measures.

- *The operational approach incorporates disaster management and emergency response systems* with assigned responsibilities, clear procedures, regular training, end-to-end early warning systems, and damage assessment tools.
- *A financial approach addresses* both short- and long-term financial needs of specific sectors.

Key Resources

Section	Resource
Water Supply and Wastewater Systems	*Cities and Flooding: A Guide to Integrated Flood Risk Management for the 21st Century.* World Bank 2012.
Energy and Communications	*Community Greening: How to Develop a Strategic Energy Plan.* U.S. Department of Energy 2009.
Transportation Systems	*Effects of Catastrophic Events on Transportation System Management and Operations—Comparative Analysis.* U.S. Department of Transportation 2004.
All sections	*Keeping the Country Running: Natural Hazards and Infrastructure. A Guide to Improving the Resilience of Critical Infrastructure and Essential Services.* U.K. Cabinet Office 2011.

Water Supply and Wastewater Systems

Infrastructural   Social

Key Points
- Water supply and sanitation infrastructure varies in complexity based on the size of the urban area and the population served.
- The location of buildings, transmission-distribution systems, and storage facilities should avoid hazardous zones through risk assessment and risk-based land use planning.
- Redundancy—multiple systems that provide the same service—is achieved in water supply and wastewater treatment by creating secondary facilities, additional transmission-distribution pipelines, or multiple water storage facilities.
- A structural approach to increasing the resilience of water supply and wastewater systems will involve reinforcement measures, building codes, and maintenance works.
- Operational mitigation for water supply and wastewater facilities includes disaster management systems and alternative equipment (e.g., chlorine and iodine tablets, emergency water treatment generators, bottled water).

Summary
Water and wastewater systems are vitally important for public health and the quick recovery of the community and its economy. Reducing the potential for catastrophic failure of water supply and sanitation systems helps make an

urban community more resilient. The mitigation framework for risk reduction (chapter 1) uses structural, locational, operational, and financial approaches to address resilience. These approaches (see also chapter 2) generally deal with the infrastructural, institutional, economic, and financial components of resilience. This chapter reviews water supply and sanitation systems and suggests concrete steps for enhancing their resilience.

Water supply and sanitation infrastructure varies in complexity based on the size of the urban area and the population served. In many urban areas where such projects are needed, water and sanitation systems are at best partially planned and have many ad hoc and improvisational elements. As a result, only some receive adequate services. Though water and sanitation systems are vulnerable to a wide range of natural hazards, particularly flooding, there are many options for enhancing their resilience. The goal for urban planners is to understand all the water supply and sanitation systems in an urban area and draw up clear strategies to address deficiencies.

Overview: Water Supply and Sanitation Systems

Although urban water supply systems vary in complexity, they all have a source, transmission-distribution infrastructure, and storage facilities, which should include capacity to treat water so as to convey purified water to users. Complex water supply systems will have treatment facilities, often near the source, that convey the water through pipelines or aqueducts to individual homes. Simpler transmission-distribution systems may consist only of pipelines from individual wells. Most urban infrastructure projects will be a mix of complex and simple transmission-distribution systems.

Sanitation systems, typically called wastewater systems, operate the opposite of water supply, conveying wastewater from individual buildings through sewers to a sewage treatment plant. Sewers may either combine human waste with storm water runoff or convey the two streams separately. Combined sewers require more resources to process and treat water but are often still used in areas that do not process wastewater or because separated sewers are complex and resource-intensive. Processing wastewater can involve primary, secondary, and tertiary treatments which will determine the quality of the treated water. Depending on the quality of water treatment, if the treated water is not fit for human consumption, it may be returned to rivers or oceans but away from human populations.

Water Supply and Distribution

Sources for water may be single wells, aquifers, rivers, or lakes. Transmission infrastructure will consist of the pipeline required to convey water and a mechanism to move it through gravity or hydraulic pressure. Storage facilities can be large or small municipal storage tanks, individual jugs, or even the water source itself. Water can be purified at the source, in transmission, or in storage facilities. There are many forms of water treatment, but chlorine is most prevalent in the developing world. Because most urban water supply projects will be a combination of planned and unplanned systems, it is critical to understand how both systems work throughout the urban area.

When evaluating the resilience of water supply, it is critical to understand *long-term demand*. Projecting future water demand against total supply over 10 or 20 years will give a more complete view of the actual capacity of a body of water or an underground aquifer to supply water to an expanding urban area. Larger urban areas may already have multiple sources of water supply, which is a form of resilience through redundancy, but sources must also be unified by an effective transmission-distribution system. Smaller and newer urban areas will most likely be exploiting surface water but may not be accessing underground aquifers, which may be a way of building in redundancy.

When dealing with transmission-distribution systems, it is critical to understand *daily and monthly demand* over the course of a year; the resilience of a system may change considerably in that time. Urban transmission-distribution systems convey water through large mains or aqueducts that spread out to smaller pipes and individual homes. These usually create pressure through gravity but where water sources are lower, hydraulic pressure may be used. Smaller urban areas generally have gravity-fed transmission-distribution systems or rely on generators for pumping. Increasing capacity to store water is important for resilient water supply systems, but so is keeping water potable. Both storage and treatment facilities will depend entirely on the water source and transmission-distribution systems. In more complex systems, large storage tanks of finished water can hold enough drinking water for the whole population for a week, but simpler systems convey water to local storage tanks that hold water for just a few families. In general, treating water at the source is more efficient from a systems perspective, but keeping that water potable may be complicated by how the water is conveyed and how it will be stored. Often it is more efficient to treat water once it has reached the storage facility. Raw water is generally treated with chlorinates to kill pathogens.

Wastewater Systems

Developed urban areas have the capacity to remove or treat wastewater. In more advanced urban wastewater systems, wastewater is separated into two systems for household/industrial and water runoff, but most systems still use combined sewer pipes. Older communities have combined sewers that require more resources to treat wastewater and so often drain sewage directly into water sources or open drainage ditches. Ideally, separate wastewater systems should treat household/industrial waste and runoff, but in practice that is not common. Separate systems can lead runoff directly to outlets but channel sanitary waste to treatment plants. Figure 3.1 illustrates a wastewater treatment process.

The steps in wastewater treatment are pretreatment and primary, secondary, and tertiary treatment. In pretreatment the water is screened to remove grit and grease. In primary treatment heavier solids are removed by settlement. In secondary treatment waterborne micro-organisms digest organic materials, which are typically discharged into water sources. Tertiary-treated water (recycled or reclaimed water), from which many remaining pollutants are

Figure 3.1 Wastewater Treatment Process

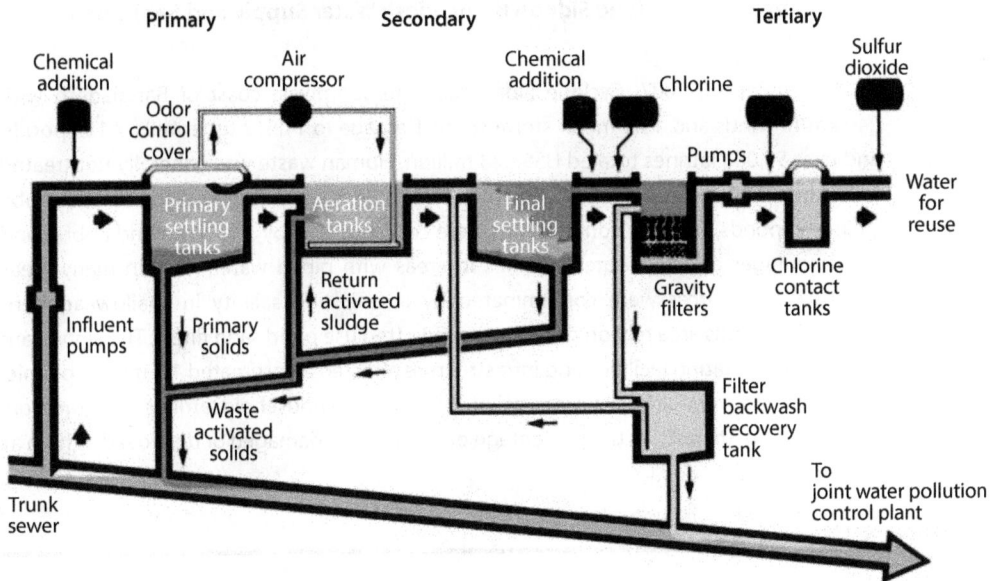

Source: New Mexico State University.

removed, is increasingly the trend because it may be discharged or used for irrigation in parks or agriculture or for industrial purposes. Where wastewater systems are more developed in urban areas, it is more common to find secondary treatments, but there are examples of tertiary treatment.

Enhancing Resilience of Water Supply and Sanitation Systems

Resilience can be increased in the water supply and sanitation systems through locational, structural, and operational approaches.

Locational Mitigation

Avoidance represents the longest time horizon; it applies to water supply systems and wastewater treatment facilities that have not yet been built. Urban planners need to ensure, through *risk assessments* and *risk-based land use planning*, that buildings, transmission-distribution systems, and storage facilities are located in areas that avoid hazardous zones (see section "Land Use Planning" of chapter 1 and sections "Risk Assessment" and "Risk-Based Land Use Planning" of chapter 2). Avoidance may not be an option when the hazard impacts an entire urban area or when the benefits of circumventing a hazardous zone are outweighed by the costs. Box 3.1 describes the impact of Cyclone Sidr in Bangladesh on water supply and sanitation facilities.

Relocation will follow the same methods as avoidance but with the increased opportunity cost of installing new infrastructure to replace current systems (see also section "Urban Upgrading" of chapter 1 and section "Urban Ecosystem Management" of chapter 2). *Redundancy*, which creates multiple systems to

Box 3.1 Impact of Cyclone Sidr on Bangladesh Water Supply and Sanitation Facilities

On November 15, 2007, Cyclone Sidr struck the southwest coast of Bangladesh with 240 km/hr winds and a six-meter storm surge. Damage to 11,612 tube wells, 7,155 ponds, and over 55,000 latrines totaled US$2.28 million. Human waste was generally not treated and waterborne disease was a major public health problem. Drinking-water sources (tube wells and ponds) in many communities were contaminated by salt water and debris, and power outages affected water supplies in areas with piped water. Also, in many areas groundwater sources were contaminated by arsenic and salinity in shallow aquifers. The people of this area rely on pond water and often use pond sand filters. The significant damage to sanitation facilities and infrastructure affected an estimated 1.3 million people. In some of the worst-affected areas, physical damage to household latrines was common, with one estimate putting the percentage of slab latrines damaged or destroyed as high as 70 percent.

Source: Government of Bangladesh, 2008.

provide the same service, is achieved for water supply and wastewater treatment by creating secondary facilities, duplicate transmission-distribution pipelines, or multiple water storage facilities. When building redundant systems, it is important to address demand should portions of the system fail, so as to ensure that there will be enough supply.

Structural Mitigation

Structural approaches seek to prepare critical infrastructure for a wide range of potential hazards when locational approaches are not feasible. As with locational approaches, risk assessments and risk-based land use planning (see sections "Risk Assessment" and "Risk-Based Land Use Planning" of chapter 2) will be the critical first step in understanding what types of hazard present risks and how critical infrastructure may be enhanced. A structural approach to increasing the resilience of water supply and wastewater systems will involve *strengthening measures* and *building codes*. This approach will be particularly effective for reducing risk from flooding, earthquakes, landslides, and storms. Figure 3.2 gives an example of mitigation infrastructure.

In the long run, water supply and wastewater treatment facilities can be strengthened by legislative action to put in place building codes that address disaster risk. Storage facilities, which can be very large, can also benefit from building codes. Strengthening can apply to buildings, transmission-distribution systems, and storage facilities. Structural analysis may suggest reinforcing retaining walls or creating floodwalls or berms around buildings, like, for example, in the case of a water treatment plant in Blair, Nebraska. In extreme cases, portions of a building or the entire building can be elevated to be higher than likely floodwaters.

Figure 3.2 Mitigation Infrastructure: Communal Toilets Elevated Against Flooding, Cambodia

Source: © Charles Scawthorn.

Transmission-distribution systems, whether above or below ground, can also be strengthened (see box 3.2). Below-ground pipes can be upgraded to withstand both a certain amount of earthquake shock and shifts as a result of

---

Box 3.2 San Francisco Water Supply Improvement Program

By 2000 many parts of the San Francisco water supply system, built in the early to mid-1900s, were nearing the end of their working life, and crucial portions crossed over or near three major earthquake faults. In 2002 San Francisco launched the $4.6 billion Water Supply Improvement Program (WSIP) to repair, replace, and seismically upgrade deteriorating pipelines, tunnels, reservoirs, pump stations, storage tanks, and dams. The program, funded by bonds issued in 2002, includes more than 80 projects throughout the service area—from San Francisco to the Central Valley—to be completed by mid-2016. One of the largest water infrastructure programs in the USA, WSIP has the following objectives:

- Improve the system to provide high-quality water that reliably meets all current and foreseeable local, state, and federal requirements.
- Reduce the vulnerability of the water system to damage from earthquakes.
- Increase system reliability by providing the redundancy needed to accommodate outages.
- Provide improvements related to water supply/drought protection.
- Enhance sustainability by optimizing protection of the natural and human environment.

Source: www.sfwater.org.

---

landslides. A backbone system can replace portions of the pipes with materials built to withstand certain forces. The cost of this option will depend heavily on the urban area. Above-ground aqueducts can, like buildings, be strengthened by reinforcement using buttresses. Storage facilities can be elevated to prevent intrusion by floodwater, but elevation can also present a risk if there is a possibility of earthquakes. Reinforcing the tank may be a viable option.

Operational Mitigation

Operational mitigation addresses the possibility of system failure and does contingency planning for the possibility of failure. For water supply and wastewater facilities operational mitigation includes *disaster management systems* and *alternative equipment*. These measures are effective against flooding, earthquakes, storms, and the majority of other natural hazards. Disaster management systems can be crucial to the resilience of water supply and wastewater facilities (see box 3.3). This type of planning can be a relatively cost-effective way to prepare for disasters. (see chapter 2 for a description of how to implement disaster management systems.)

Box 3.3 Resilience through Mutual Aid: The U.K. Water Industry

"Under the Security and Emergency Measures Direction (1998) water companies are required to provide plans to ensure provision of the water supply. In 2004, the Water U.K. Council established a mutual aid protocol for all members to ensure delivery of water by companies during an emergency. The protocol includes agreements to share emergency equipment and support affected member [companies] during incidents. This enhances the resilience and contingency options available to the industry as a whole. This protocol was amended following the lessons the industry learned from the 2007 floods. Issues addressed include number and readiness of assets, technical compatibility of assets, means of managing and deploying staff and the resilience of the scheme to cater for simultaneous events."

Source: U.K. Cabinet Office 2011, 31.

If there is a major disaster, water treatment and wastewater facilities will fail and alternative equipment will be necessary. To ensure that water is potable, either treatment tablets or finished water must be delivered to the people. Both availability and logistical capacity will be required to meet basic needs, taking into consideration that

• Chlorine and iodine tablets can kill pathogens, but sediment filters are also needed.

- Emergency water treatment generators have been successful after disasters but require fuel sources, and experts to repair them if they break down.
- Delivery of bottled water has also been successful in specific disasters but requires robust logistical capacity that is almost exclusive to militaries.

Operational measures should always be considered even when locational, structural, and financial measures have been implemented. Success may rely on a combination of measures. Box 3.4 summarizes a combination of structural and nonstructural measures for enhancing the flood resilience of houses.

Box 3.4 Making Human Settlements More Flood-Resistant

House Construction:
- Raise plinths and foundations.
- Combine a strong frame with lighter wall material that can be replaced after floods.
- Raise shelves to protect valuables.
- Use durable building materials that resist water damage.
- Plant water-resistant plants and trees as protection against erosion.
- Establish community committees to monitor construction quality and settlement planning.
- Engage in community outreach to promote hazard-resistant design approaches in future building.

Settlement Planning:
- If possible, prohibit resettlement in the most hazardous areas.
- Where feasible, improve access to safe land.
- Limit obstruction of natural channels and use absorbent paving materials and roof catchments to reduce runoff.
- Design drainage to minimize the intensity of water flows.
- Raise and reinforce access roads.
- Establish community emergency shelters and evacuation routes.
- Set up community early warning and monitoring systems to provide alerts of flood threats.

Source: Adapted from Alam, Herson, and O'Donnell 2008, 11.

Concluding Remarks

Water and wastewater systems are crucially important for public health and the quick recovery of the community and its economy. Though they are vulnerable to a wide range of natural hazards, particularly flooding, there are many options for enhancing their resilience. Understanding, anticipating, and preparing for disasters is the essence of resilience—if this is done, losses are minimized and recovery accelerated.

Energy and Communications

Infrastructural   Social

Key Points

- A combination of engineering, planning, and emergency preparedness is required to enhance resilience in the energy and communication sectors.
- Avoidance by strategic location through the use of risk assessment and land use plans is needed when installing new energy or communications systems.
- Creating secondary systems for conveying towers and cables can be a relatively low-cost option compared to post-disaster interrupted services and repair of downed lines.
- Structural mitigation may be a more practical form of building resilience into energy systems, especially when there are constraints on locating generation facilities.
- Operational approaches to energy and communication systems include building reserve capacity, alternative equipment, understanding risks to critical infrastructure, and having in place an emergency response system with effective training and procedures as well as coordination and participation of key stakeholders.

Summary

Resilience in the energy and communication sectors depends on combining engineering, planning, and emergency preparedness. There are opportunities for enhancing resilience in reducing initial losses, and operational, structural, and financial mitigation applies equally for energy and communication systems (see chapters 1 and 2 for core principles and tools). However, these systems can be quite vulnerable to particular hazards, and failures are inevitable. Local and emergency backup plans and equipment should be at the ready in order to cope with loss of power and communications for several days. The following sections give an overview of energy and communication systems and suggest practical steps for enhancing resilience.

Energy and communications systems are crucial for responding to emergencies and quick recovery of citizens and the economy. Energy in urban areas primarily concerns electric power, natural gas, and liquid fuels. The infrastructure required for each of these is essentially linear with regard to source, transmission, treatment, and distribution. Communications systems are either uni- or multidirectional but tend to be nonlinear. Broadcast radio and television are examples of unidirectional transmission and the telephone and Internet are examples of multidirectional systems. Multidirectional systems can be highly complex networks with as many "sources" as "receivers" and exponentially more paths.

Overview of Energy and Communications

Energy

Energy usage in developing cities is focused in the transportation sector; buildings and industry lag behind. Across the world urban energy demand is predominantly based on coal, oil, and gas, supplemented by nuclear, hydroelectric, biomass, and other renewable sources (IEA 2008). Demand for electricity represents nearly 13 percent of total energy demand (IEA 2008). While the energy budget is fairly consistent across all cities, usage is considerably different in the developing world. Developed nations demand more energy for buildings and industry than for transportation. Liquid fuels for automobiles and other vehicles are produced at wells and conveyed by pipeline and ship to oil refineries. The refineries distill the raw petroleum into a variety of fuels, which are then piped or carried by rail or truck to urban distribution terminals and finally to gasoline stations and other refueling depots.

Urban areas in the developing world primarily rely on fossil fuels like coal to generate electricity. Electric power systems are like water systems in that they are both source-transmission-distribution type networks. Electricity generation sources number from a few to a few dozen, and the distribution hubs within an urban area similarly number from a few to a few dozen; electricity is then conveyed to households and businesses. In urban areas with simpler systems, the generation sources can be more decentralized, with private grids run off gasoline generators or local coal markets that serve the community in a fairly resilient manner (Yates 2012).

Large-scale electricity generation begins with the transport of fuel to the power generation station. Fuel is stockpiled at the plant and then ignited. Heat converts water to high-pressure steam, which then spins a turbine generator, which converts the energy into electric power. This power is transformed to high voltage in a substation and then transmitted to urban centers over extra high voltage (EHV) transmission lines, typically carried overhead on transmission towers. At other substations near the urban centers, the EHV is transformed back to lower voltages for distribution.

Electric power networks are relatively unique as infrastructure for several reasons. For instance, electricity is conveyed very quickly over power lines. Then, electric generators and substations need a fail-safe design that automatically disconnects the system if electric power fluctuations exceed relatively small tolerances. The resilience of these systems to handle internal shock is quite high, although grids are susceptible to cascading failures when one failure leads to several, causing the system to shut down. The fail-safe protects the systems but also quickly halts delivery of electricity, which can be very important after a natural disaster.

Communications Systems

Communication systems include radios, televisions, landlines, mobile phones, and shortwave radios. Radio and television are unidirectional communication; telephones, the Internet, and shortwave radios are multidirectional. Unidirectional systems are generally centralized so they can convey a message from a single source to a large audience, but there is no mechanism to determine whether the message was received. Multidirectional systems are more decentralized, but it is clearer when a message is received.

One-way systems use a transmitter at the source that sends signals out over the air or via satellite. A television or radio then acts as the receiver of those signals and decodes the information into sound and video. Multidirectional systems have transmitters and receivers at both ends of the connection. In mobile phones the call is sent via radio waves to the nearest base station, where it is transmitted by microwave or fiberoptic cable to a central office, where it is packet-switched onward to the cell tower nearest the destination mobile phone, with the final link again by radio. Landline telephones function similarly but will either rely on physical lines to complete the connection or use satellite base stations to transfer the connection between locations.

The structure of the Internet has grown rapidly over the last several decades. Essentially it consists of the networks of Internet service providers through which traffic is routed. Telephone voice calls may now be made directly over the Internet using voice-over-Internet protocols (VoIP).

Enhancing the Resilience of Energy and Communications Systems

A combination of engineering, planning, and emergency preparedness is required to enhance resilience of energy and communication systems.

Energy Systems

Locational Mitigation: Electric energy generation and distribution systems are generally highly engineered and are usually built with hazard risk in mind, but in land use plans *avoidance* by strategic location may be needed as new systems are built (see section "Land Use Planning" of chapter 1, and sections "Risk Assessment" and "Risk-Based Land Use Planning" of chapter 2). Depending on the energy source, it may be necessary to locate a generation station inside a hazardous zone. It will be more practical to focus on siting transmission cables and towers to avoid landslide-prone and very windy areas. Electrical substations should also be sited at high elevations because they are very susceptible to flooding.

Relocation of generation stations or substations may be possible if new hazard risk is discovered, but the complexity of the infrastructure means that it will be costly; here again, transmission cables and towers might be candidates for relocation. Exceeding the demand for electricity through *redundancy* is an interesting form of locational mitigation because it does not require abandoning the infrastructure. Creating *secondary conveyance systems* of towers and cables can be a relatively low-cost option in comparison to interrupted service and repair of downed lines.

Structural Mitigation: This may be a more practical form of resilience-building for energy systems, especially since there are constraints on where generation facilities can be built. If a generation facility is in a flood or earthquake zone, strengthening the area around it with berms and ensuring that towers are supported against earthquake could be very important. Although much has been done to develop seismically resistant substation equipment, substations are still one of the most vulnerable links in the power grid. Electrical equipment is particularly vulnerable to inundation that can cause catastrophic failure. Similarly, cables and towers falling on the generation facility could shut down an electric grid for weeks after a disaster. Earthquakes can also cause secondary fires in generation facilities or as a result of fallen cables. Towers are particularly susceptible to high winds and ice storms.

Operational Mitigation: Operational approaches to energy system resilience include reserve capacity, alternative equipment, understanding critical infrastructure, and effective training and procedures. Disaster planning should always be prepared for the possibility of one or several major generating stations or transmission lines being damaged simultaneously by a natural hazard and losing function, perhaps leading to cascading failure of the entire electrical grid, but in any case resulting in partial or total loss of electric power for a region.

Because system complexity blackouts may be increasing in likelihood (Vespignani 2010), planners need to be prepared for their occurrence (Ball 2011; Bruch et al. 2011). To preclude a cascading failure, utilities operate with sufficient *reserve capacity* to cope with reasonably foreseeable sudden loss of supply. *Spinning reserve* is immediately available additional generator capacity in terms of rotational momentum of the generator and steam or hydro flow that can be quickly applied to the turbine. However, spinning reserve is expensive[1] and operators normally minimize it as much as possible. Box 3.5 describes the 1998 and 2006 blackouts in Auckland, New Zealand.

Alternative equipment that includes *quick-start capacity*, like hydroelectric power or gas, can be an effective bridge while other utilities are repaired. However, at peak consumption periods, these assets will typically already be on line, meaning the system will not have much excess capacity. If possible it is also wise to build *reserves of alternative fuels*, like gas or petroleum, and store them outside the urban area. It may also be possible to store fuel reserves specifically for emergency responders at local gas stations. Understanding critical infrastructure through effective risk assessments and risk-based land use planning will be very helpful for understanding which sections of the urban area require energy in order to maintain basic services. *Effective training and procedures* for regular maintenance of system control equipment and training of operators may make it possible to isolate system faults quickly enough to prevent them from dragging down the entire system (see chapter 2, section "Community and Stakeholder Participation").

Communications Systems
Locational Mitigation: In land use plans, avoidance of hazardous zones is important for transmitting and receiving towers for both unidirectional and multidirectional types of communication, and also for the switches that operate telephone systems. Depending on the type of hazard, towers might be placed either at high elevations to protect against flood damage or at lower elevations to protect again high winds. As with most approaches, there are important trade-offs to

Box 3.5 Auckland Blackouts, 1998 and 2006

With about 1.4 million residents (31 percent of the national population), the Auckland metro area is the largest urban area in New Zealand.

In 1998 almost all the power used downtown was electricity supplied by four power cables, two of them past their replacement date. One of the cables failed on January 20 and another on February 9, increasing the load on the other two—which both failed 10 days later, leaving about 20 city blocks without power. For the first few days few businesses could operate—some brought goods out onto the street to sell, but heavy rain soon made that impractical. Generators were brought in, increasing noise levels at the shopping district. It took five weeks before an emergency overhead line was completed to restore the power supply, and for much of that time about 60,000 of the 74,000 people who worked in the area worked from home or from offices relocated to the suburbs. Some businesses sent staff to other New Zealand cities, or even to Australia. Most of the 6,000 apartment dwellers in the area had to find alternative accommodation. For a while, temporary power was supplied from large container ships in the port supplying power to the downtown grid. New power lines were strung along the power poles along railway lines.

On June 12, 2006, power in Auckland was again interrupted when a ground wire was dislodged in high winds and fell across a 220 kV line and the 110 bus bar below it, tripping both and disrupting many public services and businesses. During the blackout, which lasted up to 10 hours, suburban commuter railway services were suspended, over 300 groups of traffic lights were off, hospitals closed with only emergency service running, radio station transmitters were taken offline for a time, mobile phone and telephone service failed, people were stuck in elevators in office buildings, and end-of-semester exams at local universities were postponed. Since the central business district was without power starting in the morning rush hours, business operations and traffic were disrupted severely. Many businesses sent their staff home. The 2009 blackout caused an estimated US$52 million lost in trade.

Sources: New Zealand Herald 1998; Siemens 2006.

be weighed. Switches are particularly vulnerable to inundation and should always be at higher elevations. *Relocating* towers or switches already installed is possible but expensive. Creating *redundant* or *alternate* towers or a system of towers that have multiple uses could be an effective and practical way to address disaster risk with locational mitigation.

Structural Mitigation: If a transmitting or receiving tower is located in a high-wind, landslide-prone, or earthquake zone, reinforcing the base structure is highly recommended. Similarly, a switch built at lower elevations and that is susceptible to water inundation should be surrounded by berms to protect it against possible floods.

Operational Mitigation: Operational mitigation for communication systems requires planners to assume that communication systems will fail catastrophically immediately after a disaster and the electric grid will not be operating. *Disaster management systems* that assign responsibility over emergency contingency plans

---

Box 3.6 The Relevance of Social Networks to Disasters

Several studies investigated the use of Twitter and Sina-Weibo, another microblogging site, after major earthquakes in Chile and China. Messages posted on Sina-Weibo mainly fell into five categories: opinions (33 percent); situation updates (25 percent); general earthquake-related (18 percent); emotion-related (16 percent); and action-related (4 percent).

In another study Twitter responses were also analyzed to determine the veracity of the information that emerged after the 2010 Chile earthquake. The findings revealed that the propagation of tweets that correspond to rumors differs from tweets that spread factual news because the Twitter community tends to question and deny rumors more than news. The conclusion was that it is possible to detect the credibility of tweets with 70–80 percent accuracy.

Source: Acar and Muraki 2011.

---

within different city neighborhoods are essential. *Effective training* and procedures and alternative equipment are the most effective tools here. Box 3.6 discusses the relevance of social networks to disasters. *Planning* should stress low-tech solutions like motorcycles or bicycles at pre-arranged collection points for emergency responders to use so that critical information can be conveyed quickly and effectively to the right people. Alternative equipment, such as shortwave radios and cell-on-wheels (COWS), which provides mobile service using a self-contained trailer, can allow emergency responders and residents to communicate across larger areas.

Concluding Remarks

Modern societies are highly dependent on energy, particularly electric power, and have very low tolerance for loss of communications, so both are crucial for a resilient society. Energy systems are similar to water networks in the sense that they are linear, which suggests that similar measures can be employed to enhance resilience. Because communication systems are nonlinear, they present different problems. Failures of these types of infrastructure are inevitable after a natural disaster, and local emergency backup plans and equipment should be ready in order to cope with loss of power and communications for several days or a week. Box 3.7 describes resilience standards for the U.K. energy and communication sectors.

Transportation Systems

Infrastructural   Social

Key Points

- Risk assessments and risk-based land use planning help urban planners to site transportation systems in safe locations.
- The complexity of road transportation systems requires planners to focus on infrastructure that will be used to evacuate affected populations and transport emergency responders and critical supplies.

**Box 3.7 Resilience Standards for Communications and Energy Infrastructure
in the United Kingdom**

The U.K. Cabinet Office makes the following recommendations:

For mobile communications towers: "BS8100 provides a design standard for communications towers within the mobile and broadcast industry. Factors taken into account are the life-time of the structure, the geographic location, i.e., vulnerability to hazards, and consideration of other infrastructure in the area. Hence, mobile communication towers are designed to withstand wind, debris, and other natural hazards and as a result are rarely disrupted by the weather in the U.K."

For electrical equipment: "Electrical equipment, such as transformers and circuit breakers, are vulnerable to temperature extremes, which can lead to power outages. The design standard IEC 61936-1:2010 provides common rules for the design and the erection of electrical power installations so as to provide safety and proper functioning for the use intended. IEC 61936-1 specifies a temperature range within which component parts of the electricity network should be designed to operate; for example, outdoor components should function at ambient air temperatures of between −25 and 40°C as calculated over a 24-hour period. Recorded extreme U.K. temperatures remain within this range; thus components designed to this standard would be expected to continue to operate during periods of extreme weather in the U.K. In addition, critical circuits will have two levels of redundancy so that in the event of any minor faults the service will remain operational."

The U.K. energy sector under the direction of the Energy Networks Association (ENA) produced an *Engineering Technical Report on Resilience of Flooding of Grid and Primary Substations* (ETR 138). The electricity transmission and distribution industry has set out target levels (standards) of resilience for different assets within the sector, which includes a risk-based target of the 1 in 1,000 (0.1 percent) annual probability flood for the highest priority assets within critical national infrastructure. Other measures to improve resilience include capacity to reconnect or provide an alternative energy supply to consumers.

Source: U.K. Cabinet Office 2011, 30, 33.

- Resilient urban planning incorporates regular maintenance and strengthening and replacement of crucial key road infrastructure like main thoroughfares, escape routes, bridges, and tunnels.
- Green infrastructure offers a suitable alternative to grey measures.
- Damage assessments help cities to prepare for road network failures.

Summary

To enhance resilience, urban planning needs to place transportation systems in safe locations and plan for recovery should the systems fail. The potential for catastrophic transportation system failure can be mitigated through structural, locational, operational, and fiscal approaches to address resilience (see chapters 1 and 2). The following sections give an overview of transportation systems and make recommendations for concrete steps to enhance their resilience.

All transportation systems have two fundamental dimensions, passenger and freight, and both are essential to resilient recovery. Transportation networks, which are almost exclusively nonlinear, can make a significant impact immediately before and after a natural disaster to which emergency planners must pay special attention. A single mitigation strategy will not be sufficient to allow critical goods and services to continue moving throughout an urban area after a disaster. Failure of road networks can have serious consequences, and through impacts on supply chains can also affect not just whole regions but also global trade and commerce. Climate-induced forces can also include, for example, temperature change, changing precipitation levels, wind loads, sea level rise, storm surges, and wave height (Meyer 2012).

Overview of Transportation Systems

Transportations systems are vital for the quick recovery of the community and its economy. The following sections describe the key types of transportation systems.

Road Transportation

Effective urban planning over several generations can produce road networks that can withstand significant loads in terms of both heavy freight and density of vehicles. These networks provide passenger and freight service simultaneously. In many countries urban road networks are highly redundant and can be quickly reconfigured if a portion of the system is damaged. Planned road networks rely on a series of alternatives to flow traffic effectively around hazards like flooding.

Urban expansion has put enormous stress on road systems as communities expand without regard to planning. Ad hoc roads can quickly become major routes that divert traffic into bottlenecks. Moreover, many urban regions will have critical bottlenecks where a bridge, tunnel, or mountain pass constricts all or most traffic into a narrow section of the road network that has limited capacity. These bottlenecks are typically the main network vulnerabilities. Power supply outages can also severely disrupt traffic management, though in an emergency they can be replaced with police on the street.

Rail Transportation

Rail systems are vital to most economies because they move bulk commodities in quantities that are not otherwise moved feasibly on land. Likewise, in most urban regions commuter rail is vital for moving people. However, these systems are much less interconnected than road systems and are typically confined to a few rights-of-way. If a disaster cuts these pathways, rail will typically be severely curtailed if not totally interrupted. Urban areas also present bottlenecks for rail lines as they pass through densely populated areas and intersect with roads. This can cause multiple failures across a number of sectors, including energy and communication when they intersect. Railway systems are also vulnerable to disruptions in power supply that occur elsewhere in interlocking networks.

Building Urban Resilience • http://dx.doi.org/10.1596/978-0-8213-8865-5

Dedicated backup generators may help mitigate this, but generators also depend on fuel supply.

Air Transportation

Most urban regions have only one or two major air transport hubs, but they will also have smaller airfields used by general aviation and the military that can be used as alternate sites. The main vulnerability for air transportation is the air traffic control (ATC) system, the networked series of ground controllers who observe aircraft locations and movement via radar and hand off to neighboring ATC centers as aircraft move from one area of control to the next. The system is entirely reliant on electric power and communications. Airports, particularly at night, are highly reliant on electric power for runway and taxiway lighting as well as radar, communications, and other needs, though they often have their own backup power.

Water Transportation

Water transportation almost exclusively addresses inland and ocean cargo. The only exception is services that ferry people. Modern marine cargo facilities are typically highly concentrated, with all but the largest ports often having only one major container port and a few oil or liquid natural gas (LNG) terminals.

Except for bulk goods like oil, coal, or wheat, most ocean cargo today is moved by large container ships, which in most ports are confined to a relatively narrow dredged channel that allows for their deep draft so they can reach ocean terminal piers and quays for loading and unloading. On the shore will be a large container yard and often warehouses. Some ports specialize in multimodal operations, where containers are loaded directly from long dedicated trains to ships and vice versa. Vessels on inland lakes and rivers are typically smaller ships and barges, which still account for an enormous amount of cargo.

Oil and LNG terminals typically consist of a pier or dolphin (a floating or fixed offshore structure) from which the liquid cargo is piped to onshore storage tanks. For petroleum, a refinery is often located next to the terminal. Inland as well as ocean marine facilities are often vulnerable to storm surge, flooding, earthquakes, and tsunamis. Where the sea level may rise due to climate change, they will have disproportionately higher vulnerability.

Enhancing the Resilience of Transportation Systems

Transportation systems are vulnerable to a wide range of natural hazards. While not all disaster risk can be prevented or anticipated, there are many opportunities to reduce the initial loss, disruption, and damage and to encourage a quick reconstruction and recovery.

Road Transportation

Locational Mitigation: The complexity of road transportations systems requires that urban planners focus on critical infrastructure that will be used for evacuation of affected populations and transportation of emergency responders and

Figure 3.3 Hurricane Evacuation Routes in Texas, United States

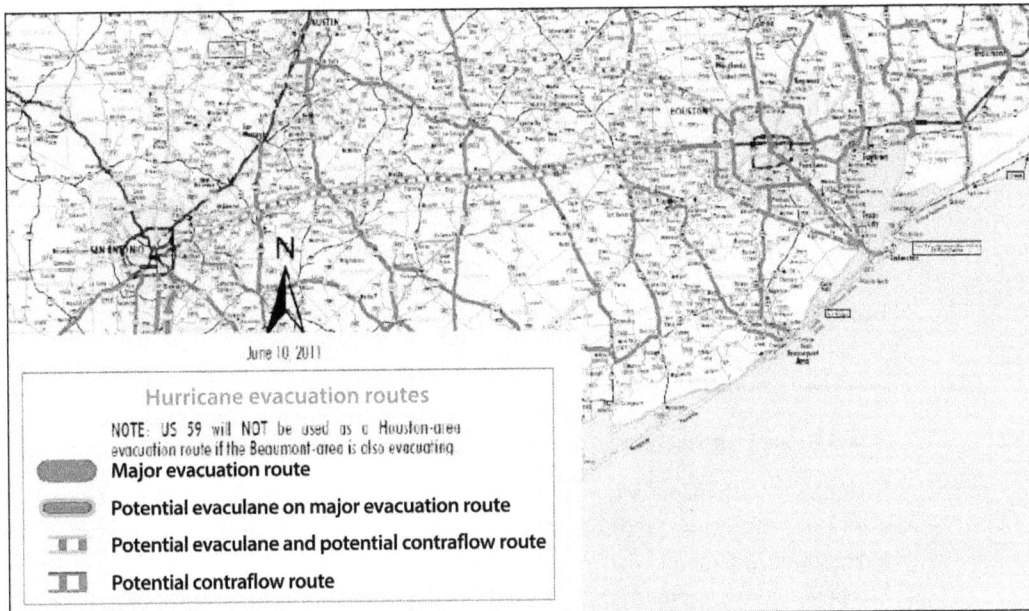

Source: Texas Department of Transportation.

critical supplies (see figure 3.3). When new road systems are planned, avoiding areas in lower elevations will keep roads from being inundated during floods. It is equally important to locate critical roads away from steep slopes so that they will not be swept away by landslides. This is another area where *risk-based land use planning* and *effective zoning* regulations can be effective. (See also section "Land Use Planning" of chapter 1 and sections "Risk Assessment" and "Risk-Based Land Use Planning" of chapter 2.)

Although mitigating risk should be a priority, other objectives might compete in a rapidly expanding urban area. Not only natural hazards but also the number and location of bridges and tunnels should be addressed. Because communities in urban areas are based on networks, an approach combining *redundancy* and *relocation* will most likely be needed. Once new redundant roads are in place, instead of removing unwanted infrastructure, older infrastructure can be given lower priority in emergency planning.

Structural Mitigation: Resilient urban planning incorporates regular *maintenance, reinforcement,* and *replacement* of key road infrastructure, such as main thoroughfares, escape routes, bridges, and tunnels. Roads can be buttressed underneath paved areas as well as protected by floodwalls or drainage ditches. Drainage ditches are often placed beside roads to control wastewater and storm runoff. However, planners must be careful not to overstress systems already in place. Experts should inspect bridges and tunnels to understand the geological underpinnings of critical infrastructure. Widening roads above expected demand is another way to create safe and effective routes should mass evacuation be necessary. Planting trees along roads to creating bioswale and rain gardens and using porous pavement can also be effective ways to make use of *green infrastructure* (see box 3.8) to strengthen road foundations and flood control. (For more on use of green infrastructure, see also section "Urban Ecosystems" of chapter 1 and section "Urban Ecosystem Management" of chapter 2.)

Operational Mitigation: Preparing for the failure of road networks depends on capacity to create reliable *damage assessments*. Disasters call for both high- and low-tech solutions. Purchasing high-resolution imagery from satellites can give emergency managers quick access to the state of road systems in a very large area, but they can also be very expensive (see also section "Data Gathering, Analysis,

---

Box 3.8 Green Infrastructure and Urban Transportation Systems

In cities, surface transportation networks (roads, railways, sidewalks, parking lots, alleys, and port infrastructure on land) account for a significant amount of imperviousness, which increases surface runoff, which in turn increases vulnerability to floods. Green infrastructure can be a suitable approach to increasing resilience because large amounts of funding are available from both local transportation departments and private system operators for both capital projects and repair, maintenance, and upgrading. Thus green infrastructure resilience measures can be incorporated into both new projects and retrofits of large impervious areas.

Among factors to be considered in taking a green infrastructure approach to transportation projects are these:
• Resilient land transportation systems, because they cover so much space, should ideally be designed to avoid high-hazard areas, particularly at critical points like bridges and tunnels.
• Because storage of rolling stock is generally less constrained by the alignment of the transportation network, it can be located in lower-hazard sites.
• Vegetation and shading along road and rail lines can decrease the expansion and contraction caused by extreme temperatures. Fewer cyclic stresses slow deterioration and make transport infrastructure more reliable.
• Although informal settlements tend to be located on marginal lands, the transportation network still needs to serve these areas to ensure they have evacuation routes during emergencies or disasters. Additional benefits are better access to markets and jobs for informal settlers.
• Ideally, a process should be institutionalized to coordinate the project plans and scheduled capital improvement projects of different departments to identify how both public and private investments in green infrastructure can achieve such benefits as storm water control, landslide mitigation, and heat island reduction.
• Methods should be available to determine what percentage of total project cost is represented by green infrastructure investments, and how this compares to traditional infrastructure (e.g., green infrastructure can be used to reduce the amount of concrete and asphalt needed for paving).

and Application" of chapter 2). Decentralized assessments can be made by training individuals to make quick damage assessments and deliver them to emergency planners. This requires more time, but less money. Once damage assessments are complete, there must be a way to effect critical repairs by clearing roads and replacing pavement or dirt where roads are impassable. One high-tech solution might be to keep construction equipment on hand in case of disaster. However this can often be accomplished with simpler traditional implements. It is vital, however, to secure capacity to make repairs quickly so emergency traffic can use the roads. Box 3.9 describes incentives for emergency repairs in California.

Box 3.9 Incentives for Emergency Repairs

During the 1989 Loma Prieta earthquake the California Department of Transportation was criticized for slow repair of damaged highway overpasses. By 1994, when the Northridge earthquake occurred, CalTrans was ready: when a major overpass on the Santa Monica freeway was heavily damaged, CalTrans implemented emergency repair contracts that included an "A+B" clause. A "cost-plus-time" bidding procedure had selected the lowest bidder based on a combination of the contract bid items (A) and the amount of time (B) needed to complete the project or a critical portion of it, and the contract encouraged speedy repair by offering bonuses (incentives) for early completion and assessing fines (disincentives) for late completion. The incentives ranged from $20,000 to $200,000 per day. As a result, on five major projects contractors finished anywhere from 8 to 74 days early, and received a total of over $23 million in bonuses—and no penalties.

Sources: DeBlasio et al. 2002, 2004.

Rail Transportation
Locational Mitigation: The type of rail network makes a difference for urban planners. In most of the developing world, rail networks consist of a single line arriving and departing from an urban area. Other regional, national, or international authorities control these networks. Urban planners should work with these agencies to build resilience together. Where there are intra-urban rail networks, planners may have greater responsibility. Those where rails are both above and below ground rails are necessarily more complex but will also tend to be easier to regulate. In any case, rail is unique in that planners must understand the vehicles as well as the infrastructure.

Future rail networks will benefit greatly from *avoidance* approaches to ensure that tracks are laid at higher elevations and away from structures, natural or manmade, that could damage the system in a disaster. *Relocation* will most likely be longer-term, although more practical once adequate funding is secured. Rather than being discarded, older tracks should be kept in good repair as a redundancy. In this case, fences might discourage people from uprooting the tracks for profit.

Structural Mitigation: Besides observing normal train operations, a system for assessing track quality is very important. *Strengthening* measures will necessarily involve repairing not only the tracks but also the foundation below them. Where rail is located in hazardous zones, tracks might be raised or reinforced. Floodwalls or lowering the elevation of the area around the tracks may also be an option. Green infrastructure (see also section "Urban Ecosystems" of chapter 1 and section "Urban Ecosystem Management" of chapter 2), such as trees planted a safe distance from the tracks, may reduce flood vulnerability. Strengthening measures should also make it possible for railways to carry more weight after a disaster that affects critical supply chains.

Operational Mitigation: Early warning systems and effective *communication* allow trains to take precautions during a natural disaster (see also section "Disaster Management Systems" of chapter 2). During an earthquake (see figure 3.4), storm, or flood, stopping or reversing the course of a train can minimize damage. Similar to the road network context, institutional capacity to quickly prepare damage assessments is vital.

Figure 3.4 A New Zealand Railbed after an Earthquake

Source: © American Geophysical Union.

Air Transportation

Locational Mitigation: Air transportation will have varying degrees of importance depending on the location of other types of transportation to handle critical supplies for an urban area. Using avoidance or relocation, to place airports outside hazardous zones is best for keeping airport infrastructure safe from flooding and landslides. As with rail transportation, relocating an airport may allow planners to use the previous airport as a redundancy, but it is also possible to make use of smaller airfields, clear fields for lighter aircraft, and even use major road infrastructure as a redundancy. It may be important to create redundancies for the control systems that allow aircraft to land, because they are vulnerable to earthquake, power outages, and other hazards.

Structural Mitigation: Since airport damage is commonly caused by flooding, it may be mitigated by reinforcing floodwalls and berms. Because of their central importance, building berms around the base of traffic control towers is particularly important.

Operational Mitigation: Early warning systems can provide precious time for aircraft evacuation before a natural disaster. Regular *damage assessments* of transportation systems by trained responders can provide local authorities with tools to prioritize repairs and create strategies after a disaster. Also, the ability to quickly reconfigure a system after a major disruption can make it possible for aircraft to operate at near normal conditions. Understanding the runway lengths and maximum weight capacities of smaller airfields located near an urban area can be very important so that they can be used effectively in the case of an emergency. This not only requires advance planning, it also relies on well-trained responders who can quickly come up with a good strategy to deal with a crisis situation. Box 3.10 describes the air transportation lessons learned from Hurricane Katrina.

Water Transportation

Locational Mitigation: Water transportation infrastructure systems often have to be located within zones that are vulnerable to flooding or other hazards like earthquakes, storms, and landslides, so the traditional avoidance, redundancy, and relocation may not be possible. There may also be an acceptable level of locational risk associated with this type of infrastructure. When possible, water transportation infrastructure should not be located on or near steep slopes, so avoidance of these areas is recommended.

Structural Mitigation: Structural mitigation of marine facilities should include *strengthening* the ground adjacent to the water where the soil might be weak: cranes and other large machinery should also be reinforced against earthquakes and high winds. Central offices or operations centers should have floodwater and earthquake protection. It may also be possible to create green infrastructure (see also section "Urban Ecosystems" of chapter 1 and section "Urban Ecosystem Management" chapter 2) that protects against floods near impervious transportation surfaces (see box 3.8). Surface transportation networks in cities account for a significant amount of imperviousness that increases surface runoff and thus heightens vulnerability to floods. *Green infrastructure* can be a suitable approach

Box 3.10 Air Service Lessons from Hurricane Katrina, 2005

In the years leading up to Katrina, before an approaching storm each airline independently selected the time for its last flight, with some choosing to cease operations sooner than others. As it became available this information was provided to the Emergency Operations Coordinator at the Louis Armstrong New Orleans International Airport (LANOIA) for dissemination to the community. The operations plan was flexible enough to allow for the specific conditions of each storm. The plan permitted airlines to fly as long as they and the FAA tower deemed weather conditions safe for travel.

Immediately before Katrina, many airlines continued operations until about 4:00 pm, Sunday, August 28, 2005. Because the planning window before Katrina was relatively short, about 400 ticketed passengers were stranded at the airport as Katrina made landfall. It is estimated that another 10,000 visitors who were unable to secure flights returned to shelter in downtown hotels. Post-Katrina, the airport was used as a nexus for evacuation and recovery operations, and some 30,000 evacuees were processed. An old well on the property provided potable water and a small generator provided limited electricity.

Source: Amdal and Swigart 2010.

to resilience, and there is often funding available that can be leveraged to incorporate green infrastructure resilience measures into both new projects and retrofits.

Operational Mitigation: Early warning systems designed to give watercraft and water transportation facilities enough time to either evacuate or prepare for an imminent hazard is likely a practical and effective operational mitigation strategy. As with other transportation sectors, quick damage assessments and the ability to communicate information promptly to emergency planners will be crucial for returning facilities to operation.

Concluding Remarks

Transportations systems are vital for quick recovery of the community and its economy. Though these systems are vulnerable to a wide range of natural hazards, there are many ways to enhance their resilience and to reduce the initial loss. Table 3.1, which summarizes lessons learned from the 2005 Hurricane Katrina, provides good examples of ways to improve transportation resilience.

Further Reading

- *Geo-hazard Management in the Transport Sector* (World Bank 2010).
- *Flood Risk Management Approaches as Being Practiced in Japan, Netherlands, United Kingdom, and United States.* (USACE 2011).
- *Cities and Flooding: A Guide to Integrated Urban Flood Risk Management for the 21st Century.* (World Bank 2012, chapters 1, 2, 4, 6).

Table 3.1 Pre- and Post-Disaster Transportation Policies Summarized

Pre-Katrina	Post-Katrina
Facility design assumed adequate flood protection.	All critical building systems are designed to be flood-resistant (i.e. elevated).
Allow evacuees to seek shelter in upper levels of selected buildings.	Vertical evacuation is not an option.
Shelters of last resort were utilized.	Shelter of last resort is not an option.
Onsite asset protection.	Movable assets were moved to destinations out of harm's way.
Evacuation response plan was limited.	The City-Assisted Evacuation Plan (CAEP) is now operational.
No public transit was available for out-of-city destinations.	CAEP uses RTA, Amtrak, and private carriers.
Memoranda of Understanding (MOUs) were limited.	New MOUs allow for maximum utilization of federal assets.
Policy making did not consider transportation resilience.	Recent transportation policies and practices (like CAEP) reflect some degree of resilience.
Communication systems were limited.	There has been little change, though out-of-area cell phones provide backup communication.
There were few offsite operation centers.	Offsite operation centers have been established.
Communication and coordination between transportation providers was minimal.	Improvement has been limited.
The Metropolitan Planning Organization was used selectively as a resource base for data and intergovernmental networks.	The Metropolitan Planning Organization's pre-storm data and governmental/technical networks serve as valuable post-storm assets.

Source: Amdal and Swigart 2010.

Note

1. Keeping excess steam readily available requires burning extra fuel and is like keeping a large amount of cash in a checking account to preclude an overdraft—in other words, it is less than optimum efficiency of asset use.

References

Acar, A., and Y. Muraki. 2011. "Twitter for Crisis Communication: Lessons Learnt from Japan's Tsunami Disaster." *International Journal of Web Based Communities* 7 (3): 392–402. http://www.inderscience.com/info/inarticletoc.php?jcode=ijwbc&year=2011&vol=7&issue=3.

Alam, K., M. Herson, and I. O'Donnell. 2008. *Flood Disasters: Learning from Previous Relief and Recovery Operations.* Geneva/London: ProVention/ALNAP.

Amdal, J. R., and S. L. Swigart. 2010. "Resilient Transportation Systems in a Post-Disaster Environment: A Case Study of Opportunities Realized and Missed in the Greater New Orleans Region." Final report, Gulf Coast Research Center for Evacuation and Transportation Resiliency, LSU/UNO University Transportation Center, New Orleans, LA.

Ball, P. 2011. "Crisis Response: The New History." *Nature* 480: 447–48.

Bruch, M., V. Münch, M. Aichinger, M. Kuhn, M. Weymann, and G. Schmid. 2011. "Power Blackout Risks Risk Management Options, Emerging Risk Initiative—Position Paper." CRO Forum: Amsterdam. http://www.thecroforum.org/publication/powerblackoutrisks.

DeBlasio, A. J., T. J. Regan, M. E. Zirker, K. Fichter, and K. Lovejoy. 2004. "Effects of Catastrophic Events on Transportation System Management and Operations—Comparative Analysis." Final report, U.S. Department of Transportation, Washington, DC.

DeBlasio, A. J., A. Zamora, F. Mottley, R. Brodesky, M. E. Zirker, & M. Crowder. 2002. Effects of Catastrophic Events on Transportation System Management and Operations, Northridge Earthquake, Jan. 17, 1994, p. 68. U.S. Department of Transportation.

Government of Bangladesh. 2008. *Cyclone Sidr in Bangladesh: Damage, Loss and Needs Assessment for Disaster Recovery and Reconstruction.* Government of Bangladesh: Bangladesh.

IEA (International Energy Agency). 2008. *Worldwide Trends in Energy Use and Efficiency: Key Insights from IEA Indicator Analysis.* OECD/IEA: France.

Jha, A., J. Lamond, R. Bloch, N. Bhattacharya, A. Lopez, N. Papachristodoulou, A. Bird, D. Proverbs, J. Davies, and R. Barker. 2011. "Five Feet High and Rising: Cities and Flooding in the 21st Century." Policy Research Working Paper 5648, World Bank, Washington, DC.

Meyer, M. D. 2012. "Design Standards for U.S. Transportation Infrastructure—The Implications of Climate Change." Transportation Research Board, Georgia Institute of Technology, Savannah, GA. http://onlinepubs.trb.org/onlinepubs/sr/sr290Meyer.pdf.

New Zealand Herald. 1998. "Summary: Ministerial Inquiry into the Auckland Power Supply Failure." July 21. http://www.nzherald.co.nz/energy/news/article.cfm?c_id=37&objectid=3400502.

Siemens. 2006. "Former Blackouts Worldwide: Power Transmission and Distribution (PTF)." Website article, November.

U.K. Cabinet Office. 2011. *Keeping the Country Running: Natural Hazards and Infrastructure. A Guide to Improving the Resilience of Critical Infrastructure and Essential Service.* http://www.cabinetoffice.gov.uk/resource-library/keeping-country-running-natural-hazards-and-infrastructure.

USACE (United States Army Corps of Engineers). 2011. *Flood Risk Management Approaches as Being Practiced in Japan, Netherlands, United Kingdom, and United States.* Washington, DC: USACE.

Vespignani, A. 2010. "Complex Networks: The Fragility of Interdependency." *Nature* 464: 984–85.

World Bank. 2012. *Cities and Flooding: A Guide to Integrated Urban Flood Risk Management for the 21st Century.* Washington, DC: World Bank/IBDR. https://www.gfdrr.org/gfdrr/urbanfloods.

Yates, J. 2012. "Coal Reigns in Emerging Market Countries." *Emerging Money*, July 9.

Disaster Definitions and Classifications

The Centre for Research Epidemiology of Disasters (CRED) defines a disaster as "a situation or event which overwhelms local capacity, necessitating a request to a national or international level for external assistance; an unforeseen and often sudden event that causes great damage, destruction and human suffering."

For a disaster to be entered into the CRED database, at least one of the following criteria must be fulfilled: 10 or more people reported killed; 100 or more people reported affected; declaration of a state of emergency; call for international assistance.

The Emergency Events Database (EM-DAT) distinguishes two generic categories for disasters, natural and technological; the natural disaster category is divided into 5 subgroups, which in turn cover 12 disaster types and more than 30 subtypes (see the figures that follow). The subgroup definitions are

- Geophysical: Events originating from solid earth (earthquake, volcano, movement of dry mass).
- Meteorological: Events caused by short-lived/small- to medium-scale atmospheric processes, lasting from minutes to days (storm).
- Hydrological: Events caused by deviations in the normal water cycle or overflow of bodies of water caused by wind set-up (flood and movements of wet mass).
- Climatological: Events caused by long-lived medium- to macro-scale processes, in the spectrum from intraseasonal to multidecadal climate variability (extreme temperatures, drought, wildfire).
- Biological: Disaster caused by the exposure of living organisms to germs and toxic substances (epidemic, insect infestation, animal stampede).

Information in this appendix is adapted from the Centre for Research Epidemiology of Disasters website and publications.

Figure A.1 Natural and Technological Disaster Classification

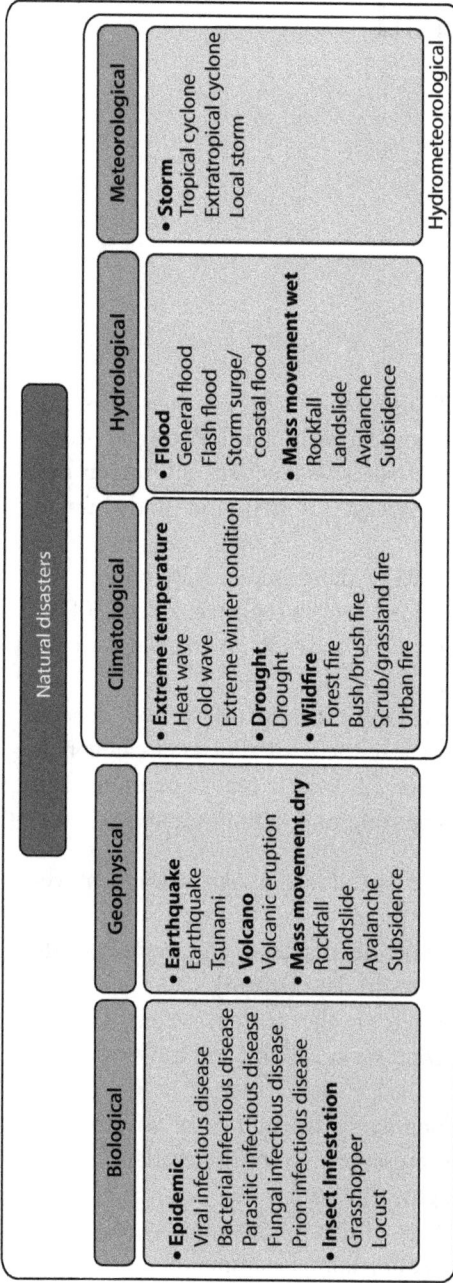

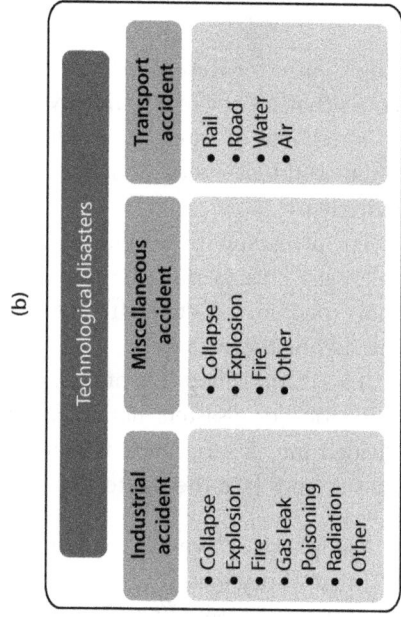

(a)

Natural disasters

Biological	Geophysical	Climatological	Hydrological	Meteorological
• **Epidemic** Viral infectious disease Bacterial infectious disease Parasitic infectious disease Fungal infectious disease Prion infectious disease • **Insect Infestation** Grasshopper Locust	• **Earthquake** Earthquake Tsunami • **Volcano** Volcanic eruption • **Mass movement dry** Rockfall Landslide Avalanche Subsidence	• **Extreme temperature** Heat wave Cold wave Extreme winter condition • **Drought** Drought • **Wildfire** Forest fire Bush/brush fire Scrub/grassland fire Urban fire	• **Flood** General flood Flash flood Storm surge/ coastal flood • **Mass movement wet** Rockfall Landslide Avalanche Subsidence	• **Storm** Tropical cyclone Extratropical cyclone Local storm

Hydrometeorological

(b)

Technological disasters

Industrial accident	Miscellaneous accident	Transport accident
• Collapse • Explosion • Fire • Gas leak • Poisoning • Radiation • Other	• Collapse • Explosion • Fire • Other	• Rail • Road • Water • Air

Figure A.2 Natural Disaster Subgroup Types

Disaster Generic Group	Disaster Group	Disaster Type	Disaster Subtype	Disaster Sub-Subtype
Natural disaster	Geophysical	Earthquake	Ground shaking	
			Tsunami	
		Volcano	Volcanic eruption	
		Mass movement (dry)	Rockfall	
			Avalanche	Snow avalanche
				Debris avalanche
			Landslide	Mudslide Lahar Debris flow
			Subsidence	Sudden subsidence
				Long-lasting subsidence

Disaster Generic Group	Disaster Group	Disaster Type	Disaster Subtype	Disaster Sub-Subtype
Natural disaster	Meteorological	Storm	Tropical storm	
			Extra-tropical cyclone (winter storm)	
			Local/convective storm	Thunderstorm/lightning
				Snowstorm/blizzard
				Sandstorm/dust storm
				Generic (severe) storm
				Tornado
				Orographic storm (strong winds)

figure continues next page

Figure A.2 **Natural Disaster Subgroup Types** *(continued)*

Disaster Generic Group	Disaster Group	Disaster Type	Disaster Subtype	Disaster Sub-Subtype
Natural disaster	Hydrological	Flood	General (river) flood	
			Flash flood	
			Storm surge/ coastal flood	
		Mass movement (wet)	Rockfall	
			Landslide	Debris flow
			Avalanche	Snow avalanche
				Debris avalanche
			Subsidence	Sudden subsidence
				Long-lasting subsidence

Disaster Generic Group	Disaster Group	Disaster Type	Disaster Subtype	Disaster Sub-Subtype
Natural disaster	Climatological	Extreme temperature	Heat wave	
			Cold wave	Frost
			Extreme winter conditions	Snow pressure
				Icing
				Freezing rain
				Debris avalanche
		Drought	Drought	
		Wildfire	Forest fire	
			Land fires (grass, scrub, bush, etc.)	

figure continues next page

Figure A.2 Natural Disaster Subgroup Types *(continued)*

Disaster Generic Group	Disaster Group	Disaster Type	Disaster Subtype	Disaster Sub-Subtype
Natural disaster	Biological	Epidemic	Viral infectious diseases	
			Bacterial infectious diseases	
			Parasitic infectious diseases	
			Fungal infectious diseases	
			Prion infectious diseases	
		Insect infestation		
		Animal stampede		

Disaster Generic Group	Disaster Group	Disaster Type	Disaster Subtype	Disaster Sub-Subtype
Natural disaster	Extra-terrestrial	Meteorite/ asteroid		

Checklist for Infrastructure Owners and Operators

The following questions can be helpful for private individuals or organizations that own or operate urban infrastructure. They are designed to take full account of critical infrastructure that might be compromised by disaster. This approach could be used as part of a community and stakeholder participation program, as discussed in chapter 2.

This checklist has been adapted from *Keeping the Country Running: Natural Hazards and Infrastructure—A Guide to Improving the Resilience of Critical Infrastructure and Essential Services*, published by the United Kingdom Cabinet Office in 2011.

Identify Risks

STEP 1: Determine critical infrastructure necessary to continue operations.
STEP 2: Determine critical infrastructure within your supply chain.

Understand Hazards

STEP 3: Identify hazards of greatest concern to your critical infrastructure and supply chains.

> *Questions*
> 1. *Have you worked with external agencies to assess the natural hazard risks to your organization's critical infrastructure? [Examples: disaster management agency, chamber of commerce, local authorities, environmental agency, geological survey.]*
> 2. *Does the location of your critical infrastructure increase the risk from natural hazards?*
> 3. *Who are your key suppliers and customers? Do they deliver an essential service to your community?*

Assess Risk and Understand Vulnerability

STEP 4: Determine how resilient your critical infrastructure would be to the hazards of greatest concern, taking into account location, structural design, and redundancies.

Questions

1. *Is it cost-effective to move critical infrastructure to a safer location?*
2. *Is it possible to reinforce, retrofit, or otherwise strengthen critical infrastructure to make it more resilient to the hazards of most concern?*
3. *What redundancies can you build in so you will be able to continue operations?*

STEP 5: Determine your organization's level of risk.

4. *Could a natural hazard bring on a surge in demand for your services? If so, will you be able to manage it?*
5. *Have you worked with partners in your supply chain to understand their vulnerability to natural hazards? How could their disruption affect your organization?*
6. *Have you worked with emergency responders and other agencies on how they can offer assistance when service is disrupted by a natural disaster?*

Build Resilience

STEP 6: Determine the level of risk to infrastructure critical to your organization that is acceptable.

Questions

1. *What is the acceptable level of risk for your organization?*
2. *Given specific risks, is your organization willing to accept them, mitigate them, or halt services?*
3. *Does your organization's governing body understand the risk of natural hazards disrupting services?*
4. *Has the governing body formally accepted certain levels of risk?*

STEP 7: Determine what level of resilience is required and what resilience strategy will be adopted.

5. *Given the hazard profile of your area over the next 5–10 years, does your strategy for resilience need to evolve?*

STEP 8: Embed resilience at the core of your strategic decision-making processes.

6. *Is your organization's resilience strategy championed at the governing level?*
7. *Has the governing body committed resources to improve resilience?*
8. *Has the governing body approved contingency plans?*

Building Urban Resilience • http://dx.doi.org/10.1596/978-0-8213-8865-5

STEP 9: Engage with emergency responders in areas where you operate to deliver services.

     9. *Is there a plan in place to manage any of the following:*
  - *Loss of primary transport routes?*
  - *Reduced staff availability?*
  - *Impaired site access?*
  - *Loss of primary or alternative power?*
  - *Loss of primary and alternative water supply?*
  - *Increased demand for health and emergency services?*
  - *Increased demand for your services?*
  - *Supply chain disruption?*

    10. *Have these plans been shared with emergency responders and supply chain partners?*

    11. *Does the board seek assurances at least annually on how resilient critical infrastructure is to disruption from natural hazards?*

    12. *Do you have a resilience-oriented education and awareness program in place within your organization?*

    13. *Have key staff been trained to implement emergency and business continuity plans?*

    14. *Is there evidence that disaster resilience has been included in your organization's strategic decision-making and investment plans?*

Evaluate Resilience

STEP 10: Challenge, test, and exercise your organizational resilience strategy.

    Questions

    1. *Have you reviewed your organizational resilience strategy?*

    2. *Have you identified and tested any assumptions that underpin your strategy?*

    3. *Do you have a simulation program in place that addresses the risk from natural hazards? Has it been approved by the board? Do board members take part in simulation exercises?*

    4. *Have you done simulation exercises for more than one type of disruption at any one time, e.g., loss of primary transport routes coupled with loss of power and water supplies?*

    5. *Are plans tested at least annually? Have findings been recorded and lessons learned?*

    6. *Were supply chain partners and emergency responders included in these exercises?*

    7. *Were findings shared with the board, supply chain partners, emergency responders, regulators, and the government?*

    8. *Have you taken part in tests or exercises run by your supply chain or emergency responders?*

APPENDIX C

Comparison of Spatial Plans for Urban Infrastructure

Table C.1 Comparison of Spatial Plans for Urban Infrastructure

Broad approach	Important terms and approaches	Strengths	Weaknesses and contingencies
• Smart growth and transit-oriented development	• Smart growth • Compact development • Integrated development • Mixed-use development • Intensification • Coordination • Transit-oriented development	• Encourages inter-sectoral and inter-agency links • Encourages links between planning and implementation • Improves sustainability • Improves public transport • Strong transport–land use links • Can slow urban sprawl	• Good links difficult to achieve • Assumes significant capacity and organization • Poor or narrow implementation undermines prospects • Popular support difficult to achieve due to conflicting views and lifestyles • Claimed benefits contested
• Integrating land use and transport	• Bus rapid transit (BRT) • Corridors and axes; integrated rail redevelopment • Linking economic activities to transport type • New transport/land use models	• Improves public transport • Promotes use of public transport • Reduces energy and improves efficiency • Enhances transport–land use links • New models enable better understanding of patterns	• Heightened property prices on transport axes can marginalize the poor • Required integration can be difficult to achieve • Needs good understanding of social and economic dynamics and space—difficult to achieve • Land use–transport links undermined by different logics, institutional divides • New models still data-hungry, aggregated, distant

table continues next page

Table C.1 Comparison of Spatial Plans for Urban Infrastructure *(continued)*

Broad approach	Important terms and approaches	Strengths	Weaknesses and contingencies
• Strategic spatial planning and infrastructure planning	• Strategic plans • Infrastructure plans • Transport–land use links	• Can give long-term direction to development • Can avoid inequitable and unsustainable development • Avoids fragmented development	• Conditions required to work are demanding, difficult to achieve • Analysis perhaps not credible • Inter-sectoral coordination • Stakeholder involvement and buy-in • Regular review • Internal champions • Special agencies
• Integrated urban development and management plans	• Multisectoral investment plans (MSIPs) • Physical and environmental development plans (PEDPs)	• More flexible, less data-demanding, and easier to prepare than master plans • Participatory • Helps to manage urban growth when resources and capacity are scarce • Can be used iteratively in decision-making process	• Problematic if seen in static or narrow way • Inter-sectoral cooperation hard to achieve • Can be countered by political decision making
• Strategic structure planning	• Integrative framework • Long-term vision	• More flexible, less data-demanding, and easier to prepare than master plans • Participatory • Multifaceted approach • Combines short-term actions with long-term planning	• Required political and stakeholder buy-in may be difficult to achieve • May still be relatively technocratic • May not provide enough detail for some decisions
• Linking spatial planning to infrastructure planning	• Integrated development plans • Spatial frameworks	• More flexible, less data-demanding, and easier to prepare than master plans • Participatory • Gives direction to infrastructure planning • GIS-based models can be used as input	• Consistency in policy and coordination between agencies difficult to achieve • Can be too broad to be useful • May be contradicted by the market
• Linking megaprojects to infrastructure development	• Urban regeneration • Multifunctional	• Powerful driver in urban form • Evolving approaches allow linking to planning over the long term • Builds cooperation between sectors and agencies	• Megaprojects often politically driven and one-off; approach is hard to achieve • Level of integration and cooperation difficult to achieve

Source: UN-HABITAT. 2009. *Planning Sustainable Cities: Global Report on Human Settlements* (p. 161). London: Earthscan Publications Ltd.

Data Collection Guidelines

Terms of Spatial Data Delivery and Sharing

Promoting data accessibility is an important component of any technical disaster or climate risk project. To ensure sustainability of project results, all data collected and created should be preserved, consolidated, and transferred to stakeholders upon project completion in a well-known or standard electronic format. Specifically the following terms should apply:

Licensing: Because all data procured and developed for a project is done on behalf of key stakeholders, all licensing agreements should be made similarly.

Vector data: Geospatial vector data must be converted into a standard Open Geospatial Consortium (OGC) or other well-known format, such as shape file, keyhole markup language (KML), geography markup language (GML), and well-known text (WKT). Other formats should only be used with approval. All files must include projection parameters.

Raster data: Geospatial raster data should be converted into a standard OGC or other well-known format, such as geoTiff, JPEG, JPEG2000, ERDAS img, ArcInfo ASCII or Binary grid, MrSid. Other formats should only be used with approval. All files must include projection parameters.

Tabular data: Tabular data should be converted into a readily accessible and well-known format, such as comma-separated values (CSV), tab delimited text file, or spreadsheet. Other formats should only be used with approval.

Media/method of transfer: All data sets should be transferred on permanent media, such as CD/DVDs or flash drives. Data sets that exceed the capacity of these should be provided on a hard or solid-state drive, as agreed by key stakeholders.

Metadata: Detailed documentation needs to be provided for each data set. The metadata must include description, source, contact, date, accuracy, and any use restrictions. A description of attributes must be provided for vector and tabular data sets. Spatial data must include details of projection. ISO international standards should be used for all metadata.

Derived data: All derived data generated will belong to key stakeholders and must be transferred on these terms.

In addition to the above, spatial data should be made available in a web-based data management and mapping platform so that it can be made publicly available in multiple formats. The platform must meet the following requirements:

- It is web-based and accessible over the Internet.
- Allow for uploading raster and vector data and assigning rendering and classifications.
- Metadata must be entered for each data set uploaded.
- Allow for definition of users and assignment of access levels to individual layers and maps as required.
- Allow for viewing and interrogating spatial data and associated metadata.
- Allow for downloading spatial data in multiple vector and raster formats, including OGC web services.
- Allow for maps to be composed by combining multiple layers.

These services are currently provided by GeoNode in open source software. More information can be found at http://geonode.org.

Capacity Requirements for Hosting GeoNode

The GeoNode website gives the following hardware requirements for deployment of a GeoNode:

- 6GB of RAM, including swap space
- 2.2 GHz processor (additional processing power may be required for multiple concurrent styling renderings)
- 1 GB software disk usage
- Additional disk space for any data hosted with GeoNode and tiles cached with GeoWebCache. For spatial data, cached tiles, and "scratch space" useful for administration, a decent baseline size for GeoNode deployments is 100GB
- 64-bit hardware recommended

IT-related capacity within the organizations should include

- Experience with web development in Python/Django,
- Experience with geospatial programming, such as GeoServer/GeoTools, GeoNetwork,
- Experience with OpenLayers/GeoExt and PostGIS
- Understanding of the Open Geospatial Consortium (OGC) standards: Web Feature Service (WFS), Web Coverage Services (WCS), Web Map Services (WMS) and Web Processing Services (WPS).

Environmental Benefits Statement

The World Bank is committed to reducing its environmental footprint. In support of this commitment, the Office of the Publisher leverages electronic publishing options and print-on-demand technology, which is located in regional hubs worldwide. Together, these initiatives enable print runs to be lowered and shipping distances decreased, resulting in reduced paper consumption, chemical use, greenhouse gas emissions, and waste.

The Office of the Publisher follows the recommended standards for paper use set by the Green Press Initiative. Whenever possible, books are printed on 50% to 100% postconsumer recycled paper, and at least 50% of the fiber in our book paper is either unbleached or bleached using Totally Chlorine Free (TCF), Processed Chlorine Free (PCF), or Enhanced Elemental Chlorine Free (EECF) processes.

More information about the Bank's environmental philosophy can be found at http://crinfo.worldbank.org/crinfo/environmental_responsibility/index.html.

green
press
INITIATIVE

www.ingramcontent.com/pod-product-compliance
Lightning Source LLC
Chambersburg PA
CBHW080330270326
41927CB00014B/3162